Victor Arwas

ART DECO

Harry N. Abrams, Inc.

PUBLISHERS / NEW YORK

Page one
MAURICE GUIRAUD-RIVIERE: L'Enigme, Patinated bronze, exhibited at the
1925 Paris Exhibition. (Author's Collection)
Frontispiece, page two
TAMARA DE LEMPICKA: La Musicienne. Oil, 1929. (Collection Barry
Friedman, New York. Photo: Sully Jaulmes)
Overleaf, left
Sèvres vase, Clairemont shape, decoration by Jean-Baptiste Gauvenet,
executed by Charles Bihan, Works Director at Sèvres, 1924, 58 cms.
(Collection Robert Zehil, Monte Carlo)
Overleaf, right
DAUM: Deeply etched, part polished, thick-walled vase on wrought-iron
stand. (Collection Robert Zehil, Monte Carlo)

Revised Edition 1992

LIBRARY OF CONGRESS CATALOGING-IN-PUBLICATION DATA

Arwas, Victor.
Art deco.
Bibliography: p.
Includes index.
1. Art deco.   2. Art, Modern — 20th century.
I. Title
N6494.A7A65   709'.04'012   80—12363
ISBN 0—8109—1926—5

First published in Great Britain in 1992 by Academy Editions, London

Copyright © 1992 Victor Arwas

Published in 1992 by Harry N. Abrams, Incorporated, New York
A Times Mirror Company

The publisher and author are grateful to the artists and their agents who
have granted permission to use their work

For works by the following artists, copyright is as follows:
Rose Adler; Jacques Adnet; Gabriel Argy-Rousseau; Paul Bonet; Robert
Bonfils; Cassandre; Paul Colin; François Decorchemont; Robert Delaunay;
Jean-Gabriel Domergue; Michel Dufet; Foujita; René Kieffer; Kisling; Jean
Lambert-Rucki; Marie Laurencin; Emile Lenoble; André Lhote; Gustave Miklos;
François Pompon; Raymond Subes; Kees van Dongen © ADAGP, Paris and
DACS, London 1992.
Emile Aubry; André Bizette-Lindet; Demetre Chiparus; Le Corbusier; Raoul
Dufy; F-L Schmied and J Dunand; Jean Dunand; Jean Dupas; Georges de
Feure; Georges Fouquet; Jean Goulden; Louis Icart; René Lalique; Tamara de
Lempicka; Georges Lepape; Robert Mallet-Stevens; Georges Manzana-
Pissarro; Jan and Joël Martel; Chana Orloff; Jean Puiforcat; Armand Rateau;
Edouard Sandoz; Gérard Sandoz; François-Louis Schmied © DACS 1992.
Louis Süe/André Mare; Georges Cretté/F-L Schmied; René Kieffer/F-L
Schmied; Rose Adler/F-L Schmied © ADAGP/SPADEM, Paris and DACS,
London 1992.
Jacques Lipchitz © Jacques Lipchitz/DACS, London/VAGA, New York 1992.
Sonia Delaunay © ADAGP, Paris and DACS, London 1992.

Printed and bound in Singapore

CONTENTS

INTRODUCTION

The Exposition Universelle, held in Paris in 1900 to commemorate the arrival of the new century, is frequently referred to in post-World War II texts as having been the triumph of Art Nouveau. It was nothing of the kind. The architecture of the various pavilions and their internal design was regional and traditional, while their contents were so general that no single movement or tendency could hope to have any impact on the viewer. In the art section, exhibitions were designed to represent the whole of the previous century as well as the previous decade. In the decorative arts any impact the Art Nouveau designers might have had was diffused by rigid structuring of the exhibits by category, grouping glass, ceramics, metalwork, furniture, etc. Since many designers worked in more than one sphere, their works were dispersed throughout the various categories and exhibited along with a great deal of work in traditional or reproductive styles. Only the School of Nancy succeeded in showing itself as a coherent group, and that largely through the accidental occurrence of exhibiting in its own regional pavilion. Indeed, the

Above
JOHN KETTLEWELL: *A Modern Cleopatra.* Gouache and watercolour design for a fan, exhibited at the 1924 Paris Salon. (Private Collection, London)
Opposite
GERDAGO: *Exotic Dancer.* Carved ivory and polychrome cold-painted bronze on onyx base. (Private Collection, London)

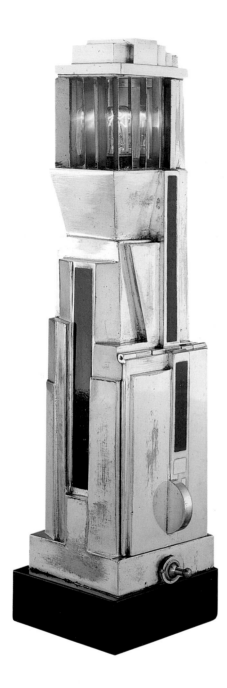

members of the School of Nancy, Gallé, Daum, Majorelle, Victor Prouvé, Vallin, Gruber, and many more, exhibited again as a group in Paris in 1903.

The Parisian designers felt the need for a loose grouping similar to that of the Nancy School which would enable them to exhibit together and, eventually, set up a new International Exhibition devoted entirely to contemporary decorative arts. In 1901 the Société des Artistes Décorateurs· (Society of Artist Decorators) was formed, grouping not only such established designers as Eugène Grasset, Hector Guimard and Eugène Gaillard, but also such younger ones as Emile Decoeur, Francis Jourdain, Maurice Dufrêne, Paul Follot and Pierre Chareau. Their intentions were to organise regular exhibitions, both in France and abroad, of decorative arts. The decorative arts had, indeed, recently been admitted to the two annual Salons, but their selection and placing was kept under the control of the painters, keeping the decorators in a subordinate position. The new society and its Salons was to promote the supremacy of the decorators. The Salons themselves were held in the Pavillon de Marsan of the Louvre, recently opened as the Musée des Arts Décoratifs by the Union Centrale.

In 1903 a further new grouping was organised under the presidency of Frantz Jourdain, and with the active help of Ivanhoë Rambosson, poet, critic and assistant director of the Petit Palais. This was the Salon d'Automne, which planned on excluding no innovation, no artistic movement, and intended to honour the independent artists who had hitherto been reviled by the various official Salons and other bodies as well as the more recognised artists. For their first Salon, held in the basement of the Petit Palais, they held a retrospective of the works of Paul Gauguin, who had recently died, while contemporary exhibits were shown under the headings of painting, drawing, watercolour, pastel, miniatures, sculpture, architecture and decorative arts. Various attempts were made to stop the Salon from opening its doors, but following its success the Municipal Council announced they could not return to the Petit Palais, while Carolus Duran, president of the Société Nationale des Beaux-Arts, announced that any of his members exhibiting at the Salon d'Automne would be promptly expelled.

A year of negotiations followed. Marcel, the new Director of the Beaux-Arts, offered the use of the Grand Palais for the Salon d'Automne. This venue, used by the two old established Salons, immediately enhanced the new Salon's prestige. Eugène Carrière, named Honorary President of the Salon d'Automne, threatened to resign from the Société Nationale des Beaux-Arts unless Carolus Duran withdrew his threat. The threat was duly withdrawn, and the Salon d'Automne was firmly established. Despite constant violent squabbling amongst its members, the Salon d'Automne succeeded in opening its doors to retrospectives of Cézanne, Puvis de Chavannes, Odilon Redon, Renoir, Toulouse-Lautrec, Manet, Ingres, Utamaro, Courbet, Carrière, Rodin, Seymour Haden, and many more, alternating the recently dead with the long-forgotten or those whose reputation had been allowed to lapse through lack of exposure. In 1904 they opened a photographic section, in 1905 a musical section, with recitals and concerts of contemporary and early music, and admitted books, bookbindings and posters. In 1906 Rodin and

Renoir were named as Honorary Presidents following the death of Carrière, and the Catalogue henceforth rejected the categorisation of entries to list all artists in alphabetical order to 'combat arbitrary and too long established discrimination between Art and those arts called minor.' The annual juries were drawn by lots, and the hanging and placing of the works given to a painter, a sculptor, an engraver, an architect and a decorator in successive years to avoid any one artistic section monopolising the best locations. No prizes were given.

'The exclusive presentation of painting, sculpture, graphics and architecture cannot nowadays give a true and complete picture of the aesthetics of an era,' wrote Frantz Jourdain in 1928 in his history of the Salon d'Automne. 'It is a fragment and not the totality of intellectual activity of a civilisation which condenses and nothing more. To grant hegemony to one art over others is to commit a grave and dangerous error.

'We did not believe in the necessity of arbitrary separations of what routine has come to call, without reason, the Major Arts and the Minor Arts, beauty placing talent in absolute equality however it manifests itself, whatever type it is. There are mediocre works and artists without value on the one hand, and masterpieces and individuals of genius on the other. That is the only rational classification one should accept. . . . We consequently resolved to return Decorative Art, inconsiderately treated as a Cinderella or a poor relation allowed to eat with the servants, to the important, almost preponderant place it occupied in the past, at all times and in all the countries of the globe.'

The intentions of the founders of the Société des Artistes Décorateurs had been to organise a new International Exhibition as soon as possible, but this was delayed by bickering amongst themselves as to its exact parameters, by lobbying various members of successive governments to accept the programme and sponsor it officially, and by preempting exhibitions held in Italy at Monza in 1909 and Turin in 1911 as well as the Brussels International Exhibition of 1910. The French Chamber of Deputies finally agreed in 1912 to hold the Exhibition in 1915, and set up an official committee to make the arrangements. Postponed to 1916, the outbreak of war in 1914 shelved the project indefinitely, but after the Armistice in 1918 it was resurrected as a way of restoring France's glory (and trading position) after the destruction suffered in the war. Announced for 1922, it was postponed to 1924 when it was realised that it would not be possible to set it up so soon because of great shortages still suffered after the war. The physical problems of construction eventually delayed the opening to 1925, a quarter of a century after the 1900 Exhibition, and its character was far removed indeed from that intended by the original planners.

One important factor remained constant. This was not to be a historical exhibition, celebrating the achievements of the past, but a forward-looking one, 'open to all manufacturers whose product is artistic in character and shows clearly modern tendencies.' The 'modern' theme was reiterated throughout, and the Exhibition Rules specified that admission would only be granted to works which fulfilled the criterion of being 'modern.' 'Whatever the reputation of the artist,

Above
JOSEF HOFFMANN: Cube table, ebonised wood and marble. (Collection Donald Karshan, Paris. Photo: Sully Jaulmes)
Opposite
MAURICE MARINOT: Internally decorated vase and bottle. (The Metropolitan Museum of Art, New York, Rogers Fund, 1970)

whatever the commercial strength of a manufacturer, neither will be allowed into the Exhibition if they submit works which do not fit the conditions outlined in the Exhibition programme.' And an Admissions Committee was set up to vet all works. As an International Exhibition, it was specifically intended to honour the Allies of the recent war, so the Soviet Union was invited even before its government was recognised by France. Germany was not invited. The other principal foe, Austria-Hungary, no longer existed, so the new republics of Austria and Hungary were invited. The United States, apparently terrified by the Exhibition's programme, declined, Herbert Hoover explaining that this was because there was no modern art in the United States. An official commission was, however, named by the U.S. Department of Commerce to observe and report on the Exhibition. Its Chairman was Charles R. Richards, Director of the American Association of Museums.

The Report, published in 1926, clearly stated that the United States had completely misjudged the French definition of modernism, and indicated that participation would at the very least have been an appropriate gesture of solidarity with a former ally. The misjudgement appears odd. As early as 1922 Edward C. Moore, Jr.—whose father was President of Tiffany and Co., and had accompanied Louis Comfort Tiffany to Paris during his seminal visits to earlier International Exhibitions—had set up a fund to enable the New York Metropolitan Museum of Art to buy 'as opportunity offers examples of the very finest quality of modern decorative arts of America and Europe.' Joseph Breck, curator of the Museum's Department of Decorative Arts, had been on buying trips to Paris in 1923 and 1924 before the opening of the Exhibition. The French definition of modernism was therefore hardly a closed book, even to those who never looked between the covers of the Decorative Arts periodicals.

It was, in fact, less of a definition than a conception, evolved over a number of years, partly in reaction to other styles and partly as a deliberate, conscious programme.

Art Nouveau, which achieved its finest creations in the last decade of the nineteenth century, only began to be popular when its creative impetus was on the decline. As many of its creators died during the first decade of the twentieth century, popularised versions of the style entered everyday life in various, often debased, forms. Art Nouveau floralism remained as a recognisable popular style throughout the 20s and 30s. The Arts and Crafts style hardly changed in England from the days of William Morris to the 20s and 30s, when the Arts and Crafts Society still flourished. Indeed, the 1924 British Empire Exhibition at Wembley and the British pavilion at the 1925 Paris Exhibition still held up the Arts and Crafts style as the paradigm of excellence in design. Scottish Art Nouveau, the rectilinear style of Charles Rennie Mackintosh, was honoured in Austria. Mackintosh exhibited at the Vienna Secession in 1900. Two years later Josef Hoffmann and Kolo Moser visited Britain for the first International 'Studio' Exhibition, stayed with Mackintosh in Glasgow, visited Charles Robert Ashbee's Guild of Handicrafts in Poplar in the East End of London, and returned to Vienna to found the Wiener

Above
ARMAND-ALBERT RATEAU: Green patinated bronze table with marble slab top, 1920-22.
(Musée des Arts Décoratifs, Paris)
Opposite
RAPHAEL DELORME: *La Robe verte.* Oil, c. 1930.
(Collection Barry Humphries, Sydney)

Werkstätte (Vienna Workshops) with the financial backing of Fritz Wärndorfer, a young banker and art collector. Inspired by the Guild Workshop system of training local craftsmen practised by Ashbee, the Wiener Werkstätte was set up as a series of well-equipped studios in which artist members of the Secession could learn and practice the various crafts in conjunction with specialised craftsmen or on their own, and in which all the various crafts could be coordinated. The dominant style in the first four years of the workshop was angular and geometric, inspired by Kolo Moser and Hoffmann. In 1906 Klimt led several of the more original artists away from the Secession, and the Wiener Werkstätte style changed to elaborate, fanciful decoration. During those first four years, however, Josef Hoffmann designed chairs, tables, lamps and flatware that are hardly distinguishable from some designed in the 20s. They are not precursors of Art Deco but full-blown Modernist works.

In 1907 the German architect Hermann Muthesius founded the Deutscher Werkbund in Munich in association with several other architects, including Henri van de Velde, Josef Hoffmann, Hans Poelzig and Richard Riemerschmid. Inspired to some degree by the theories of William Morris, the Werkbund was dedicated to improving industrial design and engineering construction by associating artists and artisans with industry. When Muthesius and his friends welcomed the machine as the only means of standardising design to enable mass-production of high quality goods and, in the process, developing its own machine aesthetic, Van de Velde broke with the group, arguing that such compromises forced the artist to abdicate his individual role in design.

Samuel Bing, founder of L'Art Nouveau, the gallery which displayed so many masterpieces of the style it gave its name to, died in 1905. His son Marcel, himself a fine Art Nouveau designer, ran the gallery until shortly before his death in 1920, but changed its character to display Persian, Greek and Egyptian antiquities. Bing's rival, Maison Moderne, founded in Paris in 1899 by Julius Meier-Graefe, a leading German art critic and editor of *Die Kunst* and *Pan*, lasted no longer. At least three of the Maison Moderne's leading young designers, Paul Follot, Maurice Dufrêne and Clément Mère, were to make new reputations as designers in the coming Art Deco style.

Art Nouveau had been violently attacked by the wholesale furniture manufacturers of the Faubourg Saint-Antoine, who saw in it a complex, highly crafted and dangerous rival to their own copies of older styles. Art Nouveau in furniture had been an attempt at re-creating style by returning to its roots in nature, and it sought to give organic shape and life to an essentially plain and inert material, wood, by treating it not as functional furniture, but as sculpture. As the originators abandoned the style, or died, the wholesalers absorbed some of the surface elements of Art Nouveau, and turned out a quantity of traditional furniture with Art Nouveauish decoration which rarely, if ever, matched the conception of the piece, but which satisfied public demand for such pieces over a number of years. French designers were totally disorientated for a while until the advent of a number of disparate occurrences were stylistically absorbed.

The liberation of colour came first, with the Fauvist exhibition at the 1905 Salon d'Automne. Four years later Diaghilev brought his Ballets Russes to Paris, and the astonishing costumes and striking colours devised by Bakst were quickly noted by critics and artists. At the 1910 Salon d'Automne Frantz Jourdain invited the Deutsche Werkbund to exhibit. Extremely well-made furniture, an adventurous use of materials and wood-stains, strong colours and coordinated style were a revelation to the Parisians, who were shocked into violent reaction. M. P. Verneuil, reviewing the exhibition in *Art et Décoration*, wrote: 'Germany seeks to create an art native to itself; but she also seeks to create an art that is contemporary, new, modern. Well, what do you see that is modern here? Actually, very little.' After a brief attack on the varied influences to be seen in the exhibits, he concluded 'can such an exhibition have any influence on French decorative art? I have no hesitation in saying no, and an absolute no. The Bavarian is certainly closer to us than the Prussian; he remains, nevertheless, Germanic. And our Latin taste can never receive any sort of sense of direction from Germanic taste. We may be able to derive some instruction from it, but never inspiration. It is a question of race. Heaviness, brutality in contrasts, too ostensible wealth, crudity of shading, can never appeal to our tastes which require suppleness, measure, grace and harmony. We can unreservedly admire the quality of workmanship, of perseverance and organisation; but we must indicate our reservations as soon as aesthetic matters come into play. . . . The men from Munich have their own qualities, the qualities of their race, we have ours. They will make a Bavarian art, which I hope will be very handsome; we, however, will make a French art.'

'This Bavarian exhibition at the Grand Palais,' wrote Frantz Jourdain in his *Le Salon d'Automne*, 'gave us a lesson in discipline which our individual and disorderly production needed; it presented the double advantage of proving the exaggeration of the dithyrambs emitted by certain overheated minds which affirmed the superiority of German taste over ours, by displaying the errors committed by our neighbours beyond the Rhine and, at the same time, stimulated our emulation by restoring our faith in ourselves, a faith which had been awkwardly shaken. It is, indeed, from that day onwards that the number of our interior designers, small until then, increased substantially, and our decorators accepted a unity of direction they had scarcely bothered with before.'

This French taste in furniture was expressed by a return to eighteenth- and early nineteenth-century styles, adapting them to contemporary modernity by stylisation. Indeed, style and stylisation were the distinguishing marks of Art Deco, which is another way of saying that surface treatment was the essence of the style, not a radical rethinking or reworking of the problems. Painting, tapestry and graphics were based partly on a return to classicism and the rotundities of Ingres, and partly on the absorption of the surface mannerisms of such avant garde movements as Cubism, Fauvism, Futurism and abstraction. It is thus easy to trace the origin of various aspects of the Art Deco movement without noticing how easily and smoothly the disparate aspects of the movement dovetail together. One reason for this ease and smoothness is the fact that the creators were artists, thought

Above, upper
CARTIER: Black onyx, agate and gold clock with 12 carved coral beads with rock crystal easel, the hands set with rose diamonds, centred with a ruby cabochon. (Courtesy Couturier-de Nicolay, Paris)
Above, lower
JEAN E. PUIFORCAT: Silver-plated clock, the central column and circular pastilles incorporating the hours in alabaster, c. 1930.

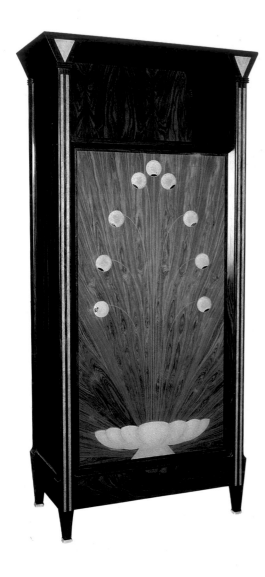

of themselves as artists, and responded as artists to their patrons; another reason was the exceptional open-mindedness and open-handedness of their patrons.

Few of the creators were craftsmen. Most had been trained as painters or sculptors, some as architects, and they conceived their designs as artists. They were, on the whole, anti-functional, constructing their creations primarily on aesthetic grounds. A chair, for instance, had to respond to their artistic demands. If, after execution, it was comfortable, well and good. If uncomfortable, this in no way detracted from its look. In the process 'sumptuous' became the keynote word for Art Deco conception. Rare figured woods were sought, rare and unusual materials such as ivory and mother-of-pearl were used for inlays, while shagreen or parchment was stretched over large surfaces. Though not craftsmen themselves, the designers employed the finest craftsmen to execute their conceptions. The craft tradition was then still strong, so there was no shortage of skilled and experienced craftsmen.

Some artisans emerged from the crafts. Some, like Clément Mère, a tabletier, adapted the techniques of their craft to the artistic demands of other disciplines. Others worked within the boundaries of their craft, but carried it beyond craft by subsuming the craft element to the artistic demands of their creativity. The result was, inevitably, totally anti-functional—porous ceramic vases through which water would spurt, glass vases of such slender forms that a single rose would topple them over, pâte-de-verre vessels in which water would ruin the inner surface, chests-of-drawers with two handles set so far apart no single person could reach both, the handles themselves often carved ivory rings connected to the drawer by silk cord, suitable only for the very occasional pull, and then only provided the drawer was empty. They were, in fact, not making vases, chests-of-drawers, chairs or desks, but art objects which adopted the surface appearance of such things. Etienne Cournault, a painter who frequently painted on mirror-glass, and built three-dimensional painted objects of no conceivable use, spoke for many in an interview reported in *Art et Décoration* in April 1931: 'I believe that an object which is useless has its own radiance, a high disinterested value. I believe in the useless, in the strange, in mystery.'

The great Parisian dress designers were among the first patrons of the Art Deco designers. Jacques Doucet was the doyen of the grands couturiers. In 1912 he abruptly sold his great collection of eighteenth-century furniture and art objects and commissioned Paul Iribe to design his new apartment, while he purchased modern paintings. Doucet's former protégé Paul Poiret had become one of the leading designers by 1910, having freed women from constricting corsets and a multiplicity of underclothes while simultaneously imprisoning them symbolically by inventing the hobble skirt. He continued the Oriental theme by introducing the feathered turban, inspired by an exhibition of Indian finery and works of art at the Victoria and Albert Museum in London. He employed Erté and José de Zamora to draw his fashions, and commissioned Paul Iribe in 1908 to design an album illustrating his style. This was so successful that he produced a further album in 1911 drawn by Georges Lepape. He was Raoul Dufy's first patron to

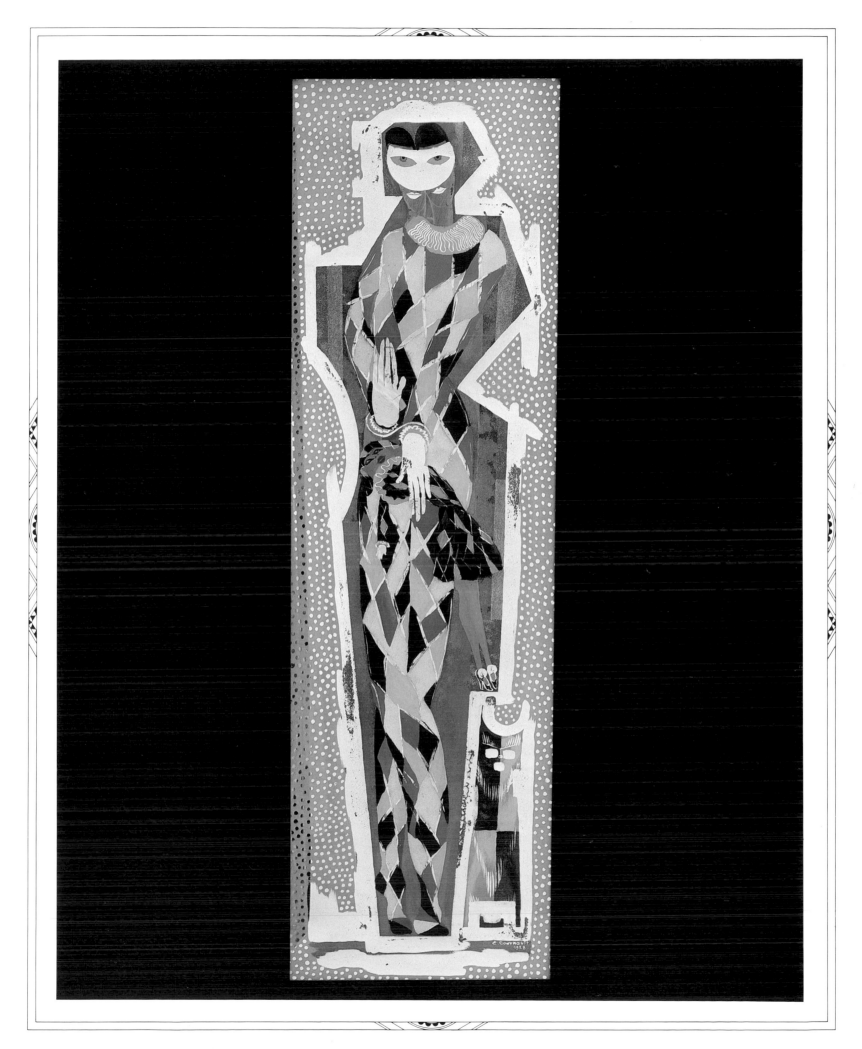

commission fabric designs, and set up the Martine School in 1912. Named after
one of his daughters, the Martine School was open to twelve-year-old local girls
who were taught the basic rudiments of drawing and painting, then taken on visits
to the countryside and the zoo and encouraged to draw and paint as naturally as
possible. Poiret chose the most striking of those often charming and naive products
and had them made up as fabrics. Some of these girls grew into fine designers in
their own right, and the Atelier Martine later produced furniture, complete interior
schemes and even perfume, named Rosine after another of Poiret's daughters.
Poiret himself collected paintings by Van Dongen, Dunoyer de Segonzac,
Modigliani, Matisse, Picasso and Utrillo, as well as sculpture by Brancusi.

Madeleine Vionnet, who created the bias cut, commissioned Jean Dunand to
decorate her house entirely in lacquered furniture, and her living room was dominated by a portrait in lacquer of her. Jeanne Lanvin had both her home and her
Salon decorated by Armand-Albert Rateau, who produced a range of bronze
lamps, tables, chairs, doors, gates, dressing tables and other items ranging from
living room to bathroom.

The most important commission of all was for Jacques Doucet's studio in
Neuilly, commissioned in 1928, when he was over seventy years old. Designed by
Ruan, the studio was furnished with unique pieces designed by Pierre Legrain,
Eileen Gray, Marcel Coard, André Groult, Rose Adler, Paul Iribe and others, and
was full of fine sculpture by Brancusi, Csacki and Miklos.

Parallel with the development of Art Deco, a ferment of other movements was
developing in Europe. In 1912 four young Czech artists formed the Prazske
Umelecke Dilny (Prague Art Workshop). These four, Pavel Jańak, Josef Chochol,
Vlatislav Hofman and Josef Gocár, had responded with enthusiasm to the Cubist
movement launched by Picasso and Braque, and had sought to translate it into
architecture. Though much of this effort was purely theoretical, they did essay a
degree of geometric design in some of the façades of buildings they designed, as
well as in a barrage that Jańak designed, but it was in the Cubist furniture
produced at the Prague Art Workshop that they expressed themselves most freely.
In an article published in 1911, 'Prism and Pyramid,' Pavel Jańak argued that only
the creator's artistic intention was to be taken into account, the technical and
functional aspects being of secondary importance. Rejecting the right angle, their
furniture was produced in split perspective, often on multiple planes, with pyramidal or crystalline shapes, frequently asymmetrical, though the designers had to
fight for their designs with the unfortunate craftsmen who had to carry them out.
'Form,' wrote Vlatislav Hofman, 'is final and superior to function.' A group of this
Cubist furniture was exhibited with the Deutscher Werkbund in Cologne in 1914.
Some of their designs were executed in ceramics and glass and produced at the
Artel Cooperative, but the outbreak of war in 1914 put an end to this venture,
and the architects never returned to Cubist ideas after the war. In the Netherlands
Theo van Doesburg founded the magazine *De Stijl* in 1917, based largely on Piet
Mondrian's theories of neo-plasticism. A group of painters, sculptors and archi-
tects soon joined under the same name to attempt a synthesis of all the arts,

including furniture, dance and theatre design. Several members designed curious, angular furniture, constructed of rigorously plain, plane wooden sections painted black, as in Felix Del Marle's pieces, or painted in strong primary colours, as in Gerrit Thomas Rietveld's Red/Blue armchair of 1918. Though Rietveld later abandoned colour, he retained the strict geometricism of shape, as in his Zig Zag chair of 1934. Though members of the De Stijl group remained relatively unknown in France, Eileen Gray's correspondence with Oud undoubtedly helped her to move away from Art Deco and towards Modernist work.

In England Roger Fry founded the Omega Workshops in 1913. Intended as a means of helping young artists to live by paying them a regular salary for carrying out decorative and design work three mornings a week, the venture was never financially viable, and was rent with fights and disagreements. During the year of its existence, however, the Workshops bought, or ordered, plain furniture which was then painted by various members, who also designed, and occasionally executed, fabrics, pottery, carpets, clothes, toys, handbags, fans and other objects. They essayed intarsia work, but lacked the technical ability to pursue it. Omega Workshops insisted on the anonymity of the individual work carried out by its artists, who included Roger Fry, Vanessa Bell, Duncan Grant, Edward Wadsworth, Henri Gaudier-Brzeska, William Roberts, Frederick Etchells and Wyndham Lewis. Bright in colour and loose in design, the products of the Omega Workshops were strongly influenced by Bakst's costumes for the Ballets Russes and the concepts of Cubism.

Henri van de Velde, who had been instrumental in developing Art Nouveau in Belgium and had worked for both Bing's L'Art Nouveau and La Maison Moderne rejected Art Nouveau early in the century, and developed a structural theory of functional form. He founded the Weimar School of Applied Arts in 1906, and joined Hermann Muthesius the following year in founding the Deutscher Werkbund. During the First World War he moved to Switzerland, later returning to Belgium. In 1919, following the end of the war, Walter Gropius founded the Bauhaus, a design school which absorbed Van de Velde's Weimar School. Each subject was taught by two teachers, an artist or theoretician, and a practical technician, and it was hoped to bring together all the arts and crafts under architecture's umbrella. The early influence of Johannes Itten, who created study programmes flavoured with mysticism, meditation, exercises, faddish diets and the wearing of robes and sandals was stopped in the 20s by the arrival of Theo van Doesburg, followed by László Moholy-Nagy. These rejected the romantic expressionism of the early years in favour of functional and rational design, simplification of structure to virtually abstract, geometric forms, and increasing dependence on machines for mass-production.

As early as 1907 Roger Marx had written that the new International Exhibition which was being planned—and which was to materialize in 1925—was to be the landmark which would 'signify the end of the contempt directed at the machine.' While the German avant garde movements were designing for the machine, the French Art Deco designers could not shake their fear and distrust of its product.

Above, upper
MAUBOUSSIN: Gold ring, c. 1930. (Author's Collection)
Above, lower
JEAN GOULDEN: Copper box decorated all over in champlevé enamel, 1925. (Galerie du Luxembourg, Paris. Photo: Sully Jaulmes)

Machinery itself was admired for its beauty and power, and many designers concurred with Marinetti's *Futurist Manifesto* when it proclaimed in 1909 that 'the splendour of the world has become enriched by a new beauty: the beauty of speed. A racing car with its bonnet wreathed with thick tubes like serpents with explosive breaths . . . is more beautiful than the Victory of Samothrace.' Almost the only supporters of design for machinery and new productions were some critics, who promptly proclaimed the failure of the 1925 Exhibition.

The Exposition des Arts Décoratifs et Industriels of 1925 consecrated the design work of those artists who had been developing their sumptuous style in the years since Josef Hoffmann had exhibited his designs. Les Arts Décos, as it was popularly abbreviated, gave its name to that style, and its parameters have largely been fixed not by what was necessarily exhibited there, but by the natural affinity of its creations as seen through the perspective of over half a century. Though many of its creations came from a variety of countries, it was essentially a French movement, developed in France and in response to the demands of primarily French patrons. A glance at the catalogues of the 1924 Wembley British Empire Exhibition or, even more surprisingly, at that of the 1925 International Exhibition of Decorative Arts of Monza, in Italy, will show how little the style had penetrated beyond the borders of France. The United States had developed a considerable body of creative designs in the geometrical style which was a component of Art Deco in the years before the First World War. Indeed, Frank Lloyd Wright had designed advanced lamps, leaded glass panels and furniture which would look modern fifty years later while the American authorities were claiming there was no 'modern' art or design in the country.

The 1925 Paris Exhibition was a uniquely effective showcase for the French designers, and most countries, participating or not, sent delegations which returned with reports, photographs and samples. A loan exhibition of items from the Exhibition toured American museums in 1926, starting at the New York Metropolitan. A year later Macy's department store organised an exhibition of Art Deco designers in conjunction with the Metropolitan, calling it 'Art in Trade.' The theme that this was modern design was so drummed that it became known in the United States as Art Moderne or, more simply, the Moderne. Yet even as it was being copied, it was being transformed to a uniquely American variation of the style. In 1929 the Metropolitan organised its own exhibition under the theme 'The Architect and the International Arts.' Under the general direction of Eliel Saarinen, eight architects each designed a complete room setting, using furniture and other components designed by them and executed by leading manufacturers. The architects, Raymond M. Hood, Ely Jacques Kahn, Joseph Urban, Ralph T. Walker, Eugene Schoen, John Welborn Root, Armistead Fitzhugh and Saarinen himself, attempted to reconcile Parisian Art Deco design with American requirements.

In France itself many leading Art Deco designers died or went out of business within a few years of the Exhibition. The smaller design firms continued to work in the Art Deco style, executing private commissions, but the larger ones found economic survival increasingly difficult in the International Depression years fol-

Above
ANDRE GROULT: Shagreen covered wood chair made for the Ambassador's wife's bedroom in the pavilion of the Société des Artistes Décorateurs at the 1925 Paris Exhibition. (Virginia Museum of Fine Arts, Gift of Sydney and Frances Lewis. Photo: Katherine Wetzel)
Opposite
SUE ET MARE: Carved ebony cabinet inlaid with mother-of-pearl, abalone and silver, 1927. (Virginia Museum of Fine Arts, Gift of the Sydney and Frances Lewis Foundation)

lowing the 1929 Stock Market crash in New York. The small group of artists who verbally rejected excess decoration and objected to ostentation confused this longing for elegant simplicity with the total rejection of decoration by Le Corbusier and his admirers, and formed a new organisation, the Union des Artistes Modernes, in 1930. Led by René Herbst, the UAM included Francis Jourdain, Hélène Henry, Robert Mallet-Stevens, Pierre Chareau, Raymond Templier, Djo-Bourgeois, Eileen Gray and Le Corbusier. Rejecting all ornamentation, they sought to use new materials, such as steel, chrome and painted metal tubes, and designed elements of furniture capable of mass-production. On the whole, however, while their simple geometrical lines and chunky shapes, allied with plain white walls created the decorative environment of the 30s, several of the artists remained attached to expensive materials, and the designs proved too individual for the industrialists of the day. As a result, some furniture by Eileen Gray and by Le Corbusier in collaboration with his cousin Pierre Jeanneret and Charlotte Perriand was not really produced in quantity until some thirty years later.

It is arguable whether there ever was an Art Deco architecture outside of the 1925 Exhibition pavilions. Robert Mallet-Stevens would be the one architect who can be said to have designed his houses within the movement, treating each house, or group of houses, as a geometrical sculpture incorporating cubes and circles, the sculptural conception extending to its interior, which he designed with friends. Pierre Chareau was more adventurous in his Maison de Verre built for Dr. and Mme Jean Dalsace in Paris between 1928 and 1931 in collaboration with Bijvoet, but was never again to have that much freedom in design. The Depression made it politic for the rich to keep a low profile, so adventurous commissions could only come from the state. The 1937 Paris International Exhibition was a fine excuse to erect monumental buildings, and the neo-classical was back in the ascendant. The rise of Fascism and Nazism brought an end to many avant garde experiments in art and education. The Vienna Secession closed its doors, the Bauhaus was closed down in 1933 and the Deutscher Werkbund disbanded. Their designers, artists and architects fled from Germany and Austria, mostly to England for a short stay in an artistically inhospitable environment, and eventually emigrated to the United States.

Neo-classical architecture in Germany under Albert Speer was dedicated to the glorification of the Third Reich. Germany's leading exiled designers combined with others of diverse origin in the United States to create the new American art, an amalgam of Art Deco, the Moderne and Modernism which was to emerge in the nation's skyscrapers, the marvellous Chrysler Building, its peak clad in aluminium, the Rockefeller Center and its crowning jewel, Donald Deskey's Radio City Music Hall. In 1934 the New York Metropolitan organised another loan exhibition of room settings, this time by nineteen designers. French Art Deco influence was almost non-existent, tubular steel and inexpensive materials dominating the designs. Modernism had arrived, and its dominance was celebrated in the 1939 New York World's Fair.

Above
PIERRE LEGRAIN: Bird cage on stand, lacquered wood, parchment, aluminium, c. 1920. (Virginia Museum of Fine Arts, The Sydney and Frances Lewis Endowment Fund)
Opposite, above
ELIEL SAARINEN: Dining room designed for the 1929 Metropolitan Museum exhibition, 'The Architect and the Industrial Arts'. (The Metropolitan Museum of Art, New York)
Opposite, below
JOSEPH URBAN: Man's Den, designed for the 1929 Metropolitan Museum exhibition, 'The Architect and the Industrial Arts'. (The Metropolitan Museum of Art, New York)

THE EXPOSITION DES ARTS DÉCORATIFS ET INDUSTRIELS, PARIS 1925

The location of the 1925 Exhibition was extensively debated, and a variety of sites mooted, including the Ile de Puteaux, Vincennes, the Porte Dauphine, the Zoo and even as far as Versailles. In the end, the centre of Paris was chosen. Here, it was felt, the advantages outweighed the obvious disadvantages of the comparatively small space available and the disruption to traffic. Choosing the centre of Paris meant easy access, a beautiful site and, best of all, the use of the Grand Palais, with its 33,000 square metres of display space. Charles Plumet was chosen as chief architect for the Exhibition, with Louis Bonnier in charge of landscaping.

Plumet and Bonnier devised an overall plan whose symmetry would have done Baron Haussmann credit. The principal gate, the Porte d'Honneur, situated alongside the Grand Palais, opened onto a straight vista across the Alexandre III Bridge, down the Esplanade to the great domed building off the Invalides. The cruciform layout of the grounds was created by the River Seine, which cut across the site, and enabled pavilions to be placed along both banks.

Everything was designed to dazzle the casual visitor. The grounds were land-scaped throughout, the spaces between the pavilions being turned into dozens of individual gardens, each with its own fountains, statues and plants, flowers and shrubs laid out by a different architect so that each would have a character of its own. Large areas of the site were devoted to fair-grounds, with a mixture of mechanical whirling transports and merry-go-rounds, stalls and tents offering everything from belly dancing to shooting galleries to toffee apples. A complete toy village was built to keep children entertained, while the more sophisticated adults were offered constantly changing programmes of plays, ballets and dance

Opposite
Monumental urns clad in figured ceramics, part of the Sèvres pavilion. (Contemporary photograph)

groups, choirs, singers and comedians from a dozen countries. Various galas, special parades, beauty contests, and frequent displays of fireworks were held. The Citroën company converted the Eiffel Tower into a huge publicity exercise. 200,000 light bulbs in six different colours were installed over the whole height of the tower on all four sides, and different illuminated patterns could be orchestrated from a keyboard. Nine phases were possible, showing an outline of the tower enclosing geometric arcs and circles, a shower of large stars, another of small ones, comets, animated signs of the Zodiac, dancing flames, shields with the dates 1889–1925 (1889 being the year of the Tower's inauguration), a shield containing the firm's double chevron trade mark, and finally the name CITROËN in enormous letters. Since the Tower can be seen from much of the city, and was certainly clearly visible from the Exhibition grounds, the publicity must have been sensational.

The Grand Palais, a somewhat unwieldy building with an elaborate façade in the monumental 1900 style and a curious interior metal armature, had been designed to cater for all types of exhibitions, from art to agriculture, paintings to cows. Ground and upper level were divided into two sections, one for the French, the other for foreign exhibitors, and various parts were given to different architects and designers to create appropriate settings, under the overall control of Charles Letrosne. Thus the architect Faunez with Armand-Albert Rateau as decorator designed a hall, tea room, covered garden, ballroom, dance hall, reception area and gallery in which to display different aspects of fashions. Raguenet and Maillard designed the perfumes section as a series of showcases radiating from the centre of an octagonal room, the cases crowned with a shimmering glass 'waterfall' by René Lalique. Every aspect of design was spotlighted with an appropriate exhibit, from the tabletterie, metal, glass and ceramics to musical instruments, scientific equipment, textiles, embroidery, jewellery, hairdressing, flowers, leatherwork and printing. Since the regulations did not allow display of raw materials, the section designers often used the most ingenious methods to bring these into exhibition, though few can have been as successful as Patout and Goumain who decorated the walls of the carpentry and furniture sections with an abstract composition made up of veneers of the most luxurious patterned and figured woods set between gilded pilasters. On the upper floor Alfred Agache and Maurice Neumont designed a complete street, the latest design in shop windows alternating with displays of posters. Stage designs were re-created, a small hundred-seat theatre was set up to show different stage and lighting effects, and examples of star dressing rooms were designed by Paul Poiret, Jeanne Lanvin and others. Photography and the cinema were also highlighted.

The huge monumental staircase which divided the building was the scene of an extraordinary gala on June 16th, 1925. Preceded by a banquet, a show was held on the staircase with over 2,000 participants. Members of the audience paid an enormous admission fee, and were seated on somewhat uncomfortable little gilded chairs set in the hallway at the foot of the stairs. Introduced by a fanfare from trumpeters in mediaeval costume, the opening 'Vision of the East' was danced by students and athletes. This was followed by a number from Loïe Fuller's

Above
ROBERT DELAUNEY: *La Tour Eiffel*. Oil, exhibited at the 1925 Paris Exhibition.
Opposite
Plan of the 1925 Exhibition grounds.

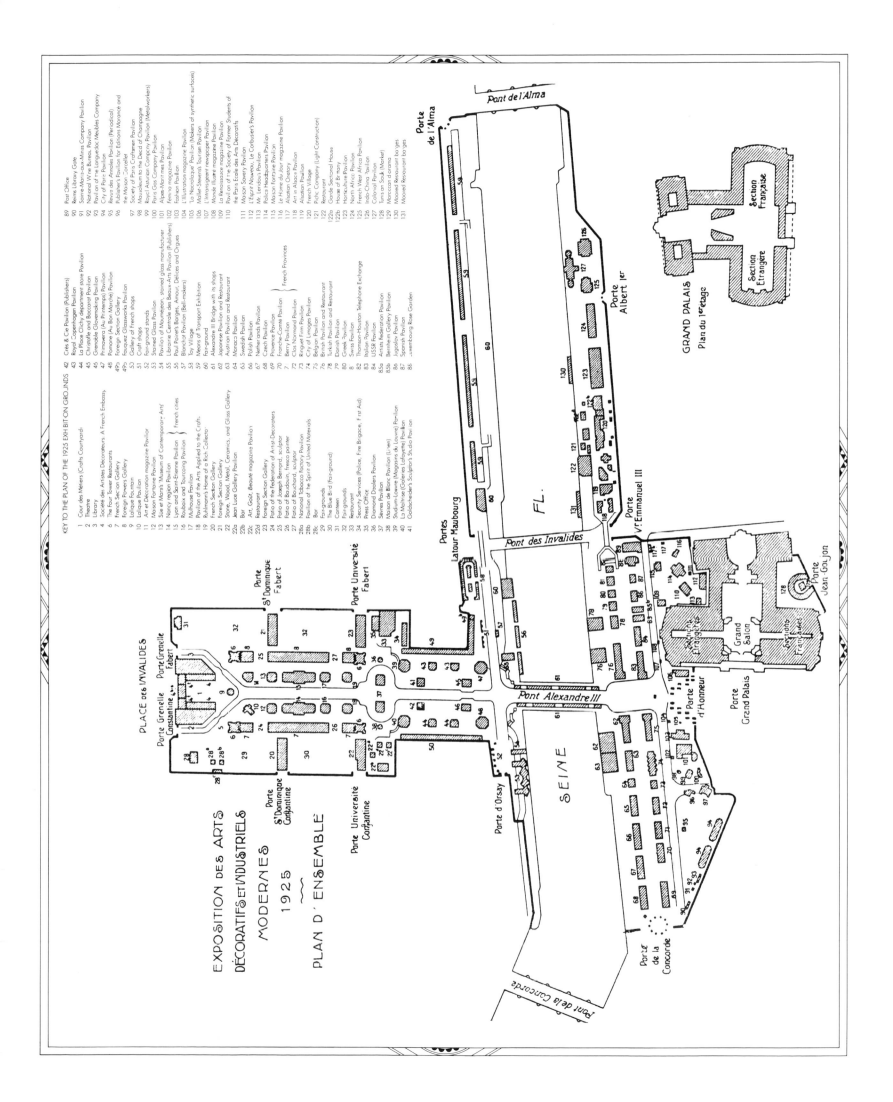

EXPOSITION DES ARTS
DÉCORATIFS ET INDUSTRIELS
MODERNES
1925

PLAN D'ENSEMBLE

GRAND PALAIS
Plan du 1er étage

Section Française
Section Étrangère

KEY TO THE PLAN OF THE 1925 EXHIBITION GROUNDS

1 Cour des Métiers (Crafts Courtyard)
2 Theatre
3 Library
4 Société des Artistes Décorateurs: A French Embassy
6 The Four Tower Restaurants
7 French Section Gallery
8 Foreign Powers Gallery
9 Lalique Fountain
10 Lalique Pavilion
11 Art et Décoration magazine Pavilion
12 Maison Fontaine Pavilion
13 Sèvres and Saint-Étienne Pavilion
14 Nancy region Pavilion
15 Lyon and Saint-Étienne Pavilion
16 Roubaix and Tourcoing Pavilion
17 Mulhouse Pavilion
18 Pavilion of the Arts Applied to the Crafts
19 Ruhlmann's Home of a Rich Collecto'
20 French Section Gallery
21 Foreign Section Gallery
22 Stone, Wood, Metal, Ceramics, and Glass Gallery
22a Jean Luce Gallery Pavilion
22b Bar
22c Art, Goût, Beauté magazine Pavilion
22d Restaurant
23 Foreign Section Gallery
24 Patio of the Federation of Artist-Decorators
25 Patio of Joseph Bernard, sculptor
26 Patio of Bouduoin, fresco painter
27 Patio of Bouchard, sculptor
28a National Tobacco Factory Pavilion
28b Pavilion of the Spirit of United Materials
28c Bar
29 Fair-grounds
30 The Blue Bird (Fair-ground)
31 Fair-grounds
32 Canteen
33 Fair-grounds
34 Security Services (Police, Fire Brigade, First Aid)
35 Press Office
36 Diamond Dealers Pavilion
37 Sèvres Pavilion
38 Maison de Blanc Pavilion (Linen)
39 Studium-Louvre (Magasins du Louvre) Pavilion
40 La Maîtrise (Galeries Lafayette) Pavilion
41 Goldscheider's Sculptor's Studio Pavilion

42 Cres & Cie Pavilion (Publishers)
43 Royal Copenhagen Pavilion
44 La Place Clichy department store Pavilion
45 Christofle and Baccarat Pavilion
46 Grenelle Glovemaking Pavilion
47 Primavera (Au Printemps) Pavilion
48 Pomone (Au Bon Marché) Pavilion
49a French Section Gallery
49b Foreign Section Gallery
50 Gallery of French shops
51 Craft shops
52 Fair-ground stands
53 Stained Glass Pavilion
54 Pavilion of Mourlejeon, stained glass manufacturer
55 Librairie Centrale des Beaux-Arts Pavilion (Publishers)
56 Paul Poiret's Barges, Amour, Délices and Orgues
57 Blanchot Pavilion (Bell-makers)
58 Toy Village
59 Means of Transport Exhibition
60 Fair-ground
61 Alexandre III Bridge with its shops
62 Japanese Pavilion and Restaurant
63 Austrian Pavilion and Restaurant
64 Monaco Pavilion
65 Swedish Pavilion
66 Polish Pavilion
67 Netherlands Pavilion
68 Czech Pavilion
69 Provence Pavilion
70 Franche-Comté Pavilion
7 Berry Pavilion
72 Clos Normand Pavilion
73 Ringuet Firm Pavilion
74 City of Limoges Pavilion
75 Belgian Pavilion
76 British Pavilion and Restaurant
78 Turkish Pavilion and Restaurant
79 Danish Pavilion
80 Greek Pavilion
8 Swiss Pavilion
82 Thomson-Houston Telephone Exchange
83 Italian Pavilion
84 USSR Pavilion
85a Artists Federation Pavilion
85b Bernheim Gallery Pavilion
86 Jugoslav Pavilion
87 Spanish Pavilion
88 Luxembourg Rose Garden

French Provinces

89 Post Office
90 Reims Library Gate
91 Soisne-Maris-aux-Mines Company Pavilion
92 National Wine Bureau Pavilion
93 Pavilion of the Languedoc Meubles Company
94 City of Paris Pavilion
95 Revue des Annales Pavilion (Periodical)
96 Publisher's Pavilion for Éditions Morance and the Maison Sorcelier
97 Society of Paris Craftsmen Pavilion
98 Mausoleum to the Dead of Champagne
99 Royal Asturian Company Pavilion (Metalworkers)
100 Paris Gas Company Pavilion
101 Alpes-Maritimes Pavilion
102 Femina magazine Pavilion
103 Fashion Pavilion
104 L'Illustration magazine Pavilion
105 La Nécrologique Pavilion (Makers of synthetic surfaces)
106 Molier-Stevens Tourism Pavilion
107 L'Intransigeant newspaper Pavilion
108 Monde Illustré magazine Pavilion
109 La Renaissance magazine Pavilion
110 Pavilion of the Society of Former Students of the Paris École des Arts Décoratifs
111 Maison Sauvrey Pavilion
112 L'Esprit Nouveau, Le Corbusier's Pavilion
113 Mr Leriduol Pavilion
114 Palacs Headquarters Pavilion
115 Maison Fontaine Pavilion
116 Le Home du Jour magazine Pavilion
117 Alsation Oratory
118 Art in Alsace Pavilion
119 Alsation Pavilion
120 French Village
121 Pichic Company (Light Construction)
122 Restaurant
122a Garde Sectional House
122b House of Brittany
123 Horticulture Pavilion
124 North Africc Pavilion
125 French West Africa Pavilion
126 Indo-China Pavilion
127 Colonial Pavilion
128 Tunis an Souk (Market)
129 Moroccan diorama
130 Moored Restaurant barges
131 Moored Restaurant barges

Opposite, top
Porte de la Concorde, designed by Pierre Patout.
The welcoming statue in the centre was by Déjean
on a plinth carved in bas-relief by Jöel and Jan
Martel. (Contemporary photograph)
Opposite, below, left
Porte d'Orsay, designed by Louis Boileau.
Watercolour.
Opposite, below, right
Porte d'Orsay, the Exhibition side of the gate with
a large painted panel by Louis Voguet.
(Contemporary photograph)
Overleaf, left
Tourism pavilion, watercolour by Robert Mallet-
Stevens (106). (Musée des Arts Décoratifs, Paris)
Overleaf, right, above
The Belgian pavilion (75) designed by Victor
Horta and the Japanese pavilion (62) designed
by Shichigor Yamada and Iwakichi Miyamoto.
The Porte d'Honneur is on the extreme left.
(Contemporary photograph)
Overleaf, right, below
The Alexandre III Bridge with its shopping mall
designed by Maurice Dufrêne (61). The house-
boats were restaurants. The buildings immediately
behind them are the Turkish pavilion and its
restaurant, The Golden Horn (78).
(Contemporary photograph)

students, 'swimming' through a turbulent sea made up of an enormous gauze veil. Loïe Fuller herself danced, a personal triumph since she had been the sensation of the 1900 Exhibition. She was also the only American contribution to the 1925 Exhibition—apart, of course, from American jazz and popular music. Thirty mannequins modelled ermine coats with endless trains held by an army of page boys—when they reached the foot of the stairs, the entire staircase was covered by a solid sea of ermine. A number of tableaux followed. Each colour of 'The Rainbow' was made up of leading mannequins from each of the main haute couture houses, while other tableaux included Napoleon's 'grande armée' and a symbolic representation of the perfumes. The 'Cortège de le Parure' (Ornamental Cortege) was led by Mistinguett in very short dress, very tall headdress and long, long train, sparkling as 'The Solitaire Diamond,' while the whole troupe of the Casino de Paris appeared as gemstones and ribbons in costumes designed by Jean le Seyeux. Eva Le Galienne and her company interpreted Joan of Arc; Ida Rubinstein, clad as the Golden Archangel in the costume designed by Bakst, danced the Martyrdom of Saint Sebastian; the Paris Opéra company sang a potted version of 'Esther'; the entire company of the Comédie Française appeared and gave brief, largely mimed versions of all of Molière's plays in appropriate costume; a Spanish caprice involved hundreds of dancers with flashing teeth, liquid black eyes, waving mantillas, snapping castanets and singing by all twenty-four exponents of the role of Escamillo in Bizet's 'Carmen' from the Paris Opéra, Opéra Comique and Gaité-Lyrique theatres; a comic interlude contained all the clowns from all the circuses in and around Paris; the Hoffman girls from the Moulin Rouge were followed by the sixty 'Tiller Girls' from the Folies Bergère; the parade of 'The Queens of Theatre' consisted of sixty of the best-known actresses of the day modelling clothes by all the leading fashion houses, accompanied by as many leading actors in full evening dress. The finale was the 'Ballet of Ballets,' danced by 300 members of the corps de ballet of all the Paris companies in white tutus. It was early morning when the show ended.

Excluding the two entrances into the Grand Palais, there were thirteen gateways into the Exhibition grounds. The Porte d'Honneur was, of course, devised as the principal entrance. Designed by Henry Favier and A. Ventre, it was made up of four pairs of fluted columns on each side of the access road, each column topped by a conventionalised fountain. Each pair of columns was staggered back and connected to the next gate by a decorative openwork grille by Edgar Brandt which continued the conventionalised fountain motif. Lack of funds meant that the wrought-iron was replaced throughout by a cheap alloy, and all the metalwork was given an aluminium finish. The staggered entrances meant that six separate lines of access were available at all times, with no need for extensive queuing. The final pair of columns framed the wide access road, which was barred by a very low grille which did not interfere with the view straight down to the far end of the exhibition grounds, the horizon topped by the great dome of the Invalides. This central grille served as exit.

The second most important gateway was that at the Place de la Concorde. Pierre Patout designed a monumental ensemble, a set of eight massive flat col-

umns which framed the trees of the Cours-la-Reine. Indeed, hardly a single tree on the exhibition site was cut down. In the very centre of, and facing, the square a statue by Déjean of a welcoming woman with open arms was placed on a massive plinth with a low relief carving by Joël and Jan Martel. The effect was somewhat that of a ship's figurehead. In between the columns, potted trees and shrubs maintained the continuity of green, and the entrances were placed on either side of the Cubist menhir. At night the gate came alive: the upper sections of the columns were illuminated and appeared to float in mid-air, while the circular column-tops glowed like futuristic flying saucers. Of the other, lesser, gates, the Porte d'Orsay, designed by Louis Boileau, and treated as a huge, glorified poster, was the most interesting.

Just inside the Porte d'Honneur was the Pavillon du Tourisme, an information centre with baking facilities and ticket agency. Designed by Robert Mallet-Stevens, it was one of the handsomest buildings on the site, its cruciform landmark tower visible from most of the grounds, crowned by a plain-faced clock. The interior formed one long room with an extended counter, daylight streaming in through a continuous leaded glass window by Louis Barillet depicting an Impressionist-Cubist landscape as seen from a car travelling at 120 kilometres per hour. The four sites flanking the central road between the gate and the bridge were assigned to Italy, Great Britain, Belgium and Japan. The Japanese pavilion was picturesque; the Italian, clearly wishing to remind one of the glories of Ancient Rome, was a white mausoleum; the British was an ugly amalgam of disparate features; only the Belgian, designed by Victor Horta, showed any originality. With the plainest materials, a wood beam skeleton, plaster cladding and reinforced concrete, Horta designed a massive, impressive construction in which each of the show-rooms was enclosed with ceilings at different levels to match and frame the heights of the surrounding trees. A continuous frieze worked its way around the front section, unusual in that it was not applied to the façade, but was part of its construction, the spaces between the figures forming openings through which light dappled into the building.

The Alexandre III Bridge, built at the time of the 1900 Universal Exhibition, had its fin de siècle flavour concealed by an ingenious construction which turned it into a shopping precinct, a modern Rialto bridge for this Venice-on-the-Seine, designed by Maurice Dufrêne. Within this design each shop was fitted individually. Sonia Delaunay had her shop there, designed by Gabriel Guévrékian, and displayed a full range of her designs, fabrics, screens and clothes executed by her, furs by Jacques Heim and leatherwork by Gilbert Girau. An ingenious set of fountains was placed below the bridge. When the fountains were switched on, the bridge appeared to float above a whirling cataract of water tumbling down to the Seine, while coloured lights played across and within the sheets of water. A nautical festival was held there on June 1st, with a procession of boats disguised as butterflies, dragonflies and flowers, while a barge was set up as a floating theatre. As the Alexandre III Bridge cascades were illuminated in amethyst and gold, other fountains set up in the middle of the Seine shot up in the air, the water's surface appeared to burst into flames with low level fireworks, while an

Opposite, above
Pavilion of a Rich Collector (Ruhlmann Group), designed by Pierre Patout. The gate was by Edgar Brandt and the sculpture above the doorway by Temporal (19). (Contemporary photograph)
Opposite, below
Rear view of the Ruhlmann pavilion. The bas-relief was by Joseph Bernard, the frescoes painted by Henri Marret and the stone sculpture by Jules Jeanniot. (Contemporary photograph)

Above
The Sonia Delaunay Simultané Shop by Gabriel Guévrekian, one of the shops on the Alexandre III Bridge. (Contemporary photograph: Sonia Delaunay Archives)

Right
Two women wearing Sonia Delaunay dresses standing by one of J. and J. Martel's concrete Cubist trees in the garden designed by Robert Mallet-Stevens within the Esplanade des Invalides (1). (Contemporary photograph: Sonia Delaunay Archives)

Left
Two of Jacques Heim's models wearing Sonia Delaunay clothes, with a car painted in a Sonia Delaunay design. In the background is the Turkish pavilion. (Contemporary photograph: Sonia Delaunay Archives)

Above
La Maitrise, pavilion of the Galeries Lafayette,
designed by J. Hiriart, G. Tribout and G. Beau
(40). (Contemporary photograph)
Right
Interior view of the La Maitrise pavilion, designed
by its artistic director, Maurice Dufrêne. The
wrought-iron work was by Schwartz-Hautmont.
(Contemporary photograph)

extraordinary display of pyrotechnics lit up the sky, as searchlights lit up the banks of the river.

Once past the bridge, a long avenue led to the Invalides. All the buildings here were French. Their positioning, a symmetrical and grandiose design, did not work out in practise because there was no coordination between the various pavilion architects. While the sites were scrupulously observed, the differing scale of the buildings created a fascinating hodge-podge of styles. The first section was designed so that the pavilions of the design studios of the four great Parisian department stores, the Louvre, Galeries Lafayette, Au Printemps and Au Bon Marché, each placed at one corner of the site, would frame it by equilibrating their masses. The differing designs of these buildings, however, did not really fulfil their architectonic placing. Each formed a perfect example of Art Deco design; grandiose, with a multiplicity of planes and angles, decorated flat surfaces, new materials, but always in decorative patterns, and with the use of such traditional decorative devices as leaded glass panels, low relief stone panels, sculpture and wrought-iron, all in the new stylisation.

The Pavillon de la Maitrise (Galeries Lafayette), designed by Joseph Hiriart, Georges Tribout and Georges Beau, had won first prize in a contest organised by the store. Its main entrance, up a flight of steps, was dominated by an enormous leaded glass panel of a sunburst by Jacques Gruber; its four framing columns were topped by emblematic statues by Léon Leyritz representing fur, feather, ribbon and lace. Maurice Dufrêne, director of La Maitrise, had joined the three other architects in designing the interior, which housed a main exhibition hall, lady's bedroom, man's bedroom, dining room, library, and a small living room. On the upper floor two tea rooms framed a series of showcases. The Bon Marché's Pomone pavilion, designed by Louis Boileau, also had its principal entrance surmounted by a vast leaded glass panel, but the general effect was made less grandiose. The interior, designed by Pomone's director, Paul Follot, comprised an entrance hall, dining room, study, smoking room and lady's boudoir on the ground floor and two bedrooms on the upper floor. The Printemps Primavera pavilion, designed by Sauvage and Vybo, consisted of a low circular outer wall topped by a reversed funnel-shaped dome covered in pre-formed pierced ceramic cladding set with glass lenses by Lalique, the gigantic entrance flanked by two massive pillars topped by plants. Indeed, plants were used throughout this building, with colourful flowerheads surrounding the structure at ground level and at the level of the base of the dome. The Studium-Louvre pavilion, designed by A. Laprade, was a more conventional octagonal structure, whose popularity was largely due to the first floor flower-decked terrace which enriched the building, and for which Laprade had designed massive carved stone urns topped with carved stylised flowers.

Even more gigantic urns were to be found in the central area given to the Manufacture Nationale de Sèvres. Here the architects Pierre Patout and Ventre, not wishing to break the perspective down the central avenue, had designed two matching pavilions joined by a virtually non-floral stone and terrazzo garden with a central fountain. Regional pavilions as well as the pavilions attributed to Foreign

Above
Primavera, pavilion of the Grands Magasins du Printemps, designed by Sauvage and Vybo (47). (Contemporary photograph)

Left
Façade of one of the twin pavilions of the Manufacture de Sèvres, designed by Pierre Patout and André Ventre (37). (Contemporary photograph)

Below
Dining room setting in the Sèvres pavilion designed by René Lalique, who also supplied the illuminated boxed ceiling, the table in palisander and glass and the glass tableware. The forest design was incised into the marble-clad walls. (Contemporary photograph)

Opposite, above
Studium-Louvre, pavilion of the Grands Magasins du Louvre, designed by A. Laprade (39). (Contemporary photograph)

Opposite, below
The Lalique fountain. Behind it is the entrance to the Crafts Court (9). (Contemporary photograph)

Powers, flanked by large areas devoted to amusement parks, led to the Crafts Courtyard. Designed by Charles Plumet as a Roman atrium, it had a central fountain by Pierre Poisson and vast mounted oil paintings lining the outside walls like frescoes, leading to a series of exhibition rooms.

The Société des Artistes Décorateurs had been largely instrumental in promoting the setting up of the Exhibition. As its name indicated, the Exposition des Arts Décoratifs et Industriels was expected to highlight both the decorative and the industrial arts. In the latter case, it had somehow been assumed that artist and manufacturer were going to get together in the months leading to the opening and would produce a number of joint ventures. Hardly anything of the kind took place. Manufacturers showed little interest in such expensive projects of dubious financial promise, while most artists reacted with extreme suspicion to any overtures from industrialists. A number of members of the Société were, of course, already engaged on projects of their own or had been commissioned to produce schemes, but no collective project existed which could bring together all the members as a group, and the funds for such a project were not available.

The Société eventually appealed to Paul Léon, Director of the Beaux-Arts, who was also assistant Commissioner General for the Exhibition. The Chambers of Deputies and Senators had voted some credits to the Beaux-Arts to subsidize various Art School and other participants to the Exhibition. Léon promised the Société a million francs. While the sum appeared sizable at first, it was soon realised that if the Société were to build a pavilion of its own there would be no money left over to furnish and decorate it. The Société's three vice-presidents, Charles Hairon, Henri Rapin and Maurice Dufrêne returned to Paul Léon. Charles Plumet, who was in Léon's office at the time, happened to mention that part of the exhibition rooms around the Crafts Courtyard had not yet been allocated. Henri Rapin suggested that the Société would be prepared to submit a project in accordance with the Exhibition's programme: a completely furnished and equipped prototype for a French Embassy. The quasi-official character of the project brought an immediate offer of two wings of the Crafts Court, and it was agreed that the subsidy would be used to decorate and furnish them. Any items not previously sold would become the property of the state. To avoid any internecine fighting, every artist decorator, both members and non-members of the Société, was invited to submit detailed projects for the twenty-four rooms, vestibules and passage ways. Each participant was entitled to vote on all projects and each had two votes, one of which he was entitled to cast for his own. Each designer then had to choose collaborators to supply all the other items of decoration necessary for each theme, pictures, glass, sculpture or pottery, rugs, wallpapers, fabrics and light fittings. One wing was devoted to the official side of the Embassy, with various reception rooms, the other to the private side, with bedrooms for the Ambassador, his wife and his child, a bathroom, a gymnasium and a music room. Both wings had a study-library, dining rooms and smoking rooms. A list of the architects, designers, ceramists, glassworkers, metalworkers, tabletiers, painters, sculptors, silversmiths and lacquerers who participated in this project is an almost complete list of Art Deco designers with a mild sprinkling of traditionalists

Opposite, above
The Cours des Métiers (Crafts Court) designed by Charles Plumet. The fountain in the centre had bas-relief carvings by Pierre Poisson, while the vases were by Jean Dunand. The exhibition space behind the large paintings was used by the Société des Artistes Décorateurs (4). Above is the Bordeaux Tower (6) which housed a restaurant. (Contemporary photograph)

Opposite, below
One of Paul Poiret's barges, decorated by his Atelier Martine, being towed to its mooring beyond the Alexandre III Bridge. The scaffolding used in the erection of the shopping arcade is still up. Paul Poiret himself is standing on the bridge wearing a white suit. (Contemporary photograph: Hugues Autexier and François Braunschweig Collection, Paris)

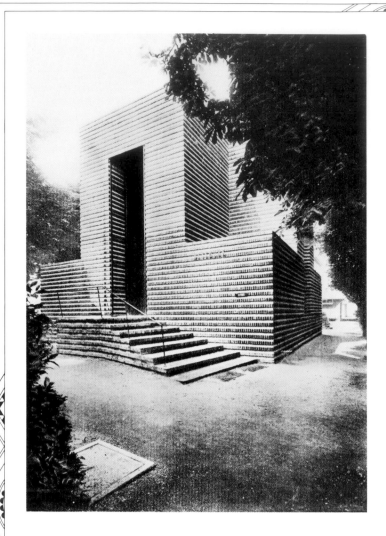

PAYS-BAS

who had made their name in the Art Nouveau movement and changed with fashion.

The transverse axis of the exhibition grounds was created by the Seine itself, with most of the foreign pavilions lining its banks and floating restaurants and other barges moored at intervals. Many of the foreign pavilions went for the picturesque and evocative. Some few proved original. Kay Fisker's Danish pavilion was an uncompromising and impressive creation. Basing his ground plan on the Danneborg Cross, Fisker designed a plain, sober building made up of alternating rows of red and white bricks, giving shape to the whole without extraneous decorations or accretions, the entrance being merely a tall gap. J. F. Stael's Dutch pavilion, with its low brick walls, undecorated save for the openings of boxed, satin-surfaced glass, was given an Oriental flavour by an enormous roof, softly curving sides ending with a gentle upward curve, the roof resting lightly on the walls because the load was carried by concealed internal columns. The self-contained effect was emphasised by a continuous very low brick wall surrounding the structure which enclosed a flowerbed; yet the whole was given an attractive welcoming feel by having its access flanked by two extended brick-enclosed pools leading to the one touch of whimsy, a doorway whose straight lines broke into curves topped by flattened circular sections. The Czech pavilion, designed by J. Gocár, was a fairly plain building made dramatic by its angular façade, shaped like the prow of a vessel; hills of shaped concrete partly covered by large slabs of red glass. On top of the building a statue of *Genius* by Jan Stursa extended the structure's height, while at the base a large low relief panel of a heraldic lion diminished it.

Certainly the most unusual of the foreign pavilions was that designed by Melnikov for the USSR. A plain timber framework, painted red and white, enclosed a rectangular exhibition area whose entire façade consisted of plate glass. To the side of this, the entrance opened onto a staircase which led up to the first floor, then down again on the other side, the staircase bisecting the display area on a diagonal, forming two triangles. The staircase, open to the sky, was surmounted by alternate panels forming decorative X shapes which gave some protection from sun and rain. Dominating the pavilion was a wooden tower with plain upright beams interconnected on inclined planes, above which waved the flag of the USSR. Though simplified in form, this structure was clearly related to Tatlin's various towers, either built or projected.

Among the more interesting of the French pavilions was that of the Diamond Dealers, designed by Lambert, Sacké and Bailly in a style very similar to that of Bruno Taut's revolutionary Glass House, built for the first Deutscher Werkbund Exhibition held in Cologne in 1914. Taut's prismatic dome was, however, replaced by one inspired by a cushion-cut diamond, while glazed panels framed and decorated Y-shaped panels which took the place of glass bricks. Another curious building was the pavilion built for the publishers Crès & Cie by Joseph Hiriart, Georges Tribout and Georges Beau, in which the façade consisted of the representation of three partly opened books, spine outwards, connected to each other by two entrances with decorative wrought-iron gates by Schwartz-Hautmont. The inside, designed by Francis Jourdain, included decorative panels by the painter Maurice Asselin, a leaded glass window by Jacques Gruber, tapestries and hangings by Mme Pangon, and sculpture by Yvonne Serruys.

Scandals were never too far from the Exhibition. A theatre was to be built on the Esplanade of the Invalides to house plays, mimes, puppet shows, ballets, modern dance, folk groups, symphony orchestras and chamber music groups from some thirty countries. The architects, Auguste and Gustave Perret and André Granet, designed a functional, multi-purpose theatre, with all seats racked for the best possible sight-lines. Its special and distinctive feature was a triple stage designed by Auguste Perret. Within the proscenium arch framed by four columns, a central stage was flanked by two further stages, placed at angles to the central one. This gave maximum flexibility both in positioning the actors and in rapid changes of scenery. The Belgian architect Henri van de Velde, who had earlier attacked Perret's design for the Champs-Elysée Theatre, stating this was copied from his own design, published a pamphlet accusing Auguste Perret of plagiarism in his triple stage design. Van de Velde was to receive no more satisfaction in this accusation than in the earlier one: a long investigation of the antecedents of triple stage designs by Ivanhoë Rambosson in *Comoedia* was to clear Perret of the charge of plagiarism. Perret himself, interviewed in the magazine *L'Amour de l'Art*, having briefly surveyed the history of multiple stages in various countries, rejected Van de Velde's claim for his theatre at Cologne in 1914: 'Does he think he designed a triple stage at Cologne? All we see there is a single stage divided into three by false mobile columns—It's a stage setting! Mobile columns! Hollow!... and with a prompter inside!!!! Does the Weimar aesthetician, using such means, pretend to ARCHITECTURE!'

A major scandal broke over the *L'Esprit Nouveau* pavilion. Le Corbusier and Amédée Ozenfant had launched their 'Purist' movement in 1918 as a rationalisation of Cubism, their aim being 'the purging of the plastic vocabulary by sweeping out parasite words.' Two years later they launched the magazine *L'Esprit Nouveau* (The New Spirit) as a vehicle for this idea. Le Corbusier wrote: 'A house is a machine for living in.' He did not trouble to hide his contempt for decorative art. 'Decorative art' he wrote, 'as opposed to the machine phenomenon is the final twitch of the old manual modes; a dying thing. My conception was thus to show something conceived for the machine, thus conceived for mass-production. The house is a cell within the body of a city. The cell is made up of vital elements which are the mechanics of a house. These elements can each in turn be a purely original cell, viable, human, useful to each and every one: standardised. Decorative art is anti-standardisational. Our pavilion will contain only standard things created by industry in factories and mass-produced; objects truly of the style of today. Works of art of high emotive potential will be paintings and sculptures by those contemporary artists who have so brutally, though so magnificently innovated the art of our era. The cell which is a home remains similar in its essential function whether it is located in a city or the suburbs, whether it is rented within a

block of flats or a cottage in a garden-city. My pavilion will therefore be a cell extracted from a huge apartment building. . . . And this same pavilion, used to demonstrate big city habitat, will be sold and planted in the suburbs as a villa.'

Le Corbusier and his cousin, Pierre Jeanneret, elaborated a complex programme involving their projected pavilion and a new urbanisation project based on the proposition that the car had destroyed the concept of the big city. 'The "street" is only a mummified grimace faced with the phenomenon of the car. The city is no more than an anachronism menacing our physical and moral health.' In January 1924 they applied to the Exhibition organisers for the allocation of a plot, and revealed their programme to the Chief Architect. Charles Plumet and Louis Bonnier were horrified, and they attempted to persuade Le Corbusier and Jeanneret to modify their plans. The Ruhlmann group was building the pavilion of a rich collector. Süe et Mare's Compagnie des Arts Français was building a Museum of Contemporary Art. Why should L'Esprit Nouveau not build the home of an architect? Le Corbusier refused. 'Why of an architect?' he wrote. 'My house is everybody's, anybody's; it is the house of a polite man, living nowadays.'

Their programme was withdrawn, and Le Corbusier made vague promises calculated to placate the organisers, submitted no plans, answered no queries. He had been allocated a fairly large plot tucked away between two wings of the Grand Palais. Le Corbusier complained that its location made the pavilion impossible to see from a distance, and also complained about the poor landscaping in his area. The building itself, a solid construction of concrete, steel and glass, was only begun in April 1925, and was the last to be erected on the exhibition grounds. 'L'Esprit Nouveau is a magazine with no assets,' wrote Le Corbusier, 'but its pavilion is fifty times bigger than those of either L'Illustration or L'Intransigeant.'

Trees on the exhibition grounds could not be cut down. Le Corbusier built his pavilion around one tree, which grew in a courtyard area between two wings of his house, and emerged through a circular opening in the roof. The interior was stark, with plain white walls on which hung a few Cubist pictures. The split level areas were furnished only with commercially available mass-produced furniture, which was, as it happened, both dull and cumbersome. The building itself, however, was a handsome construction, light, airy and reasonably practical to live in. The officials were furious, and ordered a fence to be erected around the pavilion to conceal it. 'The controversy was painful,' wrote Le Corbusier. 'A conflict of generations. On the other side, they still believe in craftsmanship, in regionalist industries, etc.' In the end, the Fine Arts Ministry had to intervene and order the removal of the fence.

Le Corbusier was to have the last word. At the height of the Exhibition he wrote: 'Right now one thing is sure: 1925 marks the decisive turning point in the quarrel between the old and the new. After 1925, the antique lovers will have virtually ended their lives, and productive industrial effort will be based on the "new." Progress is achieved through experimentation: the decision will be awarded on the field of battle of the "new."'

Opposite, above
The Triple Stage in the Exhibition Theatre designed by A. and G. Perret and A. Granet (2). (Contemporary photograph)
Opposite, below
L'Esprit Nouveau pavilion, designed by Le Corbusier. (Contemporary photograph)

FURNITURE

Avant garde French furniture was, in 1910, still mainly in the modified Art Nouveau style, with Louis Majorelle, Mathieu Gallerey, Léon Jallot, Pierre Selmersheim, Tony Selmersheim, Charles Plumet and Théodore Lambert gradually simplifying their designs, reducing carving to small reserves and increasing the angularity of shape, a tendency which had also been followed by Henri Bellery-Desfontaines until his death in 1909. The mass of available furniture from industrial sources consisted almost exclusively of copies from the antique. A group of members of the Société des Artistes Décorateurs issued a ringing *Manifesto* in the spring of 1910, insisting that there was in existence an artistic movement that was both modern and French, yet there were only four stores in Paris selling modern French furniture as against over twenty selling imported modern furniture. Industrialists should not, therefore, hesitate to interest their customers in the current movement, as foreign competition was becoming increasingly fierce. The art of furniture and the furniture trade, long a source of revenue and prosperity for France, would otherwise find world markets definitely shut to them. This warning was brought home even more actively by the arrival of the Deutscher Werkbund exhibition at that year's Salon of the self-same society.

The French entries at that Salon included two attempts at design removed from the modified Art Nouveau of Majorelle, Jallot and Gallerey or the full-blown Art Nouveau of such members of the Ecole de Nancy as Eugène Vallin. André Groult had taken a stand in which to display his carpet and wallpaper designs and had asked his friend André Mare to design the furniture, though he did not credit him. On another stand the architect Louis Süe had joined with Paul Huillard to exhibit a dining room and a small salon. Maurice Pillard Verneuil, reviewing the Salon d'Automne for *Art et Décoration*, wrote of the first stand: 'M. André Groult proves, in his little salon, that he has a great deal of taste, that is certain. Its style is a little countrified, amusing and curious. But I regret its too obvious imitation of style. I do not deny the possible charm of such re-creations, but this is not their place, where only new efforts should be admitted and shown to the public. I would therefore only mention a fine circular carpet, in which a garland of red roses runs between baskets. Its harmony, in blues and purples, is excellent.' He was less kind to Süe and Huillard's entries: 'These are interiors for snobs, and snobs absolutely devoid of taste. What can one say about this little green and currant salon; with its ugly, heavy and ungraceful furniture; what can one say of this dining room with its absolutely blue walls, chimney with ultramarine tiles, red divan, pretentious sideboard, ridiculous table and chairs in which any research into proportions is excluded!'

A year later André Mare took two stands in his own name, designed the

furniture, and invited some of his friends to take part. Roger de la Fresnaye designed a chimney and overmantel mirror, Richard Desvallières, who was to become a leading wrought-iron designer after the war, supplied the andirons, his first exhibited work, Jacques Villon decorated the coffee set, his brother Raymond Duchamp-Villon exhibited the terracotta version of his bust of Baudelaire, and Marie Laurencin supplied the paintings; Maurice Marinot supplied vases, Georges Rouault painted plates and tiles. 'The inlaid cherrywood study presented by Mr. Mare brings us nothing very agreeable or very new,' wrote Verneuil in *Art et Décoration*. 'The white chimney stands out dryly against the rather crude blue of the ensemble. Mr. de la Fresnaye, designer of the chimney, has not over-exerted his powers of invention; and the painting of Mlle Laurencin is at the very least regrettable. . . . The dining room exhibited by Mr. Mare next to his study is, unfortunately, no happier. . . . The cherrywood furniture has neither gracefulness nor originality, and the chimney is adorned (?) with regrettable ceramics. As for the Cubist still life on the overmantel, it is of lamentable platitude and taste. It is a fine thing to seek the new, provided, however, one aims for beauty; and how far from that we are here!!!'

1912 was an important year for both Süe and Mare. Louis Süe, who came from Bordeaux and had trained as an architect, set up as an interior decorator, calling his company 'l'Atelier Français' (The French Studio). André Mare, primarily a painter, exhibited a daring conception: A Cubist House. The reality, as opposed to the concept, now appears very tame indeed. Raymond Duchamp-Villon designed the façade of the house, which was set up in the middle of the Salon d'Automne. Lintels and pediments were given trangular or prismatic shapes, but these were no more than decorative touches to an otherwise straightforward housefront. The rooms were furnished and decorated in a completely bourgeois manner, the adventurous touches being confined to paintings by Fernand Léger, Albert Gleize and Jean Metzinger.

'The bourgeois living room and bedroom of Mr. André Mare are in absolute opposition to the principles whose application seemed to lead to a renewal of furniture design by adapting it to the present conception of comfort and luxury,' wrote Emile Sédeyn in *Art et Décoration*. 'Mr. André Mare does not practise the cult of truth to materials, since he conceals the wood with paint. He relegates hygiene to a secondary position by placing the bed in an alcove. And he does not embarrass himself with simplicity, for he multiplies flowers wherever they can be put. The effect he seeks is obviously one of picturesqueness and gaiety. He achieves it.' Sédeyn found Süe and Huillard's entry 'imposing.'

A few lone critical voices approved, but most attacked. The attacks multiplied in the newspapers, in the Chamber of Deputies, and in the exhibition hall itself, where members of the public heaped verbal abuse and attempted physical assault on the structure. A self-defence force consisting of Charlotte, André Mare's wife, Gaby, Jacques Villon's wife, and Marie Laurencin was set up, and the valiant three would patrol the perimeter, armed with umbrellas to repel the more violent visitors. Mare's name had been made. The 1913 Salon brought him nothing but

Above
SUE ET MARE: Figured walnut chest-of-drawers with marble top. The bronze handles are in the shape of tassels. The piece was exhibited at the 1925 Paris Exhibition, though dating from 1923. A bronze jardinière by Edgar Brandt stands on top. (Collection Donald Karshan, Paris)
Opposite above
SUE ET MARE: Carved macassar ebony chest of drawers encrusted with a floral pattern in mother-of-pearl, abalone and silvered metal marquetry, c. 1925. (DeLorenzo Collection, New York)
Opposite below
EMILE-JACQUES RUHLMANN: 'Chinoise' model vanity table, lacquered in an abstract pattern in white eggshell and black by Jean Dunand. The accompanying chair, model 'Défences', is also lacquered by Dunand. They were first exhibited at the 1927 Salon of the Société des Artistes Décorateurs. This unique model was originally purchased by Miss Redhead. (DeLorenzo Collection, New York)

compliments for a similar display of furniture and pictures, excluding the façade and the label. Indeed, the label 'Cubist' was being transferred in the public mind to mean 'new' or 'modern.' Thus Cubist girls (with short hair) wore Cubist clothes to see the latest Cubist play.

The war interrupted everything. Süe and Mare both rejoined their units, and were brought together fortuitously after the war when Süe, Mare and Gustave Jaulmes were jointly commissioned to design a temporary cenotaph to be placed below the Arc de Triomphe and to decorate the Place de l'Etoile and the avenue des Champs-Elysées, all in connection with the victory ceremonies and parade of the Allied forces. Süe and Mare got on well together, and they transformed Süe's Atelier Français into 'Belle France,' with premises in the avenue de Friedland. A few months later they moved to the Faubourg Saint-Honoré with a new name, the 'Compagnie des Arts Français' and a whole group of collaborators in various fields, most of them Mare's old friends.

Verneuil's scathing attack on the aesthetics of the Deutscher Werkbund exhibition in the Salon d'Automne had brought out the point that the German style was not native to them, but based on the French Louis-Philippe style. 'Why Louis-Philippe?' wrote Verneuil. 'If there was ever a mean, heavy, graceless era, then that was the one! An era of petty bourgeoisism with narrow ideas, no aesthetic sense, and from which art seems voluntarily excluded. It is truly odd to choose such an inspirational source; and it singularly compromises the chances of success to bring one's efforts to birth so unfavourably.'

Two years later Mare's friend André Vera wrote a ringing manifesto announcing that a purely French style needed to be created to combat the internationalism of the products of other nations. 'Thus for furniture,' he wrote, 'we will take the advice neither of the English nor of the Dutch, but will continue the French tradition, ensuring that the new style will be a continuation of the last international style we have, that is the Louis-Philippe style.'

The Compagnie des Arts Français, generally referred to at this time as Süe et Mare, was set up to produce complete coordinated interior designs. Opposed to what they called 'the monstrous extension of any one single personality,' particularly conspicuous among Art Nouveau designers who personally designed every single aspect of an ensemble, their collectivist aims, a characteristic of most Art Deco practise, were carried out by a team which included at various times Gustave Jaulmes, Paul and André Véra, Charles Dufresne, Richard Desvallières, Bernard Boutet de Monvel, Jean-Louis Boussingault, Roger de la Fresnaye, André Dunoyer de Segonzac, Marie Laurencin, Jacques Villon, Pierre Poisson and Maurice Marinot. Their decorative schemes included furniture, fabrics, ceramics, metalwork, lighting, glass, wallpapers and carpets whose characteristics they described as 'serious, logical and welcoming,' based on tradition. Several important commissions came their way, including the decoration of the French Embassy in Warsaw, part of the French Embassy in Washington, the Parfumerie d'Orsay shop in Paris, the home of the fashion designer Jean Patou, the fitting out of the luxury class cabins on the steamship Paris and that of the Grand Salon in the steamship

Above
SUE ET MARE: Leather-upholstered macassar ebony chair from a dining room set, c. 1920. (Private Collection, London)

Ile de France, for all of which their rather pompous, inflated style was highly appropriate. Characteristic of their furniture design was the featuring of legs, most of which were apparently applied to the outside of the body, often shaped as palmettes or other very noticeable shape, either carved in wood or cast in bronze or other metal. Süe et Mare had a close relationship with the firm of Fontaine et Cie from the start. Fontaine had then been established for over one hundred years, and executed all sorts of metalwork, specialising in door and window furniture. By 1925 their catalogue included thousands of traditional patterns and as many which they commissioned from nearly all the leading designers of the century.

Süe and Mare threw themselves wholly into the spirit of the 1925 Paris Exhibition. In an attempt at moving away from the traditional display of objects solely within their classification, the Exhibition organisers had decreed that all pavilions had to be devised to a pre-agreed theme. Süe et Mare chose for their theme 'A Museum of Contemporary Art'. Süe designed two identical buildings, plain single-storey structures whose only decoration was the lettering on the façade, topped by a low dome, one building for the 'Museum', the other for the Maison Fontaine. Calling on the services of all their collaborators, Süe et Mare produced room settings of all types, the major effort going into the central rotunda which was, in fact, used as the setting for a film called *Gribiche*.

Süe et Mare specialised in turning out regular examples of 'exhibition' furniture, large, frequently bizarre conjunctions of traditional pieces with striking, but structurally irrelevant touches. They turned out a number of items with mother-of-pearl marquetry, which was a favourite technique among a number of Art Deco furniture designers, including Leleu and Ruhlmann, but their great weakness was their inability to master lacquerwork coupled with their reluctance to employ the talents of a lacquerer like Jean Dunand. They devised a cheap form of pseudo-lacquer based on cellulose paints, and examples of this have not survived well, peeling and disintegrating. An example of this is the cabinet they sold to the Metropolitan Museum.

Although great effort had gone into this 1925 display, not enough work ensued. Few important commissions came their way. They had published in 1921 the first issue of a splendid periodical called *Architecture*, with a text by Paul Valéry, original graphics, including etchings, lithographs and woodcuts, and a selection of their major designs interpreted in etching by Jacques Villon. They were never to publish a second issue. In financial difficulty, they increasingly produced less expensive designs for direct sales, but without any marked success. In 1928 the Maison Fontaine, which had helped finance them, took over the firm and Süe and Mare both left. Fontaine disposed of all the Süe et Mare designs and archives, and put Jacques Adnet in as artistic director, changing the whole direction of the firm, now known simply as the Compagnie des Arts Français, to modernism and increasing the use of metal.

The leading cabinet-maker throughout the 20s was Jacques-Emile Ruhlmann. His father, originally from Alsace, had settled in Paris and set up a building firm

Above
SUE ET MARE: Spoon-backed palisander chair, the carved back joined to the seat by a gently curved riser, c. 1923. (Collection Félix Marcilhac, Paris. Photo: Sully Jaulmes)

which prospered, and enabled young Ruhlmann to indulge in his early desire to study painting. Fastidious in his tastes, he developed a personal hobby: the design of fine pieces of furniture. He is reported to have designed his first piece of furniture in 1901, and designed the furniture for his home when he married in 1907. All were, of course, executed in his father's firm. He worked for his father, spent a long time studying the construction of furniture, the way it was assembled, the art of veneering, the distribution of weight, the suspension of doors and drawers. In 1913 he exhibited some of his designs for the first time at the Salon d'Automne, and quickly established himself as a designer of luxury furniture. As soon as the war ended he took over the direction of his father's firm, Ruhlmann et Laurent, and expanded its decorating side, with joinery and cabinet-making workshops, an upholstery department, and the equipment and trained men to carry out most operations, from bevelling mirrors to applying veneers. He was then forty years old. Ruhlmann's furniture was firmly based on eighteenth-century design, simplified and slightly distorted. He favoured exceedingly slender, tapering legs often ending in tiny ivory feet. Where a sideboard or cabinet was massive, he liked to float it in mid-air, connecting it to its base by a short central column or sets of carved or shaped connectors. Most characteristic of all was his desire to completely conceal the actual construction of the piece of furniture. Most of his furniture was executed in hardwood, preferably oak, and was then cross-bonded, that is, covered in thin strips of wood with the grain going in the opposite direction from that of the body, planed smooth, then counter-bonded with the final veneer, again with the grain running in the opposite direction to that of the supporting layer. Since the cross-bonding was devised to prevent the cracking and warping of furniture due to central heating and to the fact that hardly any of the wood available was properly seasoned, some items of furniture were made with several cross-bonded layers before the final veneer was added. The rarest and costliest woods were used for the final veneers, varying from those with spectacular figuration to those with a direct, even pattern, and they were cut and assembled in large panels which completely covered the joints and joins, giving the illusion that the piece of furniture had been carved from a single enormous block. Apparent surface joins were invariably purely decorative, and bore no relationship to the location of structural joints.

Ivory was frequently used by Ruhlmann to decorate or enhance his designs. Fluted ivory ribs, ivory feet, key plates or handles, or simple whorl or circle patterns of ivory dots set flush within the surface gave his furniture their single touch of contrast other than the veneers used. For this he employed the finest tabletiers, Georges Bastard, Mme O'Kin Simmen or Le Bourgeois. When Ruhlmann wanted lacquered furniture, he usually had this executed at Jean Dunand's workshop. Ruhlmann was referred to by his contemporaries as the Riesener of the twentieth century. During his lifetime, few authentic Riesener pieces reached the prices Ruhlmann charged. The average price of one of his beds or cabinets was frequently more than the cost of a reasonably large house.

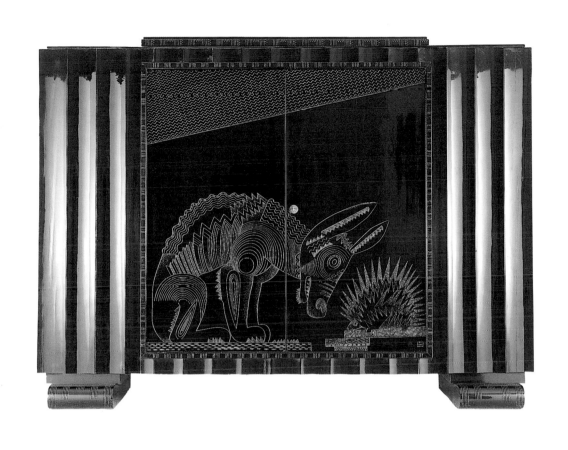

Above
EMILE-JACQUES RUHLMANN: Amboyna-wood dressing table, model 'Collectionneur', Martelet variant. The hinged central top section is covered in shagreen with an ivory surround and encrusted pattern, ivory handle and feet, c. 1925. (Collection Alain Lesieutre, Paris. Photo: Philippe Doumic)

Below
EMILE-JACQUES RUHLMANN: Amboyna-wood sofa, model 'Hanck', 1922, with ivory inlays and edges. It was exhibited at the 1925 Paris Exhibition. The model was also available in palisander and macassar ebony. (Collection Galerie Maria de Beyrie, Paris)

Ruhlmann's hand was evident throughout the 1925 Exhibition. His firm built, decorated, painted or supplied some other service to a vast number of pavilions, both French and foreign. He designed and furnished the study for the French Embassy organised by the Société des Artistes Décorateurs, and set up his own pavilion, the Hotel d'un Riche Collectionneur (Home of a Wealthy Collector). In his preface to the album published in 1926 on the subject of this pavilion Léon Deshairs wrote: 'It would have been surprising had Ruhlmann suggested building a working-class house and exhibited inexpensive furniture there. Not that he does not recognise the social usefulness of applying art to such things; not that he does not know that the simplest object, the most common material, may be ennobled by a reflection of intelligence and some talent. But other interests call to him. . . . Furniture born of his research, joined to some he admires from the production of his competitors, works of art of all types that he enjoys or would enjoy surrounding himself with, are what he conceived of grouping in the home of a hypothetical collector who would resemble him as closely as a brother.' The pavilion, designed by his close friend Pierre Patout, contained sculpture by Joseph Bernard, Antoine Bourdelle, Le Bourgeois, Temporal, Poisson, Hairon, Janniot, Déjean, Foucault, Despiau and Pompon, decoration by Francis Jourdain, Léon Jallot and Henri Rapin in addition to his own, silver by Jean Puiforcat, metalwork by Edgar Brandt, ceramics by Lenoble, Mayodon and Decoeur, lacquer and dinanderie by Dunand, glass by Décorchemont, bookbindings by Kieffer and Legrain, tabletterie by Bastard and Mme O'Kin, and paintings by a number of artists including Jean Dupas, Robert Bonfils and Gustave Jaulmes.

Ruhlmann was never parted from his sketchbooks, in which he ceaselessly explored endless variations on his designs. He was not a good draughtsman, but his shaky lines sprang from strong aesthetic convictions and will. He employed sixteen draughtsmen to work up his sketches into finished scale drawings which were then executed in one of his three furniture workshops. Writing in *Art et Décoration* in 1924, Charles Henri Besnard reported Ruhlmann's observations: 'an armchair for a living room must not be conceived like an office armchair, which in turn must be very different from an armchair for a smoking room. The first must be simply welcoming, the second comfortable, the third somewhat voluptuous. Each of these armchairs must have its own shape. The first task is to determine those shapes; created by the same artist, they will easily have that air of kinship which is the stamp of a style.' Ruhlmann undoubtedly considered that 'style' and a physical aspect that fitted its allotted role were considerably more important to a piece of furniture than its functional suitability, and he emphasised this fact by frequently putting his creations on low, velvet-covered platforms. 'What function do they fulfil?' asked Besnard in the same article. 'If the goal is an easier access to the lower parts of the piece of furniture, then this platform is unnecessary; he need only have placed this piece of furniture on longer legs. If it is a legitimate desire to protect precious wood from a conscientious servant's broom, we do not see any advantage in this raising of the floor; the feather duster which, in this case, would replace the broom would have an equally nefarious result.' In fact Ruhlmann used

Above
EMILE-JACQUES RUHLMANN: Burr walnut two-tier table on slender legs. The top is inlaid with a circle of ivory dots. (Collection Félix Marcilhac, Paris. Photo: Sully Jaulmes)
Overleaf left, above
PIERRE LEGRAIN: Oak desk and chair, made for Maurice Martin du Gard. (Collection Galerie Maria de Beyrie, Paris)
Overleaf left, below
EUGENE PRINTZ: Palmwood veneered dining room suite. (Collection Galerie Maria de Beyrie, Paris)
Overleaf right, above
EMILE-JACQUES RUHLMANN: Amboyna wood sofa, model 'Spirales', inlaid with ivory dots and an ivory spiral on each side, the thickness of the line diminishing as it approaches its centre; flat, circular silvered bronze feet, c. 1920. (Collection Alain Lesieutre, Paris. Photo: Philippe Doumic)
Overleaf right, below
EMILE-JACQUES RUHLMANN: Bar, model 'Ducharne'. The bar and stools are lacquered wood, the footrails and stool feet in chromium-plated metal, 1930. A mirrored wall-cabinet was also made en suite. (Félix Marcilhac Collection, Paris. Photo: Sully Jaulmes)

the platform to create a distancing effect, indicating that the piece of furniture was not just a sideboard, a sofa or a chest-of-drawers, but a work of art.

The Ruhlmann style was taken up by a number of other designers, most notably by Jules Leleu, who set up his own furniture workshop after the war, and exhibited in the Salons of the Société des Artistes Décorateurs from 1922 onwards, as well as the Salon d'Automne and the Salon des Tuileries. He provided some furniture for the music room and the living room of the French Embassy at the 1925 Exhibition. Less esoteric in his claims, and far less expensive than Ruhlmann, he received many important commissions, including the decoration and furnishing of several steamships and French Embassies.

The Ecole Martine was set up in 1911 by Paul Poiret in reaction to the formal teaching methods he had seen practised in the official art schools in Germany and Austria. He had seen, he wrote in his autobiography *En Habillant l'Epoque* (While Dressing the Era), 'the "Herr Professors" of Berlin and Vienna torture their students to force them to enter a new mould like an iron corset. . . . I found this work and the discipline imposed on intelligence absolutely criminal. . . . I recruited girls about twelve years old and who had finished their studies, all from working-class areas. I gave up several rooms in my house to them, and made them work after nature, without a teacher. Their parents, of course, soon found they were wasting their time, and I had to promise them wages and rewards. I rewarded the best drawings. Within a few weeks I was getting marvellous results. These children, left to themselves, soon forgot the fake and empirical precepts they had learned at school to regain all the spontaneity and freshness of their nature.' A few months later he opened the Atelier Martine, through which he manufactured and sold these new designs, transforming clothes and interior design. Some of the girls were taught to weave, others to embroider, and they produced carpets, tapestries, wallpapers and fabrics joyous with bursts of floral colour. When the girls tackled the decoration of a room, they did not produce scale drawings of a planned design, but went straight in with a ladder and pots of paint and created patterns as they went along.

Over the years some of the young Martine girls were to become full-time designers, but financial difficulties forced Poiret to close down the school, 'and these young artists full of promise had to become salesgirls in department stores or work in a bootmaker's.' Among the many who came to admire the work of the Martine girls was Raoul Dufy. He and Poiret got on very well, and Poiret set up a small studio for Dufy and hired a chemist to deal with colours, inks, and all the technical problems. Dufy began by designing fabrics in the style of the woodblocks he had devised to illustrate Apollinaire's *Bestiary*, then developed some colourful patterns. Within a year, however, Dufy was approached by the firm of Bianchini-Férier with an offer of wide facilities backed by a major industrial producer of fabrics. Poiret offered no objection, and Dufy expanded his career as fabrics designer, a career which lasted for many years parallel with his painting.

The Atelier Martine's early interior designs contained little furniture, and involved very colourful walls, rugs and fabrics, and beds, sofas or chairs heaped

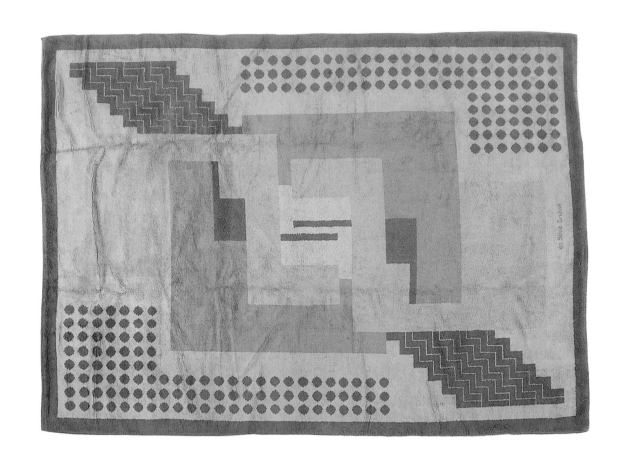

with multicoloured pillows and cushions, the typical one being a limp bolster in rich colours with long tassels. While the cushions remained Martine's trademark, Poiret soon introduced a range of furniture in uncomplicated shapes, generally cube-inspired, occasionally made of precious woods, but most often with painted surfaces, which went from solid colours with humorous, sophisticated drawings by Mario Simon, Marty or Guy Arnoux, to bright contrasts.

For the 1925 Exhibition Poiret had the original idea of converting three barges and mooring them between the Alexandre III and Invalides Bridges. 'Amour' (Love) was blue throughout, and consisted of a suite of rooms decorated and furnished by Martine. 'Orgues' (Organs) had had its interior gutted and painted white to serve as the background for a set of fourteen wall hangings he commissioned from Dufy, representing such subjects as the regatta at Le Havre, the races at Longchamps, baccarat at the Deauville casino, Paul Poiret models at the races and a reception at the admiralty. While they were being woven at Bianchini's works at Tournon, Dufy wrote a letter to Poiret: 'When I found myself facing my finished work, I was absolutely choked, as though faced by something I had never seen before, and these hangings radiate the feel of something utterly new. . . . I naturally think of you to whom I owe having entered this career which attracted me because there was so much in it to discover.' This barge was used for regular fashion parades and parties. The third barge, 'Delices' (Delight), painted predominantly in reds, was a restaurant with all the furniture, cutlery and tableware designed by Martine. Poiret counted a great deal on the success of his showing at the Exhibition, for he had recently gone through a very poor financial patch, and had lost his property on the corner of the rue Saint-Honoré which Louis Süe had refurbished for him in 1909. Since it was his office, workshop, salon, and home, he had been forced to move to a smaller house at the Rond-Point des Champs-Elysées.

'That exposition des arts décoratifs was for me a bitter disappointment,' he wrote in 1930, '(I am not even talking about the money I lost, since that is in the realm of repairable disasters), for it could in no way help the decorative arts. It opened its doors just as the Parisians who constitute the interested public were leaving for the countryside. . . . One saw at best a horde of concierges and employees avid for lights, crowds and noise rush in between nine and eleven in the evening. I had been wrong to count on the luxury clientele which flees from these popular pleasures; they did not come. It was an experience I shall remember.' As for Dufy's hangings which he was forced to sell cheaply, 'who remembers them? No one even noticed them. Public taste was not ripe, though today I could sell them for their weight in gold, so true is it that for works of art as for ideas of genius a maturity is needed for which one has to wait.' To help pay off his debts, Poiret sold off his collection of paintings which included works by Modigliani, Matisse, Dufy, Marie Laurencin, Van Dongen, Drian, Vlaminck, Valadon, Utrillo, Segonzac, Laboureur, Max Jacob, Boutet de Monvel and Picabia, Rayograms by Man Ray and sculpture by Brancusi and Pompon.

André Groult, who was to marry Poiret's sister Nicole (whose portrait was painted by Louis Süe), first exhibited at the Salon d'Automne and the Salons of the

Above
SONIA DELAUNAY: Woven carpet. (Collection Félix Marcilhac, Paris. Photo: Sully Jaulmes)
Opposite, above
IVAN DA SILVA BRUHNS: Woven wool rug, 1925, 2293.5 x 402.5 cms. (Virginia Museum of Fine Arts, Gift of Sydney and Frances Lewis. Photo: Ron Jennings)
Opposite, below
IVAN DA SILVA BRUHNS: Woven wool rug, c. 1925, 584.6 x 335 cms. (Virginia Museum of Fine Arts, Gift of Sydney and Frances Lewis)

Société des Artistes Décorateurs in 1910, having commissioned André Mare to design his first items of furniture for him. He soon developed his own style, large comfortable chairs, much drapery, coordinated colour schemes and, frequently, painted wood. The motif of the basket of flowers, so characteristic of Art Deco furniture design and decoration, and described by André Véra in his *Manifesto* as the modern equivalent of the eighteenth century's arrows, was used by Groult as early as 1910 in his design for a dining room. In 1912, perhaps encouraged by Poiret's experiments with the Martine girls, Groult commissioned a whole range of new fabric designs from Marie Laurencin, Constance Lloyd, George Barbier, Carlègle, Paul Iribe, Drésa (André Saglio), Albert André, Georges d'Espagnat, Hermann-Paul, Laprade, Lebasque, Louis Süe and Gompert. He himself designed several. All the artists responded with freedom of shape, bright colours and highly ornamental patterns.

Groult's furniture and interior designs were frequently called 'feminine' by his contemporaries, partly because of his love of curves, and partly for his frequent use of paintings by Marie Laurencin and colour schemes based on her paintings. At the 1925 Exhibition he designed room settings in the Fontaine and Christofle-Baccarat pavilions, the Musical Instruments Section in the Grand Palais, as well as the Arts of the Garden Section, and was, not surprisingly, chosen to decorate and furnish the lady's bedroom in the French Embassy devised by the Société des Artistes Décorateurs. The gentleman's bedroom, designed by Georges Chevallier and Léon Jallot, was attacked by Marie Dormoy in an article in *L'Amour de l'Art* as 'a truly funerary display chamber, as much through its colour as its lighting and the sepulchral shape of the bed.' The critic Georges Le Fèvre interviewed Groult for the June 15th, 1925 issue of *L'Art Vivant*: 'It's the Ambassador's wife's room in the Embassy at the Exposition des Arts Décoratifs. "I suppose," says he, not without candour, "that she must be very wealthy." And thus shagreen, lapis-lazuli, amazonite, ivory, ebony, horn, rose quartz are his chosen materials. He supervises the setting of his creations with tiny gestures. A phlegmatic man with a high forehead, Chinese eyes and an English smile, he caresses voluptuously the curved spine of a shagreen chest of drawers with ivory inlay. "Curved," he murmurs, "curved to the point of indecency..."'

Not all critics approved. Georges Besson, reviewing the interior decoration and furniture at the Exhibition in *Les Arts Décoratifs Modernes* wrote: 'I do not altogether like Mr. Groult's lesbian bedroom: is one of those shagreen cabinets a piece of furniture or a cello's belly? Or yet a woman's trunk? But furniture and grey and pink harmony at least make up a decorative whole with some meaning. (This empty room is as intimidating as if it were lived in).'

Paul Iribe helped create the Art Deco style in the pre-war years. Primarily an artist, he was also a fine satirical cartoonist, and illustrated Paul Poiret's first catalogue. By 1912 he was designing fabrics and wallpapers for André Groult, and was commissioned by Jacques Doucet, the dean of Paris dressmaking, to design his new apartment in the avenue du Bois after selling his collection of eighteenth-century furniture, pictures and objects. Iribe employed the young Pierre

Above
PAUL IRIBE: Mahogany armchair, c. 1912. (Private Collection, Paris. Photo: Sully Jaulmes)
Opposite, above, left
ROBERT BONFILS: *L'Afrique*. Woven cotton furnishing fabric for Bianchini-Férier, c. 1922. (Victoria & Albert Museum, London)
Opposite, above, right
PAUL IRIBE: Block-printed fabric for André Groult, 1912. (Musée des Arts Décoratifs, Paris)
Opposite, below, left
MAURICE DUFRENE: Block-printed fabric, c. 1920. (Musée des Arts Décoratifs, Paris)
Opposite, below, right
ERIC BAGGE: *L'Orage* (The Storm). Block-printed linen manufactured by Lucien Bouix, 1929. (Private Collection, London)

Above
MARIE LAURENCIN: Tufted wool woven carpet
designed for a friend who ran a concert hall, c.
1925. (Virginia Museum of Fine Arts, Gift of
Sydney and Frances Lewis. Photo: Katherine
Wetzel)

Above, left
ANDRE GROULT: Chair, the back carved as a stylised basket of flowers. (Courtesy Ader, Picard, Tajan, Paris)

Above, right
ANDRE GROULT: Ebony and satinwood chair. The back is painted with a floral spray by Marie Laurencin. This chair was awarded 3rd prize in a contest for chair designs organised by David Weill and N. de Camondo shortly before the opening of the 1925 Paris Exhibition. All the finalists exhibited their designs at the Musée des Arts Décoratifs. (Courtesy Ader, Picard, Tajan, Paris)

Below, left
CLEMENT ROUSSEAU: Ebony chair overlaid with green, pink and white shagreen. Both sides of the chairback have a radiating sun motif in shagreen with ivory fillets. The shoes are ivory and the seat is upholstered in blue silk. (Musée des Arts Décoratifs, Paris. Photo: Sully Jaulmes)

Below, right
CLEMENT ROUSSEAU: Rosewood chair inlaid with shagreen, ivory and mother-of-pearl. (Virginia Museum of Fine Arts, Gift of Sydney and Frances Lewis. Photo: Katherine Wetzel)

Legrain as his assistant. In 1914 Iribe left for the United States, where he was to work for Broadway theatres and Hollywood, designing a number of film settings for Cecil B. de Mille and others. He was to return to France in 1930, when he became very close to Chanel, for whom he designed a range of costume jewellery.

Pierre Legrain first went to work for Paul Iribe in 1908, remaining with him until he joined the army in 1914. He was therefore in contact with Jacques Doucet throughout the period of execution of the interior of the avenue du Bois apartment. Doucet had a mania for collecting. Having sold off his eighteenth-century collection and been converted to the twentieth century he promptly began to collect paintings by Matisse and Picasso and sculpture by Brancusi. He was not knowledgeable, but had a good eye for elegance and strength of design. Having discovered African art, he lost no time in collecting it and introducing his friends to it. As his collection grew, it became necessary to build a new home in which to house it. Legrain, invalided from the army, went to work for Doucet as a designer of bookbindings, a task which taught him to love covering things in beautiful hides and other precious materials. In about 1925 Doucet took over premises at Neuilly, put the architect Paul Ruau in charge of its conversion, then hired Legrain to organise its interior decoration.

Doucet's collection was no longer in accord with the bulk of Iribe's designs for the apartment, so the new Studio's style had to blend with the collection it was to house. Legrain brought in friends and designers whose work he admired to complement his own designs, and Doucet himself lectured them, made specific requests, steeped them in his requirements. On the walls were Douanier Rousseau's *Snake Charmer*, Picasso's *Demoiselles d'Avignon*, paintings by Derain, Braque, Matisse, Miró, Picabia, Ernst and Giorgio de Chirico, while sculptures by Brancusi and Zadkine waited for pedestals and everywhere were African carvings, stools, thrones and weapons.

Legrain brought in Marcel Coard, André Groult, Eileen Gray and Rose Adler. Legrain in particular devised massive pieces in macassar ebony, many directly inspired by African furniture. His fondness for covering books with rare materials led to the design of furniture similarly bound in morocco leather, crocodile or snakeskin, and the inlaid patterns were frequently derived from the patterns on African carvings. Several of the other designers working for Doucet were similarly influenced by the couturier who led them, often unwillingly, to produce their greatest designs for him. Certainly Eileen Gray was unhappy with the African-inspired side table or the Nile-inspired green and white lacquered table with lotus motifs, both among her finest creations.

Doucet's carpets were designed by artists such as Marcoussis, Miklos and Jean Lurçat, but the vein of African inspiration was to be found in other carpet designers, such as Da Silva Bruhns. Having started his professional career as a painter and interior decorator, he was commissioned by Louis Majorelle, who in the post-war years had successfully moved wholly into Art Deco design, to design some carpets for him. Finding an affinity with such design, Da Silva Bruhns studied

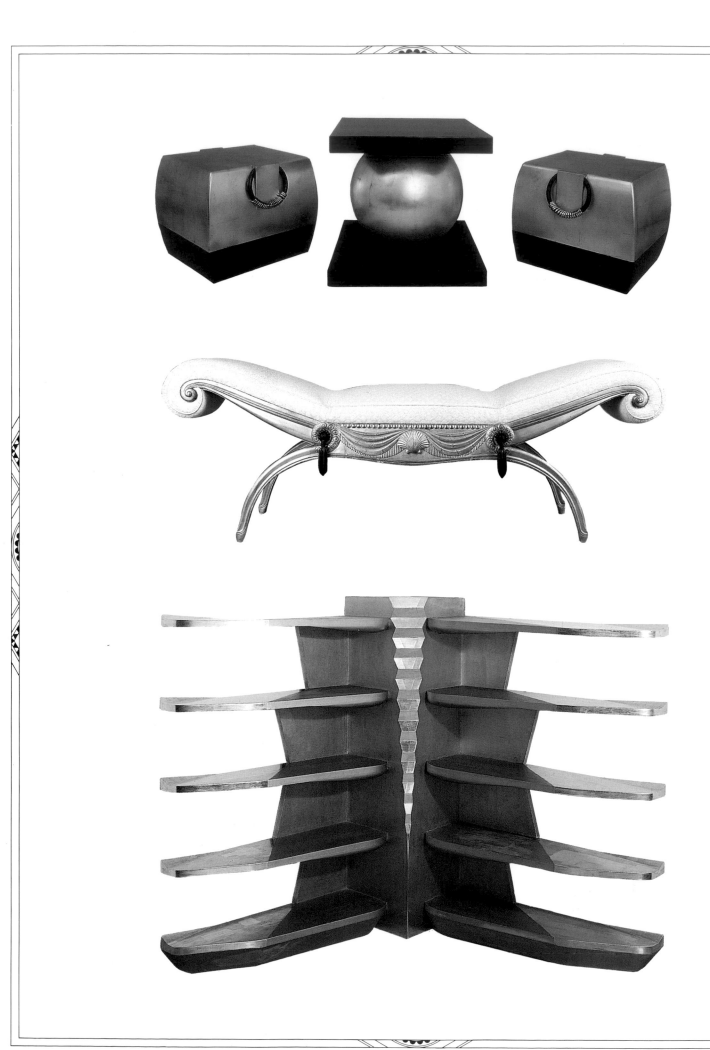

Above, left
EMILE-JACQUES RUHLMANN: Rectangular 'Lambiotte' in American figured walnut, the three panels in relief on both sides of the pedestal edged with ivory, 1929. (Collection Alain Lesieutre, Paris)

Centre
EMILE-JACQUES RUHLMANN: 'Tivo' model dressing table chair in violet wood, the low back inlaid with a decorative double swirl of ivory dots, the front shoes also in ivory, c. 1918. (Private Collection, New York)

Below, left
EMILE-JACQUES RUHLMANN: 'Ducharne' model circular pedestal table in macassar ebony, the veneer radiating from the centre, the table top and the base of the pedestal edged in gilt bronze, 1930. On the table are lacquered and dinanderie vases by Jean Dunand. (Collection Alain Lesieutre, Paris)

Below, right
EMILE-JACQUES RUHLMANN: 'Lambiotte Pare-Feu' model circular breakfast table veneered in amboyna wood inlaid with ivory. The table top is named 'firescreen' because it pivots vertically, 1929. (Collection Alain Lesieutre. Photo: Philippe Doumic)

Opposite, above
PIERRE LEGRAIN: Table and stools in black tinted sycamore and silver lacquer with black lacquer chromium-plated metal handles, 1922-23. They were made for the house of Mme Tachard at Celle Saint-Cloud, which Legrain furnished and decorated. He also landscaped the garden. (Private Collection, Paris. Photo: Sully Jaulmes)

Opposite, centre
ARMAND ALBERT RATEAU: Gilt chaise-longue. (DeLorenzo Collection, New York)

Opposite, below
PIERRE LEGRAIN: Corner bookcase in gilt wood. (Private Collection, Paris. Photo: Sully Jaulmes)

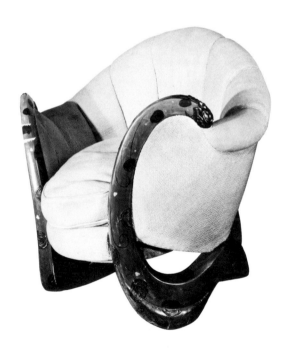

Above, upper
EILEEN GRAY: 'Bilboquet' (cup and ball) lacquered table made for Jacques Doucet. (Collection Galerie Marie de Beyrie, Paris)
Above, lower
EILEEN GRAY: Armchair with serpentine arms curving down to form the base in engraved red lacquer, c. 1912. (Galerie Vallois, Paris)

carpet-making by buying various carpets from the Middle East and taking them apart. He then trained a number of workers in the techniques he chose and set up a studio, which was more of a cottage industry, in a village in the Aisne.

A number of other furniture designers succumbed in lesser or greater degree to the temptation of African design, including Gabriel Guevrékian and Pierre Chareau. Chareau was primarily an architect, though he was only to be given the opportunity of designing a very small number of large structures. As a designer of furniture and interiors he tackled each task from the functional point of view as a structural engineer, believing each item had to be adapted to its precise function. In the war that was being waged between the purveyors of luxury furniture for the very wealthy and those who believed in the necessity for plain design for inexpensive mass-production, he was one of the leaders in attacking the precious object fit only for the rich.

At the 1925 Exhibition he was given the task of designing the study-library in the French Embassy. 'I have been entrusted with a room in the French Embassy which is a kind of private study-library,' he told Georges Le Fèvre, who reported his words in the June 15th, 1925 issue of *L'Art Vivant*. 'Contrary to what might have been expected of me, I have used extremely rare woods which are almost impossible to find, giving way to a kind of creative exaltation which has led me to carry out a real folly. But when you consider that even white wood would have been too expensive for a poor man... you can allow yourself, for once, to float into the air. Thus my woodwork is made of palmwood, a material which is simultaneously hard and soft, very difficult to work.'

His macassar ebony desk was built up in opposing planes, making it impossible to clutter up its surface with papers, which would slide to the floor. The circular room was made up of bookshelves in palmwood, broken only by a sculpture by Jacques Lipchitz and a circular carpet by Jean Lurçat while Hélène Henry supplied the fabrics. A dome-shaped ceiling reflected the light in its centre, while this could be closed off in the daytime by a panel made up of palmwood blades which could be fanned completely shut, or partly shut to dim the light.

Ruhlmann and Süe et Mare were the two largest firms of interior decorators, but there were several more, such as Dominique, Montagnac, Michel Dufet's M.A.M. and Léon Jallot and his son Maurice. Among the more interesting was D.I.M. (Décoration Intérieure Moderne) set up after the war by René Joubert and Mouveau. The latter, primarily a stage designer, left the firm in 1924 to return to the theatre, and was replaced by Philippe Petit. Highly flexible, their principal showroom in the rue du Colisée off the Champs-Elysées displayed both inexpensive furniture and the most expensive, in room settings which exhibited the full range of their offerings, including carpets, rugs, sculpture, wallpapers, panels and ceramics. Light fittings and glass came from the Cappellin and Venini firm of Murano, Italy, to whom they devoted a whole branch of the firm in the Place de la Madeleine.

Undoubtedly some of the most exciting Art Deco furniture was produced by artists who did not have large enterprises behind them. Clément Mère, who had

EILEEN GRAY: 'Lotus' dark green and white
lacquer table, made for Jacques Doucet, c. 1914.
(Collection Galerie Maria de Beyrie, Paris)
Below
JEAN DUNAND: Lacquered dressing table, c.
1926. (Private Collection, Paris. Photo. Sully
Jaulmes)

studied painting with Gérôme before going to work for the Maison Moderne, joined there with Franz Waldraff to produce elaborate bookbindings, leather panels, fabrics, ivory panels engraved and gilt; Waldraff designed elaborate prints for fabrics for several of the grand couturiers, while Mère made exquisite boxes, paper knives and bottles in wood, ivory and leather. Together they devised patterns for glass engraving for the Saint-Louis firm in Lorraine, then extended the technique to leather and other materials. Together they exhibited some furniture, but Waldraff increasingly concentrated on fabric design and stage designs, particularly for Eleonore Duse, and Mère proceeded to design and execute the most minutely detailed furniture, using rare woods, leather panels incised, etched, stained, painted and lacquered, ivory panels that were carved and stained, and enamel. The mysterious Clément Rousseau produced fascinatingly slender, swooping designs, mixing the rarest woods with ivory and shagreen, creating stylised marquetry inlays, devising amazing shapes for his patrons. There are very few of his early works available because his patrons, most notably the Rothschild family, have kept the vast majority.

Other curious and fascinating byways of Art Deco furniture include the patinated bronze furniture of Armand-Albert Rateau and the splendid lacquered furniture of Jean Dunand and Eileen Gray.

Although several designers paid lip service to the ideals of inexpensive furniture for the masses, only Francis Jourdain, son of Frantz Jourdain, the first president of the Salon d'Automne, seriously devoted his career to attempting this. Having started as a painter, he gradually essayed the decorative arts and, after gaining a Grand Prix at the 1911 Turin International Exhibition, set up his Ateliers Modernes (Modern Workshops) the following year. Designing not only furniture but wallpaper, fabrics, carpets and ceramics, Jourdain devised it all to fit the much smaller living space which modern life (and modern architects) allowed. 'We buy a table or a chest-of-drawers less for the services they might render us than for the pleasing effect we expect of such furniture when setting up our interiors,' he told René Chavance in Art et Décoration in 1922. 'It is a regrettable error. One can set up a room most luxuriously by emptying it rather than furnishing it.' He designed plain, unadorned geometric shapes using readily available, inexpensive woods and replaced costly upholstery with cane. Shortly after the end of the war he had expanded into full factory production with a separate showroom/shop.

The Art Deco style was, nevertheless, popularised not so much by the creators exhibiting in their little showrooms or in the Salons, but by the great department stores. The first to launch itself into the new decorative arts was Au Printemps, which set up a design studio called Primavera under the direction of René Guilleré, the retiring president of the Société des Artistes Décorateurs, and his wife, Mme Chauché-Guilleré, in the heady pre-war years. After the war Maurice Dufrêne, formerly from the Maison Moderne, took over the artistic direction of La Maitrise for the Galeries Lafayette in 1921. Two years later Paul Follot, another Maison Moderne designer, took over the newly founded Pomone Studio for Au Magasins du Louvre launched the Studium-Louvre under

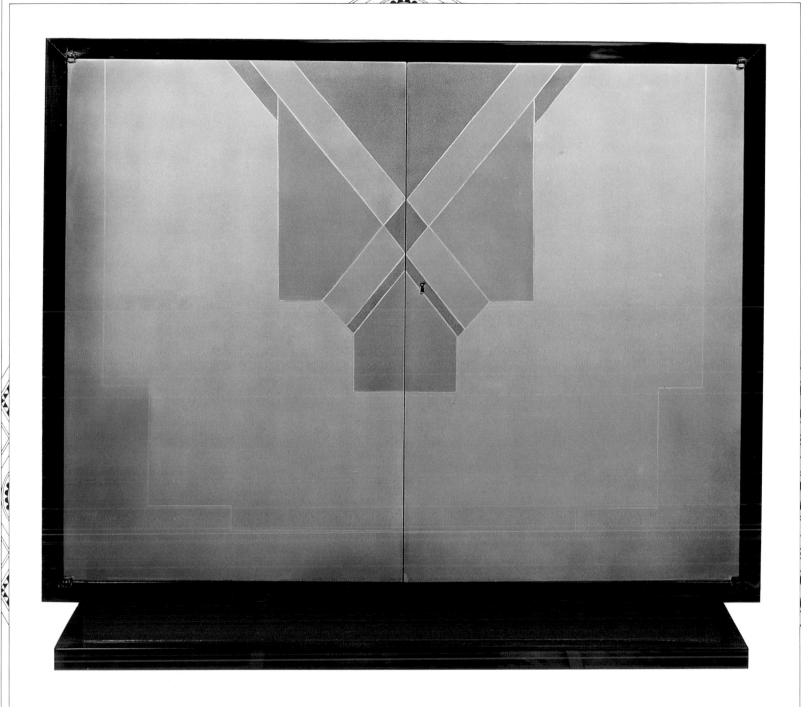

Above
LEON & MAURICE JALLOT: Cabinet lacquered
yellow, gold, grey, silver and red, probably
executed by Jean Dunand, 1929. (Private
Collection, Paris. Photo: Sully Jaulmes)
Opposite, above
PIERRE CHAREAU: Block-printed linen, c. 1927-
28. (Victoria & Albert Museum, London)
Opposite, below
PIERRE CHAREAU: Macassar ebony desk
identical with the one he designed for the study at
the 1925 Paris Exhibition. The multiplicity of
planes was intended to make it impossible to
clutter the surface. The handles are in polished
steel, 1925. (Private Collection, Paris. Photo:
Sully Jaulmes)

Above
CLEMENT MERE: Macassar ebony jewellery cabinet set with incised and lacquered leather panels and an enamelled keyhole surround on a carved rosewood base, 1923. The satinwood inside is set with an ivory medallion and incised shagreen. (Private Collection, New York)

Centre
ROSE ADLER: Macassar ebony table, the top inlaid in shagreen patterned as a stylised cityscape, the drawer pull and shoes in silver-plated and partly enamelled metal, made for Jacques Doucet, c. 1926. (Virginia Museum of Fine Arts, Gift of Sydney and Frances Lewis. Photo: Katherine Wetzel)

Below
MARCEL COARD: Rosewood sofa carved to simulate rattan, bordered in ivory and upholstered in leather. Made for Jacques Doucet, before 1929. (Virginia Museum of Fine Arts, Gift of Sydney and Frances Lewis. Photo: Katherine Wetzel)

Opposite, above
PAUL IRIBE: Chaise longue in Macassar ebony varnished black, 1914. (Collection Galerie de Beyrie, Paris)

Opposite, below
PIERRE DEMARIA: Geometric lacquered screen, exhibited at the Salon d'Automne, 1925. (Collection Galerie Maria de Beyrie, Paris)

Above
MICHEL DUFET: Armchair in lacquered and gilt wood, originally designed for Mme Duvernois and manufactured by Dufet's Company, MAM (Meubles Artistiques Modernes) until 1922. (Courtesy Mrs. Rhodia Dutet-Bourdelle, Paris)

Opposite, above
ARMAND-ALBERT RATEAU: Bedroom of Jeanne Lanvin's home, 1920-22. The blue silk lining the walls was embroidered in white and gold threads in the Lanvin workshop. (Musée des Arts Décoratifs, Paris)

Opposite, below
ARMAND-ALBERT RATEAU: Jeanne Lanvin's bathroom, tub and washstand in Sienna marble, with large wall panel in carved stucco and all fittings in bronze, 1920-22. (Musée des Arts Décoratifs, Paris)

Kohlmann, Djo-Bourgeois and Max Vibert. Designing and manufacturing a complete range of furniture and household goods in the new style, but without either the excesses of taste or the excesses of expense, these design studios succeeded in familiarising a large number of people with the broad outlines of Art Deco, and their pavilions at the 1925 Exhibition were among the most popular.

The Art Deco style in furniture was to continue in some hands throughout the Second World War and even beyond. Indeed, the average furniture shop today has a number of pieces that are no more than debased examples of the plainer Art Deco. Yet even as the Art Deco style triumphed in the 1925 Exhibition, it had only about another five years of creative activity to come. By 1930 even Ruhlmann was producing sectional plain furniture and employing metal, plastics and cellulose. Georges Besson, in his review of the 1925 Exhibition for *Les Arts Décoratifs Modernes* wrote: 'This exhibition is at least for interior decorating, the triumph of ornament, of ornament at any cost, luxurious or cheap, ingenious or ridiculous, its vulgarity diminished or transformed, but ornament nevertheless. It is the consecration of the floral stylisation that came out of Nancy, of the stylisation of 1913 (mare's arse pink), of motifs derived from Cubism, the last ornamental system used without shame by the most violent detractors of that school of painting: Let us hope that this consecration is also a funeral.' He was not far wrong.

Opposite, above
JEAN DUNAND: Polychrome lacquered fireplace. (Private Collection, Paris. Photo: Sully Jaulmes)
Opposite, below
EUGENE PRINTZ: Palmwood bookcase with brass doors encrusted with silver in a geometric pattern designed and executed by Jean Dunand, c. 1927. Each of the five doors can pivot completely round. (Private Collection, Paris. Photo: Sully Jaulmes)
Left
SUE ET MARE: Painted and gilt cabinet with lacquered doors from a design by Mathurin Méheut, marble top, c. 1920. (Collection Jean-Claude Brugnot, Paris)

METAL

Some magnificent metalwork in the Art Nouveau style was produced during the last decade of the nineteenth century. Hector Guimard, as well as designing various organic Métro entrances and grilles also designed fireplaces, balcony rails, theatre seat standards, park benches and cemetery crosses in wrought-iron. Louis Majorelle designed a full range of metalware, from railings to the most elaborate stairwells, staircases and domes. There were others too but the vast majority of ironwork conventionally produced was derivative, uninspired, overblown, overcomplicated and unattractive. Eugène Grasset, always the teacher, published a volume of simplified decorative ironwork in 1906 in the hope that it might inspire metal-workers.

The opening of the Salons to decorative art inspired a number of metalworkers to submit their designs and these opportunities exposed them to the same influences as other designers and caused them to influence each other. It also encouraged metalworkers to work closely with other craftsmen in the production of multi-media works. Thus at the 1912 Salon d'Automne a door designed by Henri Tauzin was exhibited, with ironwork by Emile Robert enclosing moulded glass panels of nudes with grotesque masks by René Lalique.

The era of the solitary creative metalworker was, however, coming to a close. New machinery was devised to simplify certain tasks, new techniques of treating metals were being perfected and the time taken to work metal was much reduced by these new aids. The problems created by the new technology were, as always, its initial and running costs, and once a metalworker had installed the machinery, he needed to work it in order to make it pay for itself. Important commissions came from the state and from architects. In both cases the commissions were frequently very precise and involved the manufacture of designs produced by the architect in charge of the project or some other outside designer, giving the metalworker no creative scope. Sometimes the designs were produced with the technical aid of the metalworker, who could thus bring his practical experience to bear on the specific commission. Very occasionally the commission gave the metalworker the oppor-tunity to produce his own design.

At the 1925 Exhibition the work of Edgar Brandt was to be seen over and over again. Henry Wilson referred to him in his report as 'the famous smith Edgar Brandt, perhaps the most famous in the world.' He executed the grilles of the Porte d'Honneur, the various doors and gates for the Ruhlmann pavilion and metal furniture and furnishings for both the Ruhlmann pavilion and the Salon d'un Ambas-sadeur where he displayed L'Oasis, a six-fold screen made of copper, brass and iron. He also provided metalwork, from grilles and gates to radiator covers, lamps, display cabinets, screens and console tables, for a number of other stands and pavilions.

Brandt served a long apprenticeship as a smith, studying not only wrought-iron but silver, gold and jewellery. His early submissions at the annual Salons of the Société des Artistes Francais always comprised both ironwork and silver jewellery, generally brooches and buckles in organic plant and floral shapes. He was awarded a Medal 3rd Class in 1905, a Medal 2nd Class in 1907 and a Medal 1st

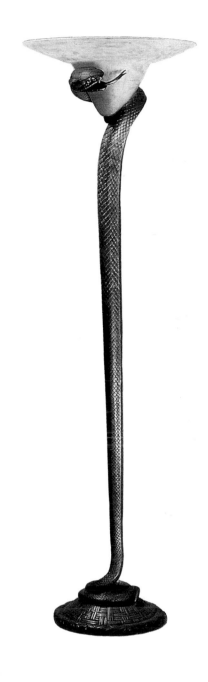

Above
EDGAR BRANDT: Cobra lamp, bronze with glass shade by Daum Frères, Nancy. The model was provided in three different heights with alternative shades in glass, alabaster and sheet metal. (Private Collection, London)
Opposite
EDGAR BRANDT: Green patinated and silver-plated radiator cover with wire-mesh backing grille. (Private Collection, London)

Class in 1908, when as a full member of the Society he became a member of the jury and was henceforth to exhibit Hors Concours. He was further honoured in 1923 when the Society awarded him its Medal of Honour. In the meantime he had also joined the Salon d'Automne and the Société des Artistes Décorateurs, becoming a member of the jury of both. He produced his own designs at various exhibitions but was always prepared to execute the designs of others. As early as 1911 at the Salon des Artistes Décorateurs he exhibited a monumental gate for the new French Embassy in Brussels, designed by its architect G. Chedanne. After the war he collaborated closely with a number of architects, particularly André Ventre and Henri Favier, the designers of the Porte d'Honneur at the 1925 Exhibition. He executed a vast number of other commissions for them as well as employing them as designers for several projects of his own.

Public commissions came his way, from monuments, including the Eternal Flame at the Tomb of the Unknown Soldier in Paris, to metalwork for the Opéra at Marseilles, the Louvre and the Banque de France in Paris. The Paris 1925 Exhibition was, however, to change his life. He had been given the opportunity to design a complete room himself at the French Embassy pavilion—and that freedom proved heady. He opened his own gallery, not merely a showcase for his metalwork, but also for glass, ceramics, jewellery, bookbinding and other crafts which fitted in with his own designs, and this attracted a number of artist-craftsmen. The Exhibition also led to his first commission in the United States, the Madison-Belmont Building on Madison Avenue at 34th Street, for which he designed the main entrance, window frames, decorative ironwork borders and grilles. For Cheney Brothers, the silk and fabric manufacturers who occupied four floors of the building, he designed a complete showroom, from doors and display racks to lighting and decorative panels. 1925 was also the year in which he opened a New York branch, called Ferrobrand Inc. on Park Avenue, though he later moved to Lexington Avenue.

Brandt was now in a dominating position as leader of the new school of metalworkers, with ateliers in Paris and New York employing a large number of craftsmen. He collaborated with architects on new buildings and monuments and with interior designers for the production of a vast range of grilles and room dividers, shelving systems, fire screens, radiator covers, console tables, stairs and balcony rails, mirrors, plant stands and lamps.

Wrought-iron lamps with cameo glass shades by Daum had been exhibited by Brandt as early as 1910, but the range of these table lamps was widened with the use of Daum glass shades of a smooth finish with opaque internal coloured swirls. He designed some lamps using reticulated glass, the shade blown into the wrought-iron armature. He also designed a number of ceiling and wall light fittings of complex metallic shapes with smooth or acid-etched shades by Daum, though he also used glass by a large variety of other makers, most notably Lalique, who produced moulded glass plaques for incorporation into elaborate chandeliers in addition to more normal shades. Brandt's most successful design was, however, the Serpent lamp, a brass snake with coiled tail resting on the corner of a brass-plated basket cover, the body extending upwards then coiling around the shade, the head staring balefully forward. The lamp was produced in three different sizes, from table lamp to standard lamp, with glass shades by Daum with the alternative of

alabaster shades. They are also sometimes found with cornet shades made of painted tin. Brandt also produced other curious designs, such as an illuminated fish tank, the glass by Daum incorporated into a wrought-iron standard.

Brandt, of course, did not confine himself to wrought-iron. He used all available metals to achieve different results, frequently combining wrought-iron with bronze, steel or aluminium and patinating metals with gold, brown, green or black. Much of the smoothness of his work was achieved by the use of autogenous soldering and he used stamping presses to repeat decorative patterns.

The interwar years were a golden age for metalwork. The spare, clean lines of architecture lent themselves particularly well to decorative metalwork and interior designers used it lavishly. Central heating radiators cried out for decorative covers. Metal furniture was made for garden use and gradually crept into the house. Indeed, the 1930s saw a surge of new metallic furniture designs which were admired for their hygienic, clean and modern lines and their imperviousness to damage inflicted by central heating. Even before the chrome-plated simplification of 30s metal furniture, Armand-Albert Rateau was designing and executing exotic bronze tables, chairs, lamps and dressing tables.

Brandt was, of course, not alone as a creative metalworker. He was the most well-known and his fame undoubtedly helped them all in making their craft an essential ingredient of any architectural or interior scheme. Notable creative metalworkers included Raymond Subes; Edouard Schenck, who was later joined by his sons; Edouard Delion; Adalbert Szabo and the brothers Jules and Michel Nics—all Hungarians who settled in Paris and became naturalised Frenchmen. Others included Paul Kis, who came from Rumania and also settled in Paris and was naturalised, Fred Perret, Gilbert Poillerat, Robert Mercoris, Richard Desvallières and Paul Laffillée and the firm of Schwartz-Hautmont—and in Lyon, Charles Piguet. All worked with and for architects, supplied ironwork for public buildings, the great transatlantic liners and the small Mediterranean and Far Eastern ships, and a number of churches and cathedrals. They also produced a vast number of smaller items for use in the house.

They were not alone in so doing—all the major firms specialising in interior decoration produced metalwork. Süe et Mare designed mirrors, lighting fixtures, fire screens and other items. They also specialised in designing complete sets of door and window furniture. Nearly all their metalwork was executed by their sister firm, Fontaine, which eventually took over Süe et Mare's Compagnie des Arts Français. Maurice Dufrêne designed a dining room in wrought-iron and glass, the sideboard and table resting on curved metal ribbons. Ruhlmann designed a wide range of metal wall and ceiling light fittings and several wall and table mirrors, the most famous of which was a silvered bronze circular mirror set on a lightly curved pedestal inspired by the shape of a steer's horns, executed by L'Art du Bronze and produced in large quantities. For the 1925 Exhibition he designed a bookcase of lacquered hammered steel sheets executed by Raymond Subes.

Metal was also used to make distinctive and unusual shopfronts. Robert Mallet-Stevens used brass plates with unconcealed rivets to create such modern structures as the Bally shoe shop in the boulevard des Capucines, which survived only slightly vandalised until fairly recently.

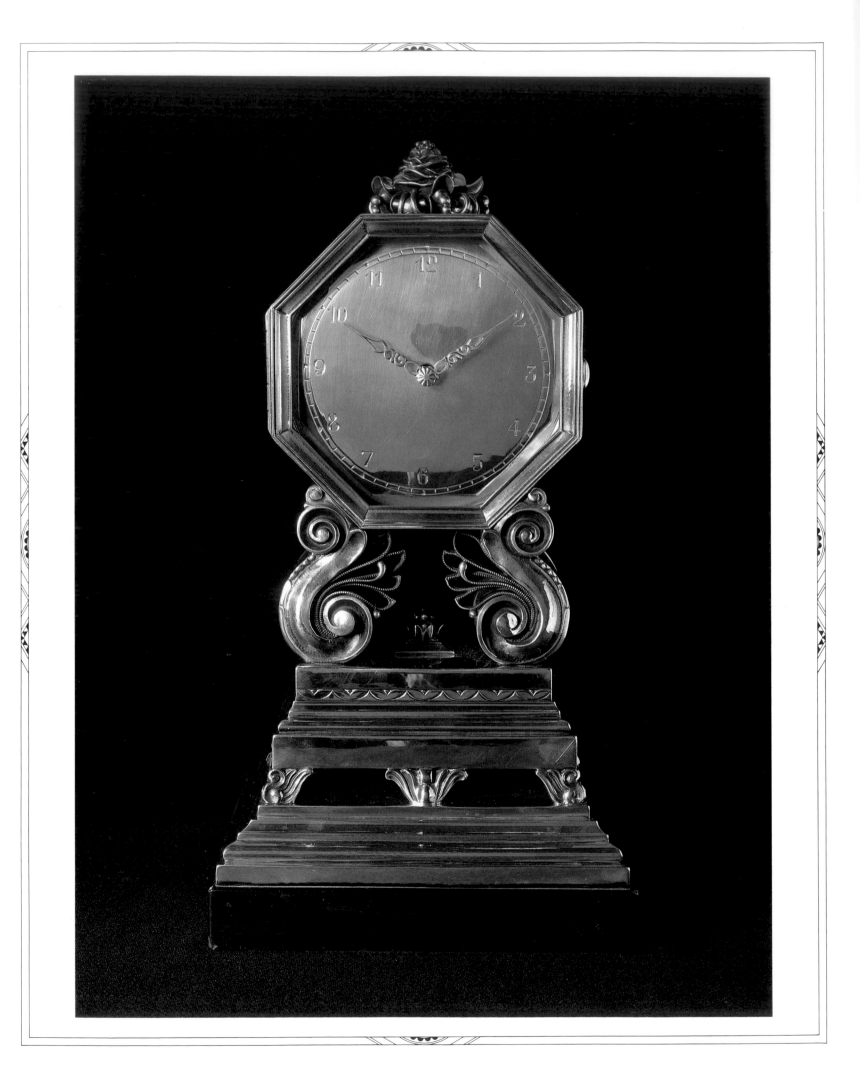

SILVER

Clean, modern lines in silver design were produced as early as 1912 by such firms as Cardeilhac, Louis Aucoc and Fabergé, who had all manufactured some splendid Art Nouveau pieces a little earlier, but the years following the 1918 Armistice saw the emergence of a number of new designers, often commissioned by established firms. Christofle, who had approached Art Nouveau with both caution and suspicion, was far more receptive to the simplicity and geometricism which went into the formation of the Art Deco style, and the firm commissioned such artists as Gio Ponti, Christian Fjerdingstad, Jean Serrière, Maurice Daurat, Gaston Dubois, Luc Lanel and Paul Follot to design for them. Many of the firm's designs were also executed in electroplate, a process they had introduced in France in 1842, and included tableware for the Normandie and other French liners. Tétard Frères, Paul Bablet and M. Gallerey followed suit, while Linzeler & Marchak commissioned the sculptor Georges Béal to design for them. Other leading manufacturers of silverware in the Art Deco style included Chapuis, Savary et Fils, Fouquet Lapar and Ercuis.

Tea and coffee sets, samovars, boxes, tureens, candlesticks, trophies, cups and cutlery were among the vast quantity of silver available. Süe et Mare produced much, often in pear-shaped curves with decorative swirls reminiscent of the Viennese designs of Dagobert Peche, though they also commissioned some handsome circular boxes from Paul Véra and Pierre Poisson, plain with a stylised head in relief on the cover. Louis Süe himself designed silver for both his own firm and for Christofle.

Undoubtedly the most important French silver designer was Jean E. Puiforcat. His father manufactured and retailed a wide range of silverware and the young Puiforcat learned the trade in his father's workshops, later studying sculpture with Louis Aimé Lejeune, himself a student of Thomas and Injalbert. At the age of seventeen Jean Puiforcat joined the army and at the end of the Great War was awarded the Croix de Guerre. He exhibited his first silver at the 1921 Salon d'Automne and at the following year's Salon; the Musée des Arts Décoratifs acquired one of his designs, a silver coffee pot with lapis-lazuli handle and finial.

Jean Puiforcat approached the task of designing silverware from an aesthetic and philosophical rather than a merely practical point of view. His starting point was Plato, from whom he 'learned of the arithmetic, harmonic and geometric mean' and the Golden Number. Harmony was only achievable through equilibrium of volumes and gracefulness of shape. Eschewing surface decoration, including the traditional hammer marks which had long been the ostentatious trademark of the handmade object, he deliberately devised large smooth areas which caught, reflected and distorted light, the light itself framing the constantly changing surface decoration. He frequently contrasted the silver finish with gilt and used crystal, lapis-lazuli,

ivory, jade and other hardstones with ebony and rare woods as handles, finials or ribs. Despite his youth, he was almost immediately hailed as a great innovator and most French silver designers followed his lead.

At the 1925 Exhibition Jean Puiforcat was a member of both admissions and prize-giving juries as well as official reporter for Metal. His designs were on view at the Puiforcat gallery at Rouard's 'Groups des Artisans Français Contemporains' pavilion, shared with the magazine *Art et Décoration,* in the French Embassy pavilion and in the display cabinets for Class 10 (Art and Industry of Metal) in the Grand Palais. The focal point of his display in the Rouard pavilion was described by Henry Wilson: 'There was a fine centre-piece with an eight-sided vase in the centre forming a fountain with jets from the four angles. The sides from which the water spouted were set with fluorspar, underneath which were placed electric lamps which shed a beautiful subdued radiance on the table when lit. At each angle of the centre vase or tank were set triangular blocks of lapis-lazuli and on either side of two subsidiary side tanks were plaques of polished lapis-lazuli. The whole effect was rich, yet restrained and beautiful.'

In 1926 Puiforcat joined with his friends Pierre Legrain, Pierre Chareau, Raymond Templier and Dominique (André Domin and Marcel Genevrière) to form 'Les Cinq', exhibiting regularly together at the Galerie Barbazange in Paris until 1928. He was one of the founder members of the Union des Artistes Modernes in 1930, but like several other founder members, his heart was not really in mass-production. The UAM's motto 'le beau dans l'utile' (beauty in the useful) clearly appealed to him but he was incapable of accepting any loss of quality for the sake of mass appeal. Ironically enough, when critics suggested that he derived some of his inspiration from the machine, he retorted angrily that 'the machine is not French—it is not French in spirit.' He was even more explicit later: 'To say I am inspired by aircraft or wireless is ridiculous. Engineers who work with figures have no chance of finding simple and pure shapes.'

Next to Puiforcat, undoubtedly the most influential silversmith was Georg Jensen. Born in Denmark, Jensen went through the long, traditional apprenticeship of the silversmith, studied, travelled and designed jewellery, silver and ceramics, before opening his own workshop at the age of thirty-eight in Copenhagen. Though he was himself a distinguished designer, he worked closely with a number of sculptors, painters and architects who designed for him. His first expansion was into Berlin, where he opened a branch in 1908. Two years later he was awarded a Gold Medal at the Brussels International Exhibition and his growing fame encouraged him to expand the number of designers and workmen. In 1919 he opened a Paris branch, in 1920 the London branch and a New York shop, and in 1930 the Stockholm branch.

The range of goods produced by Jensen was very large and included tea, coffee and lemonade sets, decanters and candlesticks, as well as several original sets of tableware and silver jewellery, occasionally set with semi-precious stones. No attempt was made to imitate expensive jewellery, so that Jensen jewellery could never be confused with costume jewellery. It was designed and crafted as an alternative jewellery, and as such was, and remains, both distinguished and popular. For a short while in the interwar years some Jensen jewellery was made in gold, but this experiment was soon abandoned.

In the 20s Jensen brought out a number of Art Deco designs, including several cocktail shakers (a completely new vessel), cigarette boxes and the distinguished 'pyramid' cutlery design of the architect Harald Nielsen.

Jean Desprès and Gérard Sandoz designed a number of individual creations, combining polished with hammered sections, studs, rivets and other decorative sections derived from industrial machinery. In England, Charles Boyton designed and executed a fine range of tableware and tea sets in strong, geometric patterns, while Walker & Hall turned out more routine, but still interestingly geometric designs.

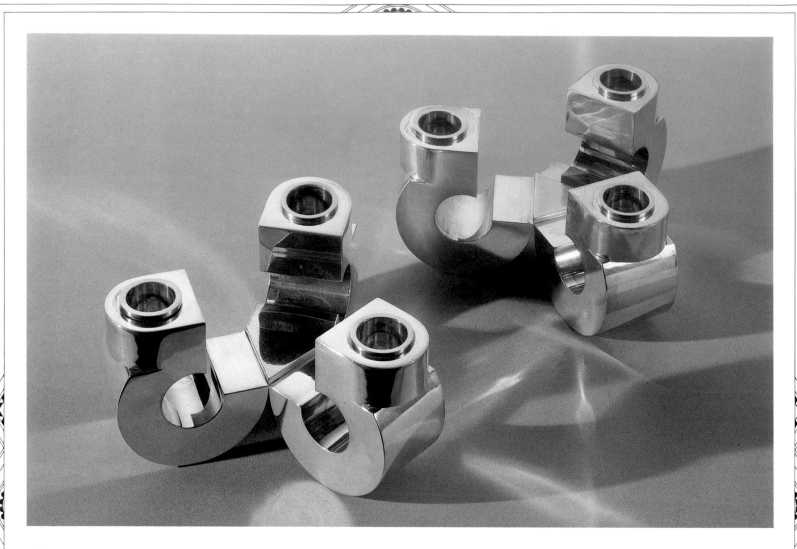

Opposite, above
JEAN PUIFORCAT: Pair of three-light silver and silver-gilt candlesticks. (Collection N. Manoukian, Paris. Photo: Sully Jaulmes)

Opposite, below
JEAN PUIFORCAT: Silver and crystal tea set made for Madame Nahmias. (Collection N. Manoukian, Paris. Photo: Sully Jaulmes)

Above
CARDEILHAC: Silver tea set with inlaid lapis-lazuli. (Private Collection, Paris. Photo: Sully Jaulmes)

Below
CHARLES BOYTON: Silver tea set with hardwood handles and finials. (Private Collection, London)

Above
JEAN PUIFORCAT: Silver and rosewood tea set with tray, 1937. (Virginia Museum of Fine Arts, Gift of Sydney and Frances Lewis. Photo: Katherine Wetzel)
Left
JEAN PUIFORCAT: Silver-gilt tableware from a dozen place settings canteen. (Editions Graphiques Gallery, London)
Opposite
JEAN PUIFORCAT: Silver table lamp for Saks Fifth Avenue, New York. (Editions Graphiques Gallery, London)

DINANDERIE, ENAMEL AND LACQUER

John Dunand, born in the canton of Geneva in Switzerland, studied drawing, carving, modelling and chasing at the local School of Industrial Arts. He wanted to be a sculptor and in 1897 was awarded a scholarship to study in Paris, where he joined two of his close school friends, the sculptor and later furniture designer Carl Albert Angst and the graphic artist François Louis Schmied. In Paris he studied in the studio of Jean Dampt, a sculptor whose commitment to direct craft work led him not only to carve ivory but to chase metal directly. An example of this was his master-piece, the group of the Chevalier Raymondin and the fairy Mélusine, the carved ivory maiden wrapped in the arms of the knight in full armour, executed in welded and chased steel. Dunand earned his living by working on the modelling and casting of the monumental winged horses which were being prepared for the new Alexandre III Bridge, which was to be inaugurated by the tsar himself, and until 1902 devoted his time entirely to sculpture.

Dunand had no illusions concerning his art. His father was also a craftsman, a goldsmelter for a watchmaking firm. Dampt taught his students that craft was the very essence of their art, made them read John Ruskin and study the work of the English practitioners of the Arts and Crafts movement. During one of his regular visits back to Geneva, Dunand studied with a local coppersmith called Danhauer and in 1903 began his own experiments with metalwork.

During the first stage of the process of dinanderie a circular sheet of copper was hammered into shape with a wooden mallet. Starting from the centre, the hammer-ing moved outwards along predetermined planes, each blow forcing the crystalline nature of the material to move forward. Large horn-shaped anvils were used, each

Above
JEAN GOULDEN: Silver-plated bronze, enamel and marble clock, 1929. (Virginia Museum of Fine Arts, Gift of Sydney and Frances Lewis)
Opposite
JEAN DUNAND: Hammered copper vase patinated with silver inlays, chased and patinated bronze snakes and wrought-iron foot, c. 1913. (Private Collection, Paris. Photo: Sully Jaulmes)

end shaped to give form to the metal which was hammered over it, the wooden mallet being replaced with a steel hammer for finer work. As each blow hardened the metal it needed to be constantly reheated to return it to a more malleable state. A vase form was created by hammering the sheet so that the outward edges gradually rose as the centre became the base. More hammering was used to elongate the neck, round the base, and to shrink or enlarge the opening, but the essence of a true dinandier's vase was that it was fashioned from a single sheet of metal, without seams, joints or solder. Soft metals, like copper, lead or pewter were most commonly used but other metals such as gold, silver, brass and steel were not uncommon. Too thin a sheet meant breaks and tears in the fabric during the hammering. Too thick a sheet meant harder and more skilled work. Since hammering the metal thinned it, pushing some of it outwards, the outer edges—which formed the neck and opening of a vase or bowl—ended up thicker than the rest of the body.

Once shaped as a vase, jardinière, plate or charger, the vessel was ready to be decorated. This was done in a number of ways: by patinating it with various formulae of acids with metallic oxides and a naked flame, thus colouring the metal green, brown or black; by gilding or silvering, the plating covering the whole surface or part of it, or even used to produce patterns; by embossing, in which the relief design was created by hammering a shaped tool held to the inner surface of the metal, forcing the outer surface to take various shapes; by chasing, carving the surface with a variety of sharp tools and a hammer; or by inlaying other metals. Using this method the design was grooved into the surface, the base of the cavity being larger than its surface opening. A softer metal plug was then inserted into the cavity and hammered in, the base of the plug spreading into the width of the cavity and holding firm. Depending on the design, the top of the plug could then be filed down to form a unity with the surface, or could be chased to a pattern. The surface could also be decorated with niello work, a practise more common in Russia, which entailed engraving the design on the surface, then rubbing in a powder made up from an alloy of copper, silver and lead mixed with sulphur when melted, then ground when cold. The decorated sections were brushed over with borax before adding the powder. When the metal was heated the composition fused and filled the engraved design. When cooled, the surface was filed off and a dark grey pattern left.

The metal sheet used was rarely more than one millimetre thick at the start, so in order to prevent distortion of the vessel when decorating, it was first filled with cement in a special composition which could easily be removed later. The whole vessel was then partly embedded into a large lump of the same cement fitted to a moveable platform. This made a large area of the surface accessible for decorating and the vessel could later be turned over and re-embedded to decorate the other side.

Dunand first exhibited a carved wood bread tray at the 1903 Salon of the Société Nationale des Beaux-Arts. The following year he exhibited a bronze bust but from 1905 onwards he began to exhibit his dinanderie-ware, which brought him increasing critical attention and sales. In 1906 he married and took the deci-

Right
JEAN DUNAND: Pair
of lacquered wood
doors. (Collection N.
Manoukian, Paris.
Photo: Sully Jaulmes)

sion to abandon sculpture and devote himself to the more craft-orientated metal-work. The shapes he devised were always natural and graceful, the design alternating between the figurative, including plants and snakes, and abstract patterns. He also took on six pupils and gave courses in sculpture, silversmithing and chasing.

In 1909 Dunand changed his forename from John to its French equivalent, Jean. He was also elected a member of the Société des Artistes Décorateurs and exhibited at the Galerie des Arts Modernes. The following year he participated in the Brussels International Exhibition.

As his fame increased, Dunand sought new ways to decorate his metalware. He had seen Japanese metal vases decorated with lacquer, but did not know how to make or apply it. His chance to learn came in 1912 when the noted Japanese lacquer artist, Sugawara, requested Dunand's help with a metalwork problem. Dunand's fee was that he be taught the art of lacquerware by Sugawara.

Lacquer is the sap of a tree, *Rhus vernicifera,* used from very early times in China over wood and other materials to give a hard, smooth, bright surface. The technique was later introduced into Japan where it was further developed. Imitations of lacquer were made in Europe and generally consisted of varnish over a gesso ground, often called 'japanning'. Real lacquer involves the application of twenty or more layers with a brush, each layer taking between one day and three weeks to dry and harden, an operation that needs to be carried out in a moist atmosphere. Each dried layer needs to be rubbed smooth before the next can be applied and the final layer is then rubbed smooth and highly polished. Natural lacquer comes in a range of tortoiseshell shades and is transparent when smoothed and polished. Colours are achieved by mixing the natural lacquer with vegetable pigments, while black is achieved by oxidising with iron. The finished lacquered surface can also be enriched by encrusting it with such materials as ivory, mother-of-pearl or metal, and it is also hard enough to be carved in intaglio. Dunand's first interest was in the application of lacquer to metal but he soon moved to its large-scale application, which meant using a soft wood base and up to forty layers of lacquer.

At the 1921 Salon des Artistes Décorateurs Dunand first exhibited a lacquered screen designed by Henri de Waroquier and his exhibition at the Galerie Georges Petit included a large group of lacquered furniture, screens, boxes and vases. This was the first of several exhibitions held at that gallery by Dunand with his friends Jean Goulden, Paul Jouve and François Louis Schmied. As Dunand's fame grew so did the orders, and his studio kept being added to in both height and floor space as he tackled increasingly larger screens and panels, including official orders for the ocean liners Atlantique and Normandie. In his workshop he designed and manufactured furniture with large, smooth surface areas for lacquering, though he also lacquered furniture for other designers, including Pierre Legrain, Eugène Printz, Jacques-Emile Ruhlmann and Jean Goulden. One of Dunand's inventions was the use of crushed eggshell set into transparent lacquer to achieve a whole new range of effects. Different results were obtained depending on whether the outside or inside of the shell was used, and on the size of the pieces.

Above
JEAN DUNAND: *Les Amoureux.* Small lacquered wood panel designed by Jean Lambert-Rucki. (Private Collection, Paris. Photo: Sully Jaulmes)
Opposite
JEAN DUNAND: *Les Amants.* Small lacquered wood panel designed by Jean Lambert-Rucki. (Author's Collection. Photo: Rodney Todd-White)
Overleaf, left
JEAN DUNAND: *Soumission.* Lacquered wood panel. (Collection Alain Lesieutre, Paris. Photo: Sully Jaulmes)
Overleaf, right
JEAN DUNAND: *L'Offrande.* Lacquered wood panel. This panel was originally designed as a firescreen for the Neuilly house of Jean-Charles Worth. (Collection Alain Lesieutre, Paris. Photo: Sully Jaulmes)

Above
JEAN DUNAND: Copper vase with four semi-circular wings, lacquered red and black. (Collection N. Manoukian, Paris. Photo: Sully Jaulmes)
Opposite
JEAN DUNAND: Hammered and lacquered vase. (Collection DeLorenzo Gallery, New York)

Right
JEAN DUNAND: Lacquered wood screen. (Private Collection, Paris. Photo: Sully Jaulmes)

Below
JEAN DUNAND: Four-leaf lacquered wood screen. (Collection Alain Lesieutre, Paris. Photo: Philippe Doumic)

Opposite
JEAN DUNAND: Cheval-glass mirror with lacquered frame and door. (Private Collection, Paris. Photo: Sully Jaulmes)

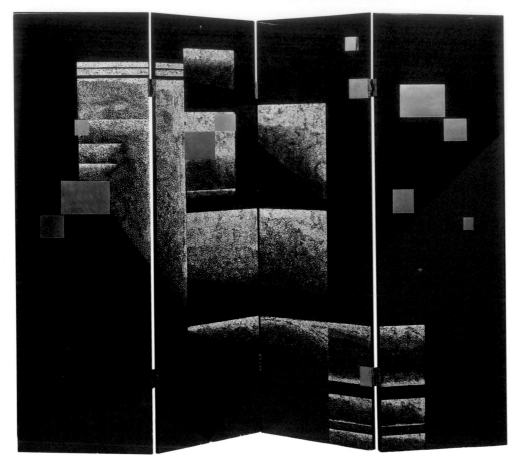

Dunand's own original panel designs varied from the figurative—including nudes, genre scenes and scenes inspired by Oriental miniatures, and a variety of animals from the naturalistic to the grotesque and humorous—to geometric patterns and abstract juxtapositions of colour and shapes. He used both styles throughout his career. He also produced a number of portraits in lacquer, some with gilt or eggshell backgrounds. For the fashion designer Madeleine Vionnet, creator of the bias cut, and the milliner Madame Agnès, he designed complete interiors. Having discovered that diluted lacquer 'took' on fabrics he painted scarves, hats, dresses, belt buckles and handbags with geometric designs for the two ladies and exhibited these items in 1925. He also lacquered small plaques for bookbindings, made jewellery, boxes and cigarette cases, and lacquered panels and sculpture, often designed by his friends. At the height of his fame he was employing about one hundred artisans, lacquerers (most of whom were Indo-Chinese), carpenters and other craftsmen.

In complete contrast to Dunand, Eileen Gray was a solitary worker. Born in Ireland of Scottish-Irish stock, she inherited the title of Baroness Gray in 1895 through her mother, granddaughter of the 10th Earl of Moray. Three years later she entered the Slade School of Art in London to study drawing. In her spare time she studied lacquering in a small workshop in Soho which specialised in the repair of old lacquer screens. In 1902 she moved to Paris, studying at the Académie Colarossi and the Académie Julian A little later she discovered the Japanese lacquerer, Sugawara, and resumed her studies of lacquer with him. After some considerable experimentation, she exhibited some of her lacquerwork at the 1903 Salon of the Société des Artistes Décorateurs, including the panel *Les Magiciens de la nuit.* From 1912 onwards she also designed a number of pieces of furniture for Jacques Doucet for his Neuilly apartment, which was being decorated under the direction of Paul Iribe. Sugawara, who initiated Dunand in the art of lacquering, worked for Eileen Gray from about 1911 to the mid-1920s. When war broke out in 1914 she drove an ambulance for a while then moved to London with Sugawara, setting up a studio in Cheyne Walk. After the Armistice they returned to Paris and in 1919 she designed a complete interior for the milliner Suzanne Talbot (Mme Mathieu Lévy), which she was to redesign a few years later.

In 1922 Eileen Gray opened her own gallery, called Jean Désert, in the rue du Faubourg Saint Honoré, where she displayed her furniture and lacquerwork, and carpets which she designed and had made in her workshop under the direction of Evelyn Wyld. In 1930 she closed down the shop to concentrate on her new love, architecture, which she had begun studying in 1924. She also started designing new, simplified items of furniture capable of mass-production, though these were only to be so manufactured when she was in her nineties.

Dunand's friend Jean Goulden came from a wealthy farming family from Alsace. He went to Paris to study medicine and there met a number of artists, with whom he felt a great affinity—and one of them was Dunand. When war broke out he joined the army as a doctor and found himself at the Macedonian front

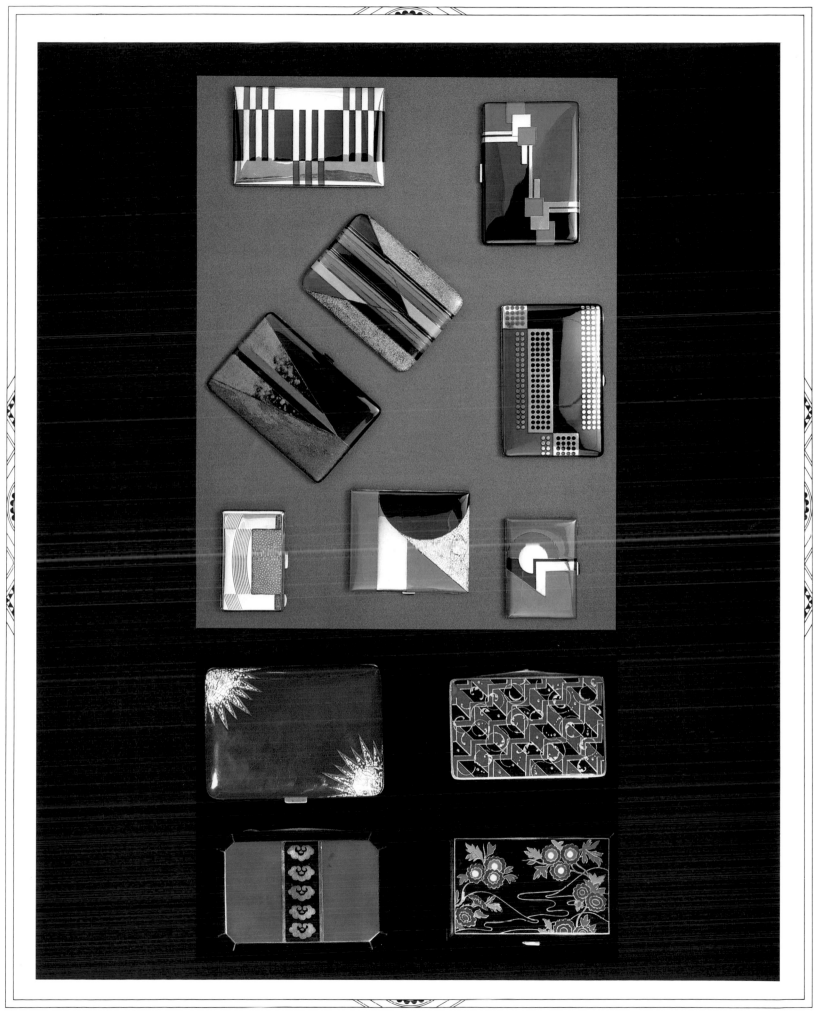

when the war ended. After the Armistice he spent several months in the monasteries of Mount Athos, where the beauty of Byzantine enamels was revealed to him. As soon as he returned to Paris he persuaded Dunand to show him the technique of champlevé enamelling, which he soon mastered and practised to the end of his life.

The studios of Dunand and his friend Schmied were in adjoining buildings and Goulden became both good friend and patron. His wealth enabled him to commission and buy works from both of them as well as from their friend Paul Jouve, the animalier sculptor and painter. Indeed, the four of them formed an intimate group which exhibited together at the Georges Petit Gallery every year between 1921 and 1932. Goulden's friendship with Schmied was further consolidated in 1925 when he married Schmied's daughter. In 1928 Goulden moved to Rheims where he continued to work until his death in 1947.

Goulden's designs were rigorously geometric—massive copper, brass or silver boxes, paperweights, candlesticks and chalices, structured like Cubist skyscrapers—decorated in gritty, mat or polished champlevé enamels. His boxes in particular provided surfaces for intricate compositions of circles, squares and triangles. He also designed enamelled plaques for bookbindings, several of which were executed for bindings designed by Schmied.

Claudius Linossier was apprenticed to a goldsmith at the age of thirteen and worked for several years with goldsmiths and silversmiths before doing a three-month stint with Jean Dunand. He settled in Lyon after the Great War and produced a wide range of dinanderie vases, bowls and plates. Using the full range of available techniques, his metalwork was rigorously geometric in design and decoration. Paul Louis Mergier, an aeronautical engineer, managed to keep up a parallel career as painter, designer and manufacturer of furniture and dinanderie, his metalwork tending to stylised figuration. Jean Serrière produced a small number of hammered copper vessels with silver inlays in addition to his work as a silversmith. Armand-Albert Rateau, who sculpted his bronze furniture, used lacquer and metallic inlays and incrustation occasionally to decorate the surfaces.

Limoges had long been famed for its enamels, and several enamellers working in the modern style set up workshops there. Abstract and floral designs in brightly coloured enamels in copper by Sarlandie are not uncommon, but the greatest enameller was Camille Fauré. Born in Perigueux in 1872, he spent a long apprenticeship before setting up his own workshop at Limoges, where he worked for some fifty years. His early work, like his post-World War II designs, involved large floral and figurative patterns, often in rich colours. He exhibited through the Paris shop, Au Vase Etrusque, and produced vases, bowls, ashtrays, boxes and other items for them. It was his geometric designs, however, which placed him as the greatest creative enameller of the Art Deco style. Using large vessels, vases, bowls or open-mouthed jardinières, the copper was then covered in multiple layers of polychrome enamels in hard, vitreous, three-dimensional geometric designs of subtle complexity and colour combinations. His friend Marty occasionally worked with him, and in a very similar style. Both produced a small number of pendants in enamelled gold, silver or copper.

Above, upper
CLAUDIUS LINOSSIER: Hammered metal vase, patinated and encrusted with niello silver chevrons and reddish copper lozenges, c. 1925, 26 cms. (Collection Alain Lesieutre, Paris)
Above, lower
CLAUDIUS LINOSSIER: Hammered and chased metal vase, polychrome patination with silver inlays, c.1925, 23 cms. (Collection Alain Lesieutre, Paris)
Opposite
Dressing table set in geometric polychrome enamel on silver glass cut with geometric patterns. Unidentified poincon. (Private Collection, London. Photo: Rodney Todd-White)

JEWELLERY

As a jeweller, René Lalique had attempted to wean fashionable women away from the traditional tyranny of the diamond and towards accepting exquisitely wrought settings incorporating such relatively inexpensive materials as enamel, glass, horn and ivory. He was never wholly to succeed. His clients included the queens of society and stage, but his greatest patron was a man, Calouste Gulbenkian ('Mr. Five-Per-Cent') of oil revenues fame, who amassed a considerable number of his jewels and other creations as display objects, not destined to be worn. Those contemporary jewellers who followed him in creating Art Nouveau jewellery, including Vever, Fouquet and Feuillâtre, also produced diamond jewellery, and it must be said that even Lalique himself occasionally used the stone. Lalique was, however, successful in showing women that well-designed, well-executed settings were of supreme importance in judging the elegance and effectiveness of a jewel. He also popularised the use of substances other than gold and precious stones. When the 20s were in full swing, Anita Loos' delicious heroine, Lorelei Lee, could echo generations of her predecessors in noting that diamonds were still indeed a girl's best friend. Yet both diamonds and their settings had changed in the last quarter of the nineteenth and the first quarter of the twentieth century. Where the jeweller of the 1870s had at his command little more than brilliant or rose-cut diamonds, the years that followed had popularised a variety of cuts, including square, emerald, pear, table, marquise and navette. The mark of the 20s was, however, the baguette, often in conjunction with other cuts or stones, its shape and sparkle ideal for the geometric shapes the jewels were increasingly adopting. Reporting on jewellery at the 1925 Exhibition for the Report of the British Department of Overseas Trade, the jeweller Henry Wilson wrote: 'Much is being made today in Paris of diamonds cut in rod form (taillé en baton ou en allumette). This has only been general for the last two years, I am told.'

Settings, too, had changed. The nineteenth-century jeweller had had to make his settings of gold, and gems had generally been mounted in cups, often foiled. Where diamonds had to be set, silver was generally used for its colour, but was highly unsatisfactory since it was both too soft and too prone to discolour, needing constant polishing. The increased use of platinum in the first quarter of the twentieth century had opened up immense new possibilities. Platinum was so strong and flexible that diamonds and other gems could be held with tiny claws and the gems isolated or clustered closely at will. Craftsmen delighted in using platinum to join separate sections of a jewel with slender rods, or to make supple, articulate bracelets or necklaces which followed the natural curves of the wearer's body.

To contrast with the arctic splendour of diamond and platinum, jewellers turned to enamel and black onyx. Rings and brooches were set with thin squares of black

Above
CARTIER: Pendant watch, the back set with a black onyx plaque, and diamonds on a silk ribbon with diamonds and onyx set in platinum. (Editions Graphiques Gallery, London)
Opposite
CARTIER: *Top* Three platinum pendants; milkmaid set with diamonds and emeralds and cabochon amethysts; owl set with diamonds, rubies and cabochon opal; robot set with baguette diamonds, cabochon amethyst and rubies. *2nd row* Diamond and platinum clip set with carved rubies and emeralds. *3rd row* Pair of earclips with diamonds and cabochon rubies and emeralds; crystal brooch with carved lapis-lazuli, diamonds and enamel. *Bottom* Platinum and diamond brooch with carved rubies and amethysts. (Private Collection, London)

onyx into which the diamond was set. Where appropriate, or where the armature was too slender to take the onyx, the metal itself was enamelled black. A touch of colour was occasionally introduced as additional contrast, tiny emeralds or rubies framing the diamond. A very similar result at less cost was achieved by replacing the diamond with a white sapphire.

Coloured gemstones were imported in quantity from Ceylon, India and Madagascar. Generally, small emeralds, rubies and sapphires were carved in rudimentary fashion in their country of origin in the shapes of leaves, fruit or flowers. These were then assembled in Paris, frequently in conjunction with diamonds and other stones, to form brooches, rings, earrings, clips and pendants in which the carved stones clustered together to form intricate polychrome figurative designs of flowers in pots, waterfalls or baskets of fruit. Cartier was one of the first to design such pieces, but other jewellers, including Boucheron, followed suit.

Fascination with the Far East was fed by adopting carved Chinese and other Oriental plaques in jade, coral or other hardstones, in platinum and diamond settings, while various precious cigarette cases, vanity cases and powder boxes were decorated with Chinese or Japanese landscapes or genre designs in lacquer, enamel or inlaid mother-of-pearl and gemstones.

Simplified geometric designs became increasingly popular as the 20s advanced. Edwardian designs were slightly adapted to eliminate the curve in favour of the straight line, but the pure circle, crescent and triangle were coming into their own in new combinations.

20s jewellery was quite distinct from pre-war jewellery. Women had changed radically. They cut their hair short, frequently sporting the 'garçonne' look: thus they had no use for hair combs, tiaras or diadems. They did not wear large feathered hats, so had no need for long hat pins. They wore short dresses with plunging necklines front and back, with short sleeves showing long naked arms which echoed the fashionable long, slender neck. So brooches were made, worn not only on the breast, but on the shoulder, the hip, the belt and on the plain little hats, including the cloche, which went with short hair. Pairs of clips were the most versatile of jewels. Clipped together they formed a brooch, separated they could be worn along the décolleté, front or back, on the lapel, on the belt or on any ornamental piece of fabric applied to the dress. Necklaces were worn, as were elaborate pendants on slender chains, long strands of pearls, and beads in coral, lapis-lazuli, nacre, jade or agate, matching, graduating or carved. The long pearl sautoirs, wrapped sometimes several turns around the neck, often ended in two long tassels, sometimes made of strung seed-pearl rows, loose or plaited. The lavallière was a loose, jewelled tie, the 'knot' a gem-encrusted pendant from which were suspended two chains of unequal length, each terminating in a setting for a large gem or cluster of gems, sometimes in tassels.

The naked arm cried out for adornment, and the jewellers responded with articulated gold, silver and platinum bracelets encrusted with cut, carved and cabochon stones in lapis-lazuli, jade, coral, onyx, agate, rock crystal, clear lead crystal and mat glass, several being worn at the same time. They were also

Right, above
RENE LALIQUE: 'Zig Zag' extensible glass
bracelet. Model 1327, first made in 1927.
(Private Collection, London)

Right, centre
BOUCHERON: Gold buckle set with diamonds
and carved lapis-lazuli, jade, onyx and coral.
Designed by Lucien Hirtz for the 1925 Paris
Exhibition. (Collection Boucheron, Paris)

Below, left
CHAUMET: *Top* Pendant and ear pendants in
jade, onyx, diamonds and pearls. *Centre*
Enamelled gold and ivory cigarette holder.
Bottom Coral bead bracelet with three onyx and
diamond sections set in platinum, 1925-30.
(Collection Chaumet, Paris)

Below, right
CHAUMET: *Top* Enamelled gold pocket watch
with diamond motif set in platinum. *Centre* Four
enamelled gold notepads with gold propelling
pencils and a circular, enamelled gold pill box set
with a mother-of-pearl and hardstone landscape
plaque surrounded by diamonds. *Bottom* Jade,
lapis-lazuli, diamonds and sapphires cigarette
case, 1926-30. (Collection Chaumet, Paris)

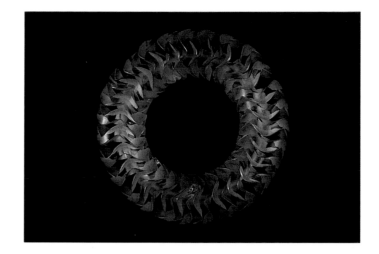

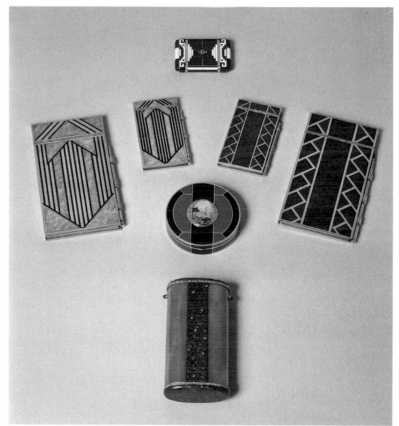

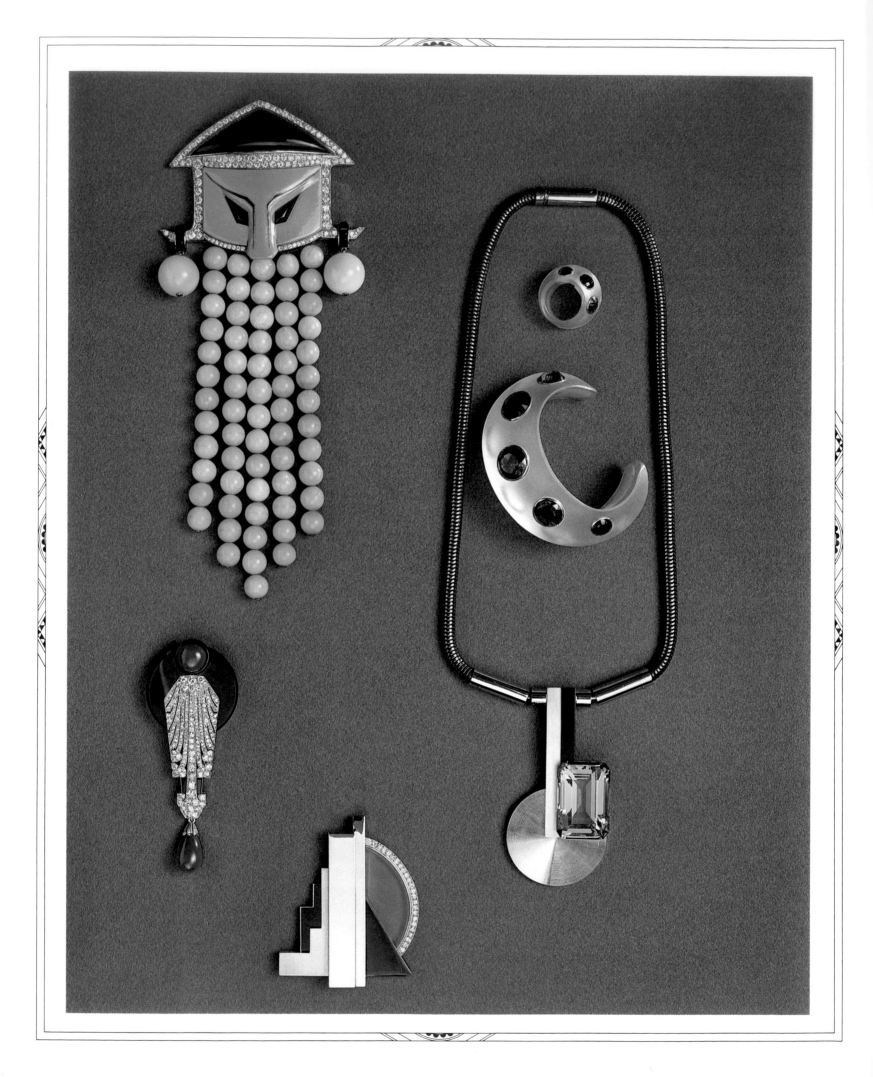

designed in such fashion that two bracelets could be clipped together to form a 'dog's collar' necklace. Bangles also came into their own, large ones to wear on the upper arms, smaller ones to wear in clusters from the wrist upwards, made of ivory, tortoiseshell, gold, silver, elephant hair wrapped in gold, enamelled, lacquered or painted. Short hair meant the ear-lobe was uncovered and long, frequently articulated ear pendants were designed in gold, silver or platinum with pearls, diamonds or coloured gemstones, though small earrings also remained in vogue.

Wristwatches became increasingly fashionable and designers produced a variety of styles, encrusted with diamonds or enamelled, contrasting different colours of gold or different finishes for platinum. The face tended to be fairly plain, black or white, fantasy confined to the numbering, while the design was concentrated on the case and bracelet. Even more fashionable were the pendant watches, attached to an extended ribbon or an interlinked articulated section, and pinned to the lapel. Since the back of the watchcase was visible it was treated as a pendant and was lifted and turned to tell the time, so the dial was normally put in upside down for the convenience of the wearer.

Art Deco jewellery was made by the great jewellery firms and by certain individual creators, though the latter frequently came from families of jewellers. All the major jewellery firms of Paris strove for luxury, the look of wealth adapted to the requirements of fashion, and they accumulated the most precious gems for use in the most stylish settings, though they were also prepared to harmonise those gems with carved hardstones and less precious, but colourful, gems. Among these old established firms were Boucheron, Cartier, Chaumet, Fouquet, Mauboussin, Mellerio and Vever, though another of the great firms, the more recently established Van Cleef & Arpels (then known as A. Van Cleef, S. & J. Arpels) produced a variety of precious vanity cases, powder boxes, lipstick cases, cigarette lighters, holders and cases. Van Cleef & Arpels, indeed, invented the precious vanity case's name when one of the firm's directors had one made for his wife, a gold case with compartments for powder, lipstick, rouge, comb, handkerchief and small change, the lid inset with a full-sized mirror. When he saw her simpering into the mirror, striking attitudes, the case thereafter became known as a 'minaudière' (a 'simperer').

George Fouquet, who had designed both Art Nouveau and traditional jewellery, launched himself into the new style with great zest. Concentric circles of diamonds and onyx, brooches and bracelets incorporating coral and enamel, combinations of enamel with jade beads, diamonds and onyx—all produced dramatic, often romantic shapes which flattered when worn and were objets d'art when in a cabinet. His son Jean Fouquet, who joined the firm in 1919 when he was just twenty years old, pioneered new, totally geometric designs which incorporated aquamarines and moonstones, rock crystal and glass, lacquer more often than enamel, engine-turned decoration, both yellow and white gold, and platinum. His designs are curiously sexless, abstract sculptures of great originality. Recognising this originality, his father had all Jean's jewellery signed 'Jean Fouquet'. Fouquet also commissioned designs from a number of fine designers, including André Leveillé, Ferté and Eric Bagge, several of whose pendants were made of mat crystal in conjunction with diamonds, onyx or coral.

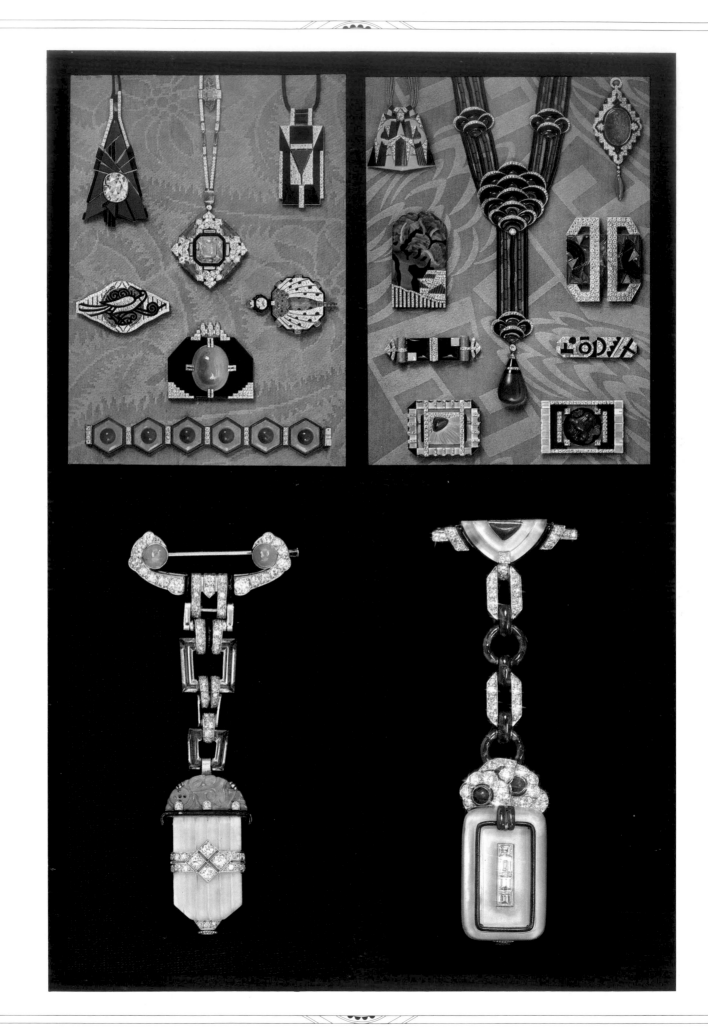

Maubossin produced some of the most colourful jewellery in the 20s, combining hardstones, faceted and cabochon gems and crystal with gold and platinum, though their designers from about 1928 onwards tended towards more chunky, machine-inspired shapes. Chief among their designers in these styles were Pierre-Yves Maubossin, Marcel Goulet and M. Vellay.

A number of firms somewhat smaller than the major ones already mentioned also produced highly stylised and stylish jewellery in the Art Deco style. They included Janesich, Dusausoy (whose chief designers were Justin and Jean Dusausoy and Mlle Chezelle), Robert Linzeler & Marchak (the latter, originally from Kiev in the Ukraine, survived on his own), Lacloche Frères (who had taken over Fabergé's London shop) and André Aucoc, an old established firm of jewellers and silversmiths with whom René Lalique had originally trained.

In addition to these, a number of other firms exhibited in the jewellery section, where the display cabinets were topped by stylish glass waterfalls by Lalique, and it became obvious that certain jewels in the windows of different manufacturers bore more than a passing surface resemblance to each other. 'The least knowledgeable visitor,' wrote Jacques Guérin in his official report, 'placed in the centre of that ellipse in which are gathered the greatest names of Parisian jewellery, could not help but be struck by the obvious kinship between many jewels, the work of different houses.' The reason was simply the old established habit of purchasing designs from individual, self-employed designers, a habit begun in the eighteenth century. These generally anonymous designers chose not to work for the jewellery firms, but to supply them with original designs. The results were that, on occasion, two or more jewellers ended up making slight variations on an identical design.

Raymond Templier's grandfather had founded the family jewellery firm. Run by his father Paul, they manufactured all Raymond's designs until 1929, when Raymond took over the running of the firm, renamed Paul and Raymond Templier.' His jewellery made full use of geometric patterns, often of great intricacy, contrasting mat and polished sections of platinum or white gold with diamonds, frequently pavé-set in swirling patterns. He used lacquer on occasions and such stones as aquamarine and haematite, as well as amber. In 1928 he designed all the jewellery worn by Brigitte Helm in Marcel L'Herbier's film L'Argent, based on Zola's novel.

Gérard Sandoz also came from a family of jewellers and watchmakers. Originally from the Jura, his grandfather Gustave had moved the business to Paris in 1865, where he had been succeeded by Gérard's father, Gustave-Roger Sandoz. Gérard was barely eighteen years old when he began to design jewellery which was manufactured by his father's firm, though he was only to devote a decade to it, ceasing to design jewellery in 1931. The last five years of that decade were his most prolific, but his designs throughout were totally inspired by the look of machinery, smooth, intricate planar structures of silver or gold in combination with flat cuts of such hardstones as haematite, onyx and labradorite, often in conjunction with rock crystal, aquamarine or citrine. He also designed a number of geometric patterns, executed in lacquer on silver cigarette cases in his father's works.

René Boivin had founded his jewellery shop and atelier in 1892, later marrying Paul Poiret's sister, Jeanne. On her husband's death in 1917, Madame Boivin took

Above, left
GERARD SANDOZ: *Semaphor*. Brooch with polished and mat platinum, diamonds, coral and jet, 1925. (Collection N. Manoukian, Paris. Photo: Sully Jaulmes)

Above, right
JEAN DUNAND: Pair of earclips and brooch in silver lacquered with a red and black geometric pattern. (Galerie Vallois, Paris)

Left
JEAN DUNAND: *Top and centre* Two pairs of silver earrings with red and black lacquer. *Bottom* Silver bracelet with red and black lacquer. All c. 1925. (Private Collection, Paris. Photo: Sully Jaulmes)

Opposite
GERARD SANDOZ: Five pendants. *Left to right* White and reddish gold set with labradorite on oxidised silver chain; silver haematite, citrine and onyx on an oxidised silver chain; yellow and white gold and onyx on carved rock crystal chain; white gold and onyx set with an aquamarine on a white gold hinged chain; yellow and reddish gold set with haematite. All c. 1928. (Private Collection, Paris. Photo: Sully Jaulmes)

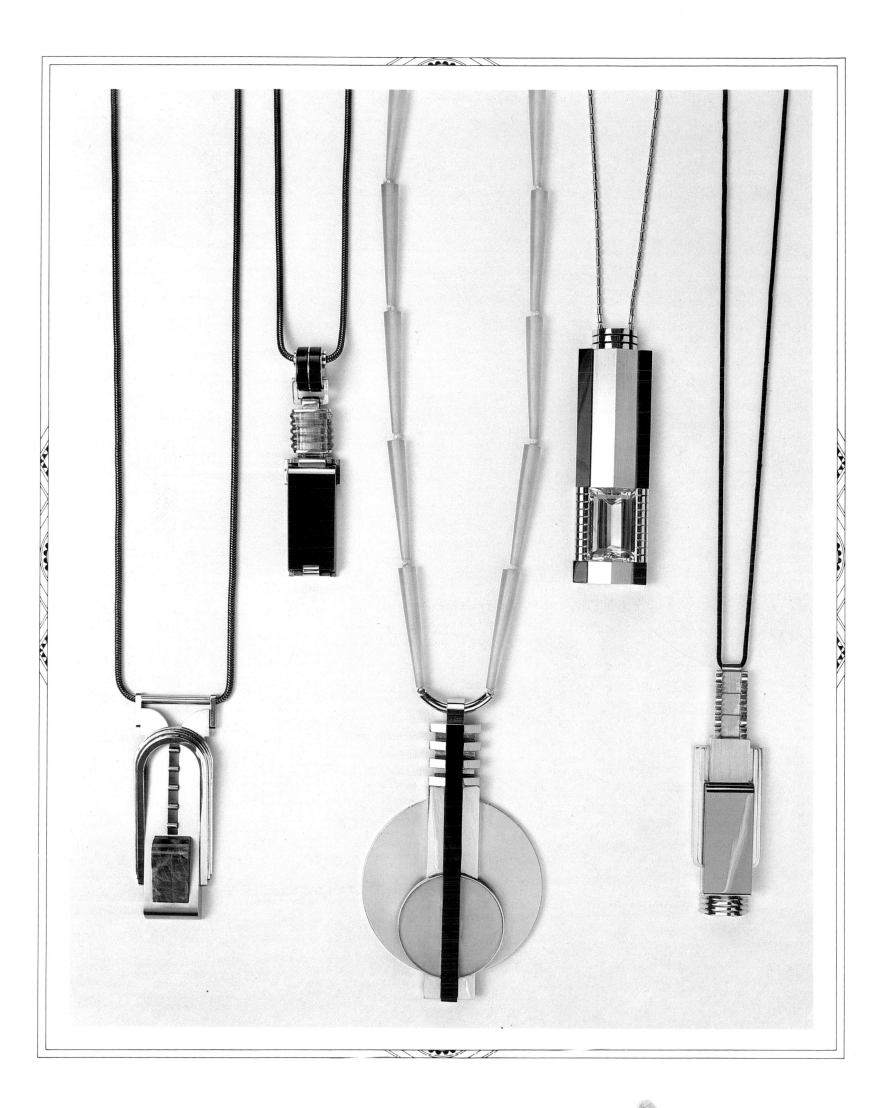

over the firm's direction for some forty years before being succeeded by her two daughters. Though Mlle Juliette Moutard became principal designer in 1933, Madame Boivin herself created most of the designs prior to that date and a number subsequently, moving from the early Art Nouveau-inspired designs to chic, stylised patterns in platinum, onyx and crystal.

Paul Brandt was a totally individual designer of jewellery. His pre-war designs, inspired by Art Nouveau, frequently married mother-of-pearl and abalone to silver and gold, but his 20s designs follow the same rigorous geometricism that inspired Jean Fouquet, Raymond Templier and Gérard Sandoz. Contrasting rectangular and triangular patterns, he often juxtaposed black onyx or black enamel with polished or mat platinum, while a recurrent motif consisted of embedding pearls into an onyx plaque, the pearls set in a diagonal or straight line.

Jean Dunand began designing and making jewellery in about 1924, varying from brooches in naturalistic, almost Art Nouveau, shapes based on plant forms to rigorously geometric ones. The latter included structured bracelets, brooches and earrings in hammered metal, as well as sets of hoops in graduated sizes, worn as sets of necklaces or bracelets. Most were lacquered in red and black patterns which alternated with the polished metal. Dunand normally used either silver or aureum, an alloy of silver with brass, giving a hard, golden metal particularly suitable for lacquering and firing. He also lacquered a number of pocket watch cases, cigarette and match cases and boxes, vanity cases and dressing-table sets. Jean Desprès also used lacquer to decorate his silver and gold jewellery, most of it in structured geometric patterns. His first uncompromisingly machine-inspired jewellery dates from about 1912, when he was twenty-three years old. As a silversmith and goldsmith, he often produced larger pieces, like chunky bracelets, in alternate hammered, roughly finished and smoothly polished sections. The lacquer on his jewellery is minimal—one or two short lines, a half curve or a small section, always contrasting with the metal. In the late 20s he began a long collaboration with the Surrealist painter Etienne Cournault, who supplied him with engraved and painted little sections of mirror-glass for insertion into rings, brooches and pendants.

Precious objets d'art were also made by the great jewellers. Cartier, directly inspired by Fabergé, produced miniature flowers in pots made of rose-quartz, nephrite, rock crystal and ivory, hardstone ashtrays and 'Kovsh' shapes, and clocks, including mystery clocks, complex colour combinations of carved quartz, hardstones and coral, set with diamonds and other gems. Boucheron, Linzeler & Marshak and Lacloche Frères were among those who also produced such objets d'art, with particular emphasis on portable cases.

René Lalique made a wide range of glass jewellery. Some were pendants moulded in relief with frogs, newts, insects, flowers, fruit, nymphs, birds or abstract patterns executed in clear or coloured glass, and hung on silk or cotton cord, usually with one or two tassels. Some of the pendants made in clear glass had nymphs, fairies or mermaids carved in intaglio, though some were only moulded. Other moulded glass sections were set into brass or silver holders to make brooches which were occasionally foiled to give the glass coloured reflections. Moulded glass

Above
Brigitte Helm in Marcel L'Herbier's film *L'Argent* wearing jewellery designed by Templier, 1928. (Contemporary photograph)
Opposite, above, left
RAYMOND TEMPLIER: Platinum brooch set with diamonds, 1928. (Author's Collection)
Opposite, above, right
RENE BOIVIN: Platinum, crystal, black onyx and enamel brooch. (Editions Graphiques Gallery, London)
Opposite, below
JEAN DESPRES: *Left* Silver, gold and black lacquer necklace. *Centre above* Brooch in yellow and white gold, silver and lapis lazuli. *Right* Silver and gold necklace. *Centre bottom left* Brooch in silver and black lacquer set with a glass panel engraved by Etienne Cournault, 1927. *Centre bottom right* Silver and enamel ring set with a similar panel. (Private Collection, Paris. Photo: Sully Jaulmes)

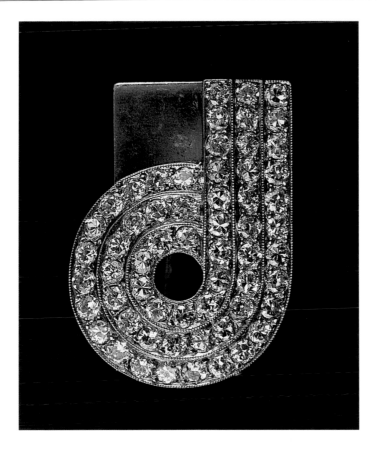

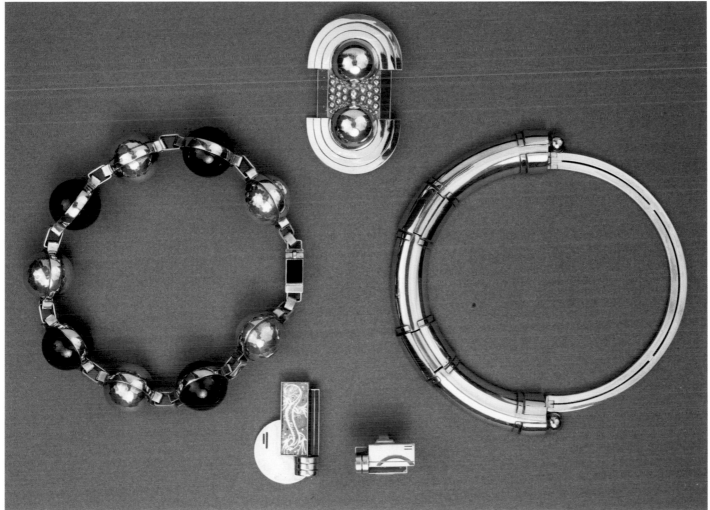

beads were strung as long necklaces, while sections of different shapes were strung together with elastic cords as flexible bracelets. Almeric Walter produced a number of pâte-de-verre pendants modelled as insects or flowers, though some of these were set in gold or silver as brooches. Gabriel Argy-Rousseau also produced a number of translucent pâte-de-cristal pendants modelled with flowers, animals, ballerinas and other subjects. Goupy and Heiligenstein designed and executed glass pendants enamelled with a variety of subjects, sometimes on both front and back.

Outside France, comparatively few designers worked in the Art Deco style. In Italy, G. Ravasco adapted his diamond-encrusted jewellery to geometric decorative patterns, alternating them with emeralds, sapphires, topaz and other coloured stones, sometimes using a little enamelling. In Britain, most of the creative designers were still working in the Arts and Crafts style, while the average jeweller turned out traditional designs. All the great Parisian houses had branches in London and New York as well as a number of other major capitals, and they were well able to cope with any demand for modern designs from the wealthy. After the 1925 Exhibition, a number of jewellers in London began designing in the Art Deco style, but the most interesting creations are often found unsigned.

In Denmark, Georg Jensen and his designers produced some very stylised, spare gold and silver brooches, rings, necklaces and pendants, many of which are still in production today. Carl Christian Fjerdingstad also designed a range of silver jewellery, often set with moonstones or amber. In the United States, Tiffany and Marcus & Co. also produced some highly stylised Art Deco jewellery, while Black, Starr & Frost and Tiffany made a number of precious boxes and clocks.

In Switzerland, much of the jewellery revolved around the watchmaking industry, which concentrated on producing small, gem-encrusted watches. Henri Blanc produced a number of very attractive small ladies' watches set into gold with cloisonné enamelled designs. In Germany, Theodore Wende and Theo Ortmann designed intricate, mechanistic constructions, while Naum Slutzki produced silver and cheap metal jewellery in striking, constructivist shapes which were more sharp and uncompromising than anything produced in France. The jewellery industry in Germany, centred on Pforzheim, went on producing large quantities of finely made traditional jewellery, and very likely executed a number of designs for some of the French firms.

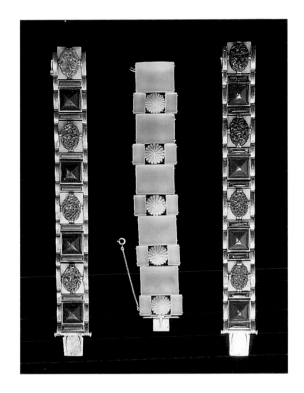

Above
MAUBOUSSIN: *Right and left* Gold bracelets set with carved jade plaques on agate and coral or lapis-lazuli pyramidal cabochons, designed by Pierre-Yves Mauboussin. The two can be connected to form a dog's collar necklace. J. KAUFFMANN: *Centre* Silver and crystal bracelet set with carved jade cabochons, 1927. (Private Collection)
Left
GEORG JENSEN: Gold brooch shaped as a stylised deer. (Editions Graphiques Gallery, London)
Opposite
RENE LALIQUE: Moulded coloured or stained glass pendants on cords, some with tassels. The central pendant is also a scent bottle. (Private Collection, London)

TABLETTERIE

Certain geographical locations specialise in the production of certain goods. Thus Lorraine in Eastern France, Bohemia in Czechoslovakia and Stourbridge in England specialised in the production of glass. For some three hundred years the Beauvaisis in France, in an area encompassing the town of Andeville and the surrounding villages of Le Déluge, Méru, Noailles and Sainte-Geneviève, specialised in the making of fans, particularly in mother-of-pearl, together with the ancillary carving of mother-of-pearl buttons. Industrialisation killed off many cottage industries and by the 1890s there were very few fan-makers left in the area as they had all gone to work in the factories.

Georges Bastard was born into one of the few surviving fan-making families in Andeville in 1881. His great-grandfather had been a noted domino-maker and his grandfather a leading mother-of-pearl carver and sculptor, successful at the 1867 Paris International Exhibition. His father maintained the tradition and from an early age Georges was initiated into the subtleties of carving and engraving rare substances. He soon realised that confining himself to traditional patterns and designs would not satisfy him and he persuaded his father to send him to Paris, where he spent four years studying at the School of Decorative Arts. He quickly absorbed the aesthetics of the Art Nouveau movement and, by the time he returned to Andeville, he had with him several hundred drawings for objects with largely floral decoration.

Back at home he perfected his technique and skill at handling the most precious and delicate of materials: ivory, mother-of-pearl, horn, tortoiseshell, coral jade, amber, rock crystal, all the hardstones and wood, studying the qualities and problems involved in turning and carving the rarest, the softest and the hardest of exotic woods, each substance requiring different skills and techniques.

Mother-of-pearl, extracted mostly from pearl-bearing oyster shells, has different aspects of luminescence, even iridescence, as well as colour and pattern, varying not only from shell to shell but particularly from species to species, coming from such widely spread areas of the world as Australia, the West Indies and the Middle East. An extremely hard substance, mother-of-pearl is cut and faceted using a variety of miniature saws and files, occasionally carved on the wheel, engraved with a burin, or graving tool, and polished with sulphuric acid. The traditional fan-makers of the region normally divided each of the many steps involved—from rough cutting, carving, assembling, polishing and engraving to finishing—among

Above
GEORGES BASTARD: Two mother-of-pearl fans, 1925. (Contemporary photographs)
Opposite
GEORGES BASTARD: Mother-of-pearl fan, 1925 and RAYMOND TEMPLIER: Table mirror in silver, the back set with gold, cornelian and niello, 1921. (The Metropolitan Museum of Art, New York, Edward C. Moore, Jr. Gift Fund, 1923 and 1925)

Above, left
GEORGES BASTARD: Carved ivory bowl,
c. 1925. (Contemporary photograph)
Above, right
GEORGES BASTARD: Thuyawood box with
carved mother-of-pearl panel set into the lid,
c. 1925. (Contemporary photograph)
Bottom, left
GEORGES BASTARD: Thuyawood box with
carved cover. (Contemporary photograph)
Bottom, right
GEORGES BASTARD: Carved rock crystal bowl.
(Contemporary photograph)
Opposite
EMILE BACHELET: *Venus and Cupid.* Carved
ivory tusk set in gilt-bronze base, c. 1934. It was
exhibited at the 1937 Paris Exhibition. (Virginia
Museum of Fine Arts, Gift of Sydney and Frances
Lewis. Photo: Katherine Wetzel)

different craftsmen, each of whom had his speciality. Individual craftsmen such as Georges Bastard learned to cope with every step of each technique they practised.

Ivory comes mainly from elephant tusks, Indian and African elephants each producing ivory with different properties. Certain sea mammals also grow tusks, particularly the walrus and the extraordinary arctic narwhal which grows one or two twisted tusks extending up to ten feet in length. The tusks are, of course, teeth in which the dentine has become extremely hard and dense. Smaller tusks come from the boar and the warthog, while the teeth of whales, hippopotami and crocodiles all provide carvable ivory. Of these, only the teeth from the hippopotamus need to have their extremely hard outer layer of enamel stripped before the dentine (or ivory) may be used. In the Stone Age ivory was used to make weapons and tools, and in the Middle Ages it was used as a prime material for carving both religious and secular subjects. It has remained in continuous artistic use from Ancient Egypt to contemporary Japan and China. In Europe the artistic use of ivory waxed and waned, but ivory remained in continuous demand for a variety of more mundane purposes—from billiard balls to brush backs, buttons and piano keys. The major source of supply for many years turned out to be the huge beds of fossil mammoth tusks which stretched from Alaska to Siberia, which were dug up some three million years after the mammoths themselves became extinct. Preserved in bogs and ice, the enormous curved tusks were frequently in perfect condition. Ivory from whatever source may be carved or turned just like wood.

The official report of the 1925 Paris Exhibition stated that between sixty and one hundred thousand elephants were destroyed every year for their tusks in Africa and Asia. Auctions were held in Antwerp and London for the world markets and the report noted the increasing prices due to the massive export of tusks to the United States. While these figures appear staggering, elephants survived in large numbers until fairly recently in African game parks, where the herds were kept fairly constant by regular culling. Unfortunately wars and poachers armed with machine guns are coming close to making the African elephant extinct. Wildlife protective legislation enacted in the United States and some other countries has done nothing to halt the slaughter. Indiscriminate banning of imports into the United States has meant the confiscation and destruction of many works of art by customs officials, while the product of the newly killed has merely been redirected to other countries.

Tortoiseshell does not come from the tortoise and is not a shell. Similar in composition to the horns and hooves of mammals, it is a multi-layered compound within the carapace of certain marine turtles, particularly the hawksbill, found in the West Indies and off the Brazilian coast, with most of its exports to Paris coming from Havana; the loggerhead turtle, found in the Far East; and the Seychelles hawksbill, found in the Indian Ocean. Each carapace carries some forty plates, varying in size and mottled in various browns, reds and yellows. The plastron, or belly, contains smaller, blonde plates. Heat is used to detach the plates from each other and these are then sorted out for size and colour. Placed in boiling water mixed with salt, the plates soften and may be moulded or welded

together to form larger pieces, ensuring there is no waste. The part opaque, part translucent material can be moulded, carved, cut or engraved. Its colours never fade and it can be polished to a brilliant lustre.

Horn may be used from a wide variety of animals such as bulls and steers. While some of it may be carved, it is generally treated like tortoiseshell, softened by heat and moulded. Horns from rare creatures such as the rhinoceros were occasionally used, when available, for a particularly luxurious piece. In recent years the rhinoceros has been brought to the verge of extinction because of the high price its horn fetches in China, where in a powdered form it is held to have aphrodysiac properties, and in Saudi Arabia and the Arabian Gulf States where the horn is prized in a dagger's hilt.

Coral is formed through the secretions of the coral polyp, a kind of sea anemone which lives in colonies which form tree-like growths which root in any hard substance on the sea bed, normally below five fathoms deep. The polyps live just under the outer skin of this bush and eat by thrusting their heads through holes in the surface. The bush itself is made of a vast number of rod-like strands. There are many different types of coral, found in reefs in the Mediterranean, around Japan, the Canary Islands, the Fiji Islands, and off the coasts of India, Formosa and other localities. Shapes of the coral bushes vary and large pieces are normally used for carving statues and other objects, while smaller pieces are used to make beads or add decorative touches to multi-media pieces. The colour of coral varies enormously, from white to deep red, with a vast number of different shades of pink. Dead colonies sometimes turn the coral brown or black, and yellow and blue coral have occasionally been found. Each shade has been given a romantic name by coral collectors. These range from Angel Skin for an almost white colour barely suffused with a pale pink blush, to Bull's Blood for a rich dark red. Coral may be sawn, filed, drilled, engraved, ground and polished. As it propagates itself easily and at a fairly rapid rate it is unlikely to run out, especially since its collection is somewhat hazardous.

Jade is a compact mineral, found in two major forms, Nephrite and Jadeite, both extremely rare and both found in a variety of colours—from the kingfisher green prized by the Chinese to various shades of grey, green, white, brown, yellow, red, blue, mauve and black. The colours are created by the presence of minute amounts of various mineral compounds. Jade is an extremely hard substance which can only be cut with a diamond, so it is not carved but ground, a long and patient process using abrasives. Paradoxically, jade is brittle and shatters easily. Most hardstones, such as the rich dark blue lapis-lazuli, frequently found with streaks of iron pyrites which look like gold, can be carved and polished. Amber, which is a fossil resin found in various, mostly translucent colours, yellow, red, brown and black, and occasionally blue and green, is extremely soft and brittle. Boiled in oil it can be bent and fused. In its normal state it can be cut, carved, ground and polished. Rock crystal is a colourless, transparent quartz. Extremely hard, it can be carved and faceted with no loss of clarity and can be polished to a brilliant finish.

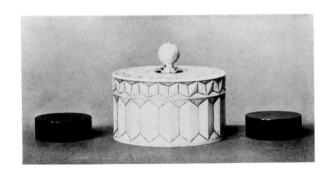

Above
GEORGES BASTARD: Two small tortoiseshell pillboxes on either side of a sectional ivory box with jade bead finial set into a silver collar, 1925. (Contemporary photograph)

Georges Bastard sent some of his creations to the 1902 Salon of the Société des Artistes Français. They made an immediate impact and he was awarded an Honourable Mention. The newspapers and art magazines took him up and several artists began to correspond with him. As he was only twenty-one years old he lacked the courage to leave home and an assured income. Four years later, however, he and his wife moved to Paris. He continued to send work to the annual Salons of the Société des Artistes Français and was awarded a 3rd Class Medal in 1908, a 2nd Class Medal in 1909, a travelling scholarship in 1910 and a 1st Class Medal in 1912. Between 1910 and 1912 he also exhibited at the Salon des Tuileries.

Bastard soon shed Art Nouveau floralism in favour of geometric design and executed a vast range of boxes, paper knives, bowls, lanterns, parasol and umbrella handles, dressing table sets and mirrors in all the available precious substances, frequently mixing them in extraordinary combinations such as ivory or ebony set with mother-of-pearl, abalone or jade. He designed and executed a wide range of jewellery, ivory bangles studded with silver or gold, gold hat pins set with jade, coral, lapis-lazuli or cornelian, elaborate hair combs, necklaces and carved beads. He also worked closely with such furniture designers as Léon Jallot, Montagnac and Ruhlmann, executing for them the exquisite handles, plaques and finials required for individual pieces. At the 1925 Paris Exhibition Bastard exhibited his individual items of tabletterie as well as supplying the accessories for many of the items of furniture on display through the various French pavilions. That year he was awarded the Légion d'Honneur.

Georges Bastard was the most versatile of the tabletiers, but there were many others. Mlle O'Kin, a Japanese lady who was to marry the ceramist Henri Simmen, was equally gifted and creative. In the pre-war years she exhibited in the various Salons with great success. After her marriage she frequently supplied exquisite carved finials and stoppers in ivory and precious woods for her husband's ceramics. Mlle E. Le Bourgeois, who normally worked in wood, carved elaborate ivory buttons, while Henri Hamm specialised in horn buttons. Charles Hairon carved intricate wooden frames, some of them for lacquer screens by Jean Dunand. Paul Liénard and Henri Vever both produced elaborate horn combs. Perhaps the most gifted was Clément Mère, who designed and executed a vast range of boxes, lamp standards, bowls and mirror frames in which he combined ivory, embossed, painted and gilt leather, various woods and enamel. He also used this whole range of materials in the furniture he designed and executed.

Several firms commissioned these and other designers to draw ranges of brush sets, hair combs, toilet sets and travelling cases. While some were executed in the rare materials characteristic of the tabletier, most were made of substitute materials: the corozo nut tree from South America—the fruit of which yields vegetable ivory; or gutta-percha, vulcanised rubber, celluloid, casein-based plastics such as galalite and lactoid, synthetic resins such as bakelite and substitutes for mother-of-pearl such as nacrite—a pearly variety of mica, or 'nacrolaque', a French cellulose-based material.

Above
MME O'KIN SIMMEN: Carved ivory stopper on glazed ceramic vase by Henri Simmen. (Collection Robert Zehil, Beverly Hills)

CHRYSELEPHANTINE STATUETTES AND SALON BRONZES

Ivory carving was first established in Dieppe in the sixteenth century. The 1685 Revocation of the Edict of Nantes, which had granted religious freedom to the Protestant Huguenots, proved a great blow, since many of the ivory carvers were Huguenots. The French Revolution was another blow, for the few remaining carvers had specialised in religious subjects, now no longer approved. Napoleon I attempted to revive Dieppe but the continuous wars during his reign led to the capture of many men from there. Paradoxically enough, many of these men practised their craft in British prison camps, and peace after the defeat of Napoleon turned Dieppe into a thriving tourist centre with the ivory carving trade orientated toward the tourist. Exceptionally fine and artistic ivory sculptors, though still working in Dieppe, did not find their work truly appreciated.

In the meantime a new centre for ivory carving had been established. Count Franz I of Erbach-Erbach, born in 1754, and himself a highly skilled ivory carver, set up a guild of ivory carvers under the instructions of his own teacher, Johann

Above
FERDINAND PREISS: *Modern Dancer*. Carved and stained ivory on green onyx base. (Author's Collection)
Opposite
FERDINAND PREISS: *Flame Leaper*. Cold-painted bronze, tinted ivory and composition flames on stepped black marble base, 34 cms. (Editions Graphiques Gallery, London. Photo: Rodney Todd-White)

FERDINAND PREISS: *Dancing Bather*
Cold-painted bronze and tinted ivory
on green onyx base, 39 cms. (Private
Collection, London. Photo: Rodney
Todd-White)

FERDINAND PREISS: *Charleston
Dancer*. Cold-painted bronze and
tinted ivory on marble base,
37 cms. (Editions Graphiques
Gallery, London)

Left
FERDINAND PREISS: *Autumn Dancer*.
Cold-painted bronze and tinted ivory
on green onyx and black marble
base, 38 cms. (Author's Collection)
Opposite
FERDINAND PREISS: *Invocation*.
Cold-painted bronze and tinted ivory
on green onyx base. (Editions
Graphiques Gallery, London)

Above
BRUNO ZACH: *The Cigarette*. Patinated bronze
and ivory on marble base, 64 cms. (Author's
Collection)
Centre
BRUNO ZACH: *The Riding Crop*. Patinated
bronze and ivory on green onyx base, 32 cms.
(Author's Collection)

Above
PIERRE LE FAGUAYS: *Message d'amour*.
Patinated bronze on marble base, 26 cms.
(Editions Graphiques Gallery, London)
Opposite
PIERRE LE FAGUAYS: *Danseuse au thyrse*. Cold-
painted bronze on stepped marble base, 28 cms.
(Editions Graphiques Gallery, London)

Left
GERDAGO: *Temple Dancer.* Polished
and enamelled bronze and tinted ivory
on green onyx base, 47 cms. (Collection
Elton John, Windsor. Photo: Rodney
Todd-White)

Opposite
JOSEF LORENZL: *Dancer.* Cold-painted
and decorated bronze by Crejo and
tinted ivory on green onyx base. (Private
Collection, London)

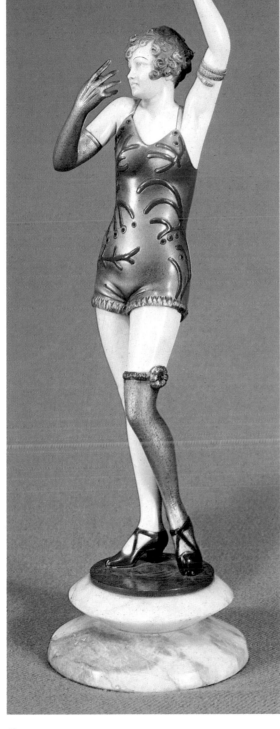

Above
DOROTHEA CHAROL: *Danseuse exotique.* Cold-painted and enamelled
bronze and tinted ivory on marble base, 40 cms. (Author's Collection.
Photo: Rodney Todd-White)
Right
GODARD: *Danseuse des Indes.* Patinated and silver-inlaid bronze and ivory
on marble base, 51.5 cms. (Editions Graphiques Gallery, London)
Opposite
SOLANGE BERTRAND: *Elégante au chien.* Polished gilt patinated and silver-
inlaid bronze and tinted ivory, 29 cms. (Private Collection, London)

Tobias Arzt. Centred in the village of Erbach on the Odenwald, the school trained sculptors to produce both artistic and useful carvings and the school's graduates set up in Erbach and neighbouring villages. In the nineteenth century Erbach specialised in ivory jewellery, often intricately carved, and frequently based on the motif of the Erbach rose, itself inspired by the earlier Dieppe rose.

It was in Erbach that Johann Philippe Ferdinand Preiss was born on February 13th, 1882, the son of the owner of the local Preiss Hotel. He was orphaned at the age of fifteen, the Hotel sold, and young Preiss and his five brothers and sisters placed with various relations and friends. Preiss, whose mother came from a family of ivory carvers, naturally gravitated towards the craft. He served a two-year apprenticeship with Phillip Willmann (1846-1910), followed by a year and a half working in Willmann's workshop before essaying a variety of jobs with different firms in different countries, acquiring experience and perfecting his technique. After a period as a modeller in Milan he joined the firm of Carl Haebler in Baden-Baden in 1905, and there met a number of young carvers from his native Erbach.

A year later Preiss moved to Berlin with one of his co-workers from the Haebler firm, a young Berliner called Arthur Kassler, and they opened a workshop under the name of Preiss & Kassler. They were reasonably successful, working as turners and carvers, but it was not until 1910, three years after Preiss's marriage, that the partners took the decision to expand. They were joined by Robert Kionsek of the Berlin bronze foundry of Gladenbeck, shortened the name of the firm to PK, hired two ivory carvers from Erbach, Ludwig Walther and Louis Kuchler, and began working on multi-media works. Preiss was artistic director, while Kassler became sales manager.

The word 'Chryselephantine' comes from the Greek and refers to the combination of ivory and gold. The monumental statue of the Athena Parthenos on the Acropolis was said to have been made of ivory and gold by Phydias. In the late nineteenth century the Belgian Congo was opened up and the Belgian government initially offered ivory free to artists for certain projects to encourage its artistic use. The first group of these sculptors using ivory as the sole or main material exhibited in the 1894 Antwerp International Exhibition and again in a separate exhibition organised by the Cercle Artistique in Brussels. The first official Chryselephantine Section was set up in the Colonial Section of the 1897 Brussels Exhibition, held in Tervueren. Several more artists were encouraged to use ivory, particularly Symbolist sculptors, who were most in harmony with the natural look of ivory. Multi-media sculpture became more adventurous. In Belgium, Egide Rombeaux carved a number of ivory nudes entwined in oxidised silver plants by Franz Hoosemans. Other sculptors combined ivory with bronze or wood, marble or rock crystal. The meaning of the word chryselephantine was soon extended to encompass any work combining ivory with some other substance.

Preiss's first known multi-media work was a small classical sculpture of a draped nude carved from different woods. His stay in Italy had given him a taste for classical figurines, and he sculpted a series of nude and partly draped Greek goddesses which were made of bronze and ivory.

Above
GUSTAV SCHMIDTCASSEL: Polished and enamelled bronze and ivory on marble base, 45 cms. (Private Collection, London)
Opposite
AMEDEO GENNARELLI: *Pigeon Voyageur*, polished silver-plated bronze on a tall, black marble base. The bronze was available in two sizes, and the marble column in three heights for the larger figure. (Editions Graphiques Gallery, London)

It was the invention of the pantograph by Achille Colas in the mid-nineteenth century that enabled sculpture to be scaled down for home use. Sculptors frequently created massive sculptures for show in the Salons: they had to be big to avoid being overlooked in the large sculpture rooms and to impress the jury with the sculptor's ability to handle size, proving he could undertake a state commission for public statuary. Most successful sculptors earned their living by selling the publication rights of their exhibits to various commercial enterprises, most of which were bronze founders in their own right. The pantograph machine was used to scale down the original to a more suitable size for the preparation of the moulds from which the bronze edition was cast. Needless to say, the cast bronzes needed a great deal of finishing by chasers before being patinated and polished. It was the development of a similar machine to deal with ivory that enabled the chryselephantine figures of the twentieth century to flourish.

The first machines, developed in 1910, were fairly simple and followed the contours of an object or statue which had previously been carved by hand, duplicating those contours onto a turner's lathe, in which was placed the block of ivory to be carved. By the mid-1920s the more sophisticated machines produced by the firms of Wenzel in Berlin, Friedrich Deckel in Munich and Kempf in Taunus, could also scale up or down in size from the original. Chryselephantine sculptures were created sectionally, which meant that the parts made of ivory were frequently small—the head and neck, separate arms and legs, and the occasional torso. Only the whitest pieces of ivory were chosen, free of striations and other blemishes.

The designer carved his original model either in sections or from a single block of ivory or wood, which was then cut into sections. A machine was then used to block out the basic shape of each section, often in fairly large quantities, while the bronze sections were cast. That is when the real work began. Each roughly prepared ivory section was then carefully carved by hand, each finger delineated, each facial feature carefully shaped. After carving the ivory was polished and various details painted, the lips pink or crimson, the cheeks rouged, the eyebrows carefully contoured, the hairs lightly coloured. The Ancient Greeks had thus coloured their ivory and marble statues, and the chryselephantine sculptors of the twentieth century followed suit.

At the outbreak of war in 1914 the PK firm employed about half a dozen ivory carvers. Preiss, Kassler and their staff all joined the army and the firm only reopened its doors in 1919. By the mid-20s they employed ten sculptors, including Walter Kassler and Philipp Lenz, who was to become Mayor of Erbach in the 30s. Their finest carver was still Ludwig Walter but he was later to set up on his own in Berlin before moving back to Erbach. His female nudes, carved from a single block of ivory, were particularly successful.

Preiss himself designed most of PK's production. Moving away from the pre-war classical models, he designed a large number of statuettes of children, clothed and naked, completely in ivory or in bronze and ivory; several all-ivory female nudes, strikingly beautiful amazons, slender in body, ecstatic in expression; chryselephantine statuettes of dancers and bathing beauties; and the Olympian series—men and women playing golf, tennis, fishing, racing, hurling a javelin or using a bow and

Opposite, above
PIERRE TRAVERSE: *Nude with Fawn.* Patinated bronze exhibited in the Goldscheider pavilion at the 1925 Paris Exhibition. (Private Collection, Scotland. Photo: Rodney Todd-White)
Opposite, below
PIERRE LE FAGUAYS: *Faun and Nymph.* Patinated bronze on marble base, exhibited in the Goldscheider pavilion at the 1925 Paris Exhibition. (Private Collection, London)

160

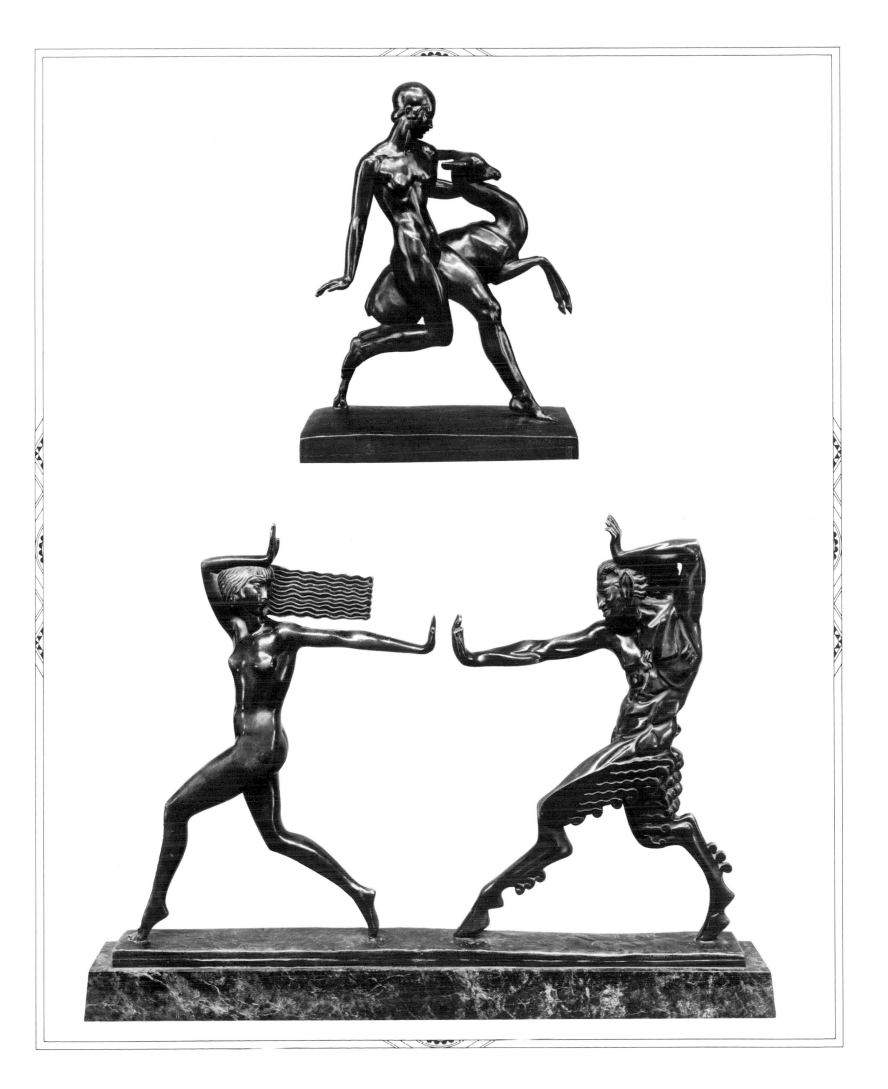

arrow. A few of his models were also produced in bronze or sterling silver. Several of the dancers were based on real people: a dancer holding up a transparent beach ball is Ada May, a C. B. Cochran dancer in *Lighter Than Air,* another statuette represents Brigitte Helm in Fritz Lang's film *Metropolis.* Similarly, several of the Olympians were based on actual sportsmen and women—the skater Sonja Henie was the inspiration for two of Preiss's statuettes. Ivory, in the post-war years, was an expensive material and Germany was already caught in the hyper-inflation spiral that was to pave the way for Hitler's coming. France and Italy, until recently at war with Germany, were closed markets. England, also a recent foe, was more sanguine about trading with Germany and soon provided the major market for her ivory and chryselephantine figures, though the German artists were frequently noted in contemporary English catalogues as being 'Austrian', apparently a less emotive origin since the dismemberment of the Austro-Hungarian Empire.

Berlin became a centre which attracted a number of artists who worked with ivory and bronze. They included Prof. Otto Poerzl, a fine carver who often produced subjects that were almost identical with those of Preiss; Dorothea Charol, who produced a number of exotic dancers in stylish poses and also designed models executed in porcelain; Rudolph Kaesbach, who carved finely detailed polychrome nudes—and many others, including Fritz Heinemann, Otto Hoffmann, R.W. Lange, Kraas and Arthur Lewin-Funcke. The PK firm commissioned figures from artists other than their own, and these included Otto Poerzl, Rudolf Belling and Philippe, an Austrian sculptor who produced highly stylised figures of women in geometrically shaped outlines, their hair fashionably cut à la garçonne.

Several of Dorothea Charol's figures are erotic in their connotations but undoubtedly the most effectively erotic artist was Bruno Zach. His long-legged perverse creatures, in stockings and high heels, with whip or riding crop, almost dressed in the frilliest of bronze underwear, or dressed from neck to ankle in a tight-fitting black leather suit, stand in awe of no man. Even his more conventional subjects have the whiff of challenge: a pert girl in buttoned boots with umbrella tucked under her arm, or an ecstatic Europa lying on the back of her enormous bull. Most of Zach's figures are patinated bronze, with a few in cold-painted bronze and fewer still in bronze and ivory. He also produced a few pornographic cold-painted bronzes depicting couples in often acrobatic, but always elegant coupling, as well as a few grotesque and humorous clown figures.

While the ivory on most chryselephantine figures was normally tinted, the bronze was either patinated—that is given a traditional brown, black, green or gilt finish using acids, metallic oxides and heat applied with a small blowtorch—or cold-painted in various colours and given a cellulose lacquer finish. Two chryselephantine artists who specialised in elaborate polychromaticism in their treatment of the bronze component were Gerdago and Gustav Schmidtcassel, who also designed their dancers in almost futuristic costumes and highly theatrical poses.

Among German workshops specialising in chryselephantine sculpture was Rosenthal und Maeder, whose artists included Prof. Poerzl, Philippe and Harders. All their sculptures are normally marked with the RuM monogram. In order to obtain the services of these sculptors the PK firm took over Rosenthal und Maeder in 1929.

The leading Austrian firm specialising in ceramics and bronze figures was Friedrich Goldscheider, who produced fine and stylish ceramics throughout the 20s and 30s. Among their artists was Joseph Lorenzl, a versatile sculptor who designed a wide range of ceramic sculptures for them and other firms, in addition to executing a large number of frequently stylised figurines in ivory, bronze and ivory, bronze or spelter. Some of his chryselephantine figures have the bronze components, normally representing the clothing, painted in elaborate polychrome patterns, presumably by a colleague, and these are signed Crejo. Several of his bronzes, finished in a mat gilt or silver, represent highly stylised female nudes with elongated limbs and simplified features, in elegant acrobatic attitudes.

Goldscheider first set up a Paris branch in 1892 to commission, manufacture and sell bronze, plaster and terracotta sculpture. This branch also included a bronze foundry. They exhibited successfully at the 1900 Paris Universal Exhibition and the annual Salons until the outbreak of war, when they were forced to close down. The bronze foundry, however, which had been set up as a separate French company under Arthur Goldscheider, survived and in the post-war years itself became an Editeur d'Art. Both the Austrian and French companies exhibited at the 1925 Paris Exhibition though the French exhibit was by far the most elaborate. Arthur Goldscheider had his own pavilion, designed by Eric Bagge, and his own team of sculptors, grouped in two artistic societies, La Stèle and L' Evolution. They included Pierre Traverse, Raoul Lamourdedieu, Pierre le Faguays and Sibylle May, who all sculpted highly stylised figures cast in bronze or bronze and ivory, while Sibylle May and Cazaux also had their figures executed in ceramic. Non-members of the two societies also designed for Arthur Goldscheider, including the Hungarian artist Alexander Kelety. In the mid-30s the Arthur Goldscheider firm closed down and most of their sculptors moved to the firm of Les Neveux de J. Lehmann.

Another leading Parisian firm was that of Etling, who distributed the works of Chiparus, a Rumanian artist settled in Paris. Chiparus had, early in his career, supplied a few models for A. Goldscheider but he soon became one of the leading artists working for Etling. He designed spectacular, hieratic figures executed in bronze and bronze and ivory, on elaborate stepped marble bases. His figures were inspired by the stage, music hall and ballet, though he also designed sentimental figures of children, religious statuary and several amusing ceramics. Another Etling artist was Claire-Jeanne-Roberte Colinet, born in Brussels, who had studied with Jef Lambeaux, and sculpted several highly charged hieratic figures. Still another was Marcel Bouraine.

Among the many French artists not attached to any one particular editor were Maurice Guiraud-Rivière (who occasionally supplied Etling with models), Andrée Guerval, who was a student of Pierre le Faguays, and Solange Bertrand.

Several of the Parisian sculptors used dinanderie techniques for decorating the bronze components of their chryselephantine statues, applying silver, copper and other metals to the surface, forming patterns with acid or burnishing, and further extending their decorative possibilities.

Above
JOSEF LORENZL: *Dancer.* Cold-painted bronze on green onyx base. (Private Collection, London. Photo: Rodney Todd-White)
Opposite
GUSTAVE POPINEAU: *Nu debout.* Silvered bronze. (Private Collection, London)

AVANT GARDE SCULPTURE

Years of struggle and creative activity eventually established Rodin as the colossus of sculpture, and his admirers hailed his work as the death of academic sculpture. The announcement proved premature and, indeed, greatly exaggerated. Academic sculpture was somewhat altered but soon resumed its central place in the scheme of things.

Aristide Maillol was at least partly responsible for this. A student of Cabanel at the Ecole des Beaux-Arts, he had rejected the academicism and classical ideals he had been taught to join with his friends Maurice Denis, Pierre Bonnard and Ker-Xavier Roussel in working in the decorative style and freedom that Gauguin and Cézanne had opened up. Yet once he had begun to sculpt, he re-created the neo-classical ideal. Inspired and creative enough to dominate this ideal, his plump, well-proportioned and massive nudes nevertheless pointed the way. The following generations of sculptors were a shade less individual, adopting a stylisation of features, pose and expression which was, in effect, the new academicism. Some, like Joseph Bernard or Charles Despiau, showed a degree of freedom in some of their works, but most sought to fix forever the eternal canons of beauty within the stylisation of the day.

Their decade was the 30s and, more particularly, those years that led to the 1937 Paris Exhibition. The old Trocadero, across the river from the Eiffel Tower, was gone and in its place arose the Palais de Chaillot with, next to it, the new twin Museums of Modern Art. The buildings were covered in sculptural low reliefs, framed in a peristyle of larger-than-life-sized statues, confronted by huge fountains with multiple sculptures. An army of sculptors worked on these major commissions. Charles Malfray, Henry Arnold, Bizette-Lindet, Carlo Sarabezolles, Evariste Jonchère, Alfred Janniot, Marcel Gaumont, Léon Drivier, Gustave Saupique, Paul Landowski, Marcel Gimond, Albert Marque, Paul Cornet, Auguste Guénot, Pierre Poisson, Henri Lagriffoul, Gilbert Privat, Louis Déjean, Albert Pommier, Paul Niclausse and Robert Wlérick were among them. The Palais de Chaillot itself housed a theatre and more museums, all well supplied with free-standing and low relief statuary.

The derision accorded this public statuary for years prevented a closer look at the more intimate works of these sculptors. There is a touch of the cold hand of classicism about them, but only a touch——most of their works retain the saving grace of humanity, and are usually graceful, sometimes stylised, often voluptuous representations of the naked human body. A closer look at the public statuary can also be rewarding. Though the cold hand is necessarily colder here because of the scale, an overwhelming impression of the kind of beauty the sculptors attempted to re-

Above
EDITH M. GABRIEL: *Standing Nude*. Bronze, 1928, 122.5 cms. (Author's Collection)
Opposite
EDITH M. GABRIEL: *Mermaid*. Alabaster, 1926. (Author's Collection)

create is itself created by the cumulative effect of their labours—a trifle laboured on occasion, yet exhilarating, whether seen at the Trocadero, the Modern Art Museums or in the Maillol garden in the grounds of the Louvre.

A tiny touch of neo-classical idealism affected some of the English sculptors of the 20s and 30s who yet worked in the Art Deco mood, many of whom studied, lived and exhibited in Paris. One of the most interesting of these was Edith M. Gabriel, who exhibited at the Paris Salons, the Royal Academy in London and the Royal Glasgow Institute of Fine Arts, working in bronze, plaster, marble, alabaster and wood. She produced intimate scenes of mothers and children as well as carvings reminiscent of Javanese art. S. Nicholson Babb, Ferdinand Blundstone, Harold Brownsword, Joseph Else, Richard Garbe, Maurice Lambert, Gilbert Ledward, Helen Mackay, William McMillan, Alfred Oakley and, particularly, James Woodford, were among her fellow members of the Royal Society of British Sculptors who produced fine Art Deco works.

The United States is such an enormous country that a vast army of sculptors was kept busy throughout the 20s, carving and modelling monuments, architectural features, fountains and memorials. Many came from Europe, others were native born, but the influence of Paris was all-pervasive. Many went to Paris to study and exhibit, many of the others studied with graduates of the Paris academies. Among the most influential teachers were the brothers Gutzon Borglum and Solon Hannibal Borglum, the former having studied at the Académie Julian before being elected a member of the Société Nationale des Beaux-Arts, the latter having studied with his brother and Frémiet in Paris. Among those who worked in the Art Deco style were Harriet Whitney Frishmuth of Philadelphia, who had studied in Paris with Rodin and Injalbert, in Berlin with Cuno von Euchtritz and in New York with Hermon MacNeil and Gutzon Borglum; and Paul Manship, a student of Solon Borglum, Isidore Konti and Charles Grafly. Other sculptors working within a similar idiom included Albert Atkins from Wisconsin; Gaetano Cecere, Karl Heinrich Gruppe, Frederick Guinzburg and Edward McCartan from New York; Duane Champlain from North Carolina; Ernest Wise Keyser from Maryland; Anna Coleman Ladd from Pennsylvania; George Lober and Wheeler Williams from Chicago; Grace Talbot and Lawrence Stevens from Massachusetts; and Hilda Lascari from Sweden; Mario Korbel from Czechoslovakia; John Brcin from Serbia; Cecil de Blaquière Howard from Canada and Carl Jennewein from Germany. The Stock Market crash, followed by the Depression, destroyed the market in their work. When, in the 30s, John D. Rockefeller Jr. built his own monument, Rockefeller Center in New York, most of the statuary commissioned for the enterprise was in the heroic style that was to become a characteristic of the New York Moderne typified by the giant figure of *Atlas* by Lee Lawrie.

Properly classical low relief panels were supplied for the Marine Museum by the brothers Jan and Joël Martel. These least conventional of sculptors had first shocked the delicate critics of the day with their concrete Cubist trees at the 1925 Paris Exhibition. These had been set in a garden designed by their friend Robert Mallet-Stevens, who was to design and build a home for them. The Martel twins, who

always worked together, experimented with every sculptural material, including bronze, aluminium, glass, sheet steel, wood, ceramic, marble and concrete. Their work ranged from small table sculptures and car mascots to massive monuments and architectural features. Their *Belfort Lion* monument was made of twisted zinc ribbons.

The Martel brothers produced many stylised sculptures of animals while remaining outside the field of animalier sculpture as such. The essence here was to stylise the treatment without affecting the recognition of the animal portrayed. One method was to streamline the animal, smoothing out both the shape and the surface. François Pompon was a master at this, achieving almost abstract shapes from his animals' outlines. Armand Petersen, Maurice Prost, Auguste Trémont, Georges-Stéphane Hilbert, Gabriel-René Lacroix, Willy-Georges Wuilleumier, Marguerite de Bayser-Gratry, Charles Artus and Gaston le Bourgeois were among those who also chose this path. The second method involved kneading the clay and retaining all the finger marks in the bronze cast. Subjects were frequently portrayed in curled-up positions in order to achieve even more massive effects. Prince Paul Troubetzkoy and Rembrandt Bugatti were the masters of this technique, while artists such as Paul Jouve and Edouard Marcel Sandoz used both techniques with equal virtuosity.

Parallel with the development of neo-classical statuary a number of individual sculptors were questioning the whole basis of their art and re-creating it in various ways. Cubist painting pointed the way to a new method of looking at reality. Rodin himself used differing sight lines to achieve impact, bringing out grotesque elements, cutting up portions of anatomy, leaving sections unfinished, seeking 'essential' (later thought of as 'psychological') truths rather than mere surface likeness. The arrival of African tribal wood carvings and bronze casts (particularly Benin ones) had as great an influence as Japanese art had had in the 1880s and 90s.

Constantin Brancusi arrived in Paris in 1904 from his native Rumania. Two years at the Ecole des Beaux-Arts did not unduly hamper him in his pursuit of simplification and purification in both his carvings and modelling. Obsessively confining himself to a handful of subjects, he reworked each one over and over again, year after year, rethinking the forms to achieve greater simplicity, reaching for the unattainable essence he saw beyond the symbol of reality. From 1907 onwards he abandoned modelling in favour of direct carving, though he lavished attention on his various casts, varying rough patches with utterly smooth polished bronze, with occasional sections of black patination. A quiet, introspective and private man, his declared aim was to bring 'pure joy'. Dismissing surface realism as 'beefsteak' he abstracted his forms to egg and cylinder shapes which, in 1920, brought him the notoriety of having his *Princess X* withdrawn from the Salon des Indépendants because its cylindrical shape appeared too phallic.

Brancusi's influence on his contemporaries was enormous, despite his discretion. His friendship with Modigliani, with whom he went to Livorno in 1909 on a visit to the painter's birthplace, encouraged Modigliani to embark on his series of carved stone heads, hieratic elongated simplifications of totem-like power and beauty. The influence of African carvings was very clear, an influence Brancusi himself accepted

Above
JAN & JOEL MARTEL: *Polyhedric Sculpture.* Wrought iron armature covered in plaster which was then covered in mirror glass, executed by Barillet, 1927. (Collection Félix Marcilhac, Paris. Photo: Sully Jaulmes)
Opposite, above, left
JAN & JOEL MARTEL: *The Belfort Lion.* Zinc sheet. (Contemporary photograph)
Opposite, centre, left
JAN & JOEL MARTEL: *Pigeons.* Bronze on black marble bases, 1924. (Collection Alain Lesieutre, Paris. Photo: Sully Jaulmes)
Opposite, right
JAN & JOEL MARTEL: *Profile Medallion.* Moulded in a caseine-based plastic (galalith) with a mat gilt finish, 1925. (Private Collection, Paris. Photo: Sully Jaulmes)
Opposite, below
JAN & JOEL MARTEL: *Steam powered Locomotive in Motion.* Polished zinc, c.1930. (Private Collection, New York)

with equanimity, frequently commenting that 'only Africans and Rumanians know how to carve wood.' Another artist influenced by his friendship with Brancusi and Modigliani as well as an ardent collector of African sculpture was Jacob Epstein. A New Yorker who had studied there and in Paris before settling permanently in England, Epstein met Brancusi, Picasso and Modigliani in 1912 when he came to Paris to carve the neo-Assyrian tomb of Oscar Wilde, erected at the Père Lachaise cemetery. On his return to England he carved a number of incredibly powerful, primitive and massive forms which outraged and horrified the delicate sensitivities of newspaper and magazine critics of the day. He alternated these with many modelled portraits which brought him acclaim. While some are fairly conventional portraits of the famous, most are among the finest portrait busts and heads of our time. Some, like the *Mask of Meum* or the portrait of Gladys Deacon, later Duchess of Marlborough, achieved a heightened stylisation both of their time and outside of time. Others are intimate explorations of character, while some of the heads of children achieve their effects through great simplification. As a founder member of the Vorticists, the British Cubists, he created one of the great objects of Cubist sculpture, the *Rock Drill* of 1913.

Raymond Duchamp-Villon spent years exploring in bronze the power of the horse, completing the final version of his *Cheval Majeure* in 1914, shortly before enlisting in the army. He was to die four years later in a military hospital. The *Cheval Majeure* remains his monument, a highly charged composite of legs, muscles and sinews, abstracted in a Cubist context. Jacques Lipchitz, a Lithuanian who went to Paris at the age of eighteen, worked as a labourer at night to pay for his studies. A friend of Modigliani and Juan Gris, he was introduced to Cubism by the latter. From 1914 onwards he created Cubist sculptures, bringing a third dimension to what was essentially a two-dimensional analysis. Though he later partly abandoned Cubism in favour of a free and more lyrical abstraction, he remained the poet of sculpture. Vincent Huidobro wrote: 'Thanks to Jacques Lipchitz, stones speak in the language of dreams and bronzes fly to the sky, lighter than butterflies' wings.'

Alexander Archipenko held his first one-man show in 1906 in his native Kiev. Two years later he left Russia for Paris. Two weeks at the Ecole des Beaux-Arts convinced him that formal teaching held nothing for him and he moved to a studio close to that of Modigliani and Léger. From 1910 onwards he exhibited his streamlined, often truncated nudes at the Salon des Indépendants and the Salon d'Automne. In 1912 he began experimenting with multi-media sculptures and painted bronzes, gradually simplifying his figures to near abstracts, relating holes and space to his compositions. Joseph Csaky came to Paris in 1908 from his native Hungary and exhibited with the Cubists at the 1911 Salon d'Automne and Salon des Indépendants. In the post-war years he developed a very personal idiom based on Cubist aesthetics but transformed by humanist concern expressed through a form of Hellenic classicism. Henri Laurens was largely self-taught, though he had had some crafts training and had attended evening classes. Friendship with Braque drew him into the Cubist group and by 1914 he was executing polychrome Cubist sculptures, working with terracotta, stone and bronze. Gustave Miklos arrived in Paris in 1909

Above, upper
EDOUARD-MARCEL SANDOZ: *Zeus en Colère.*
Patinated and silver-plated bronze. (Collection
Robert Zehil, Beverly Hills)
Above, lower
EDOUARD-MARCEL SANDOZ: *Poisson Chinois.*
Patinated bronze. (Collection Robert Zehil,
Beverly Hills)
Opposite
GUSTAVE MIKLOS: *Column.* Polychrome and
silvered wood, c. 1923. (Private Collection, Paris.
Photo: Sully Jaulmes)

from Budapest. He was just twenty-one years old and had studied with the Hungarian painter Kimnach before attending the Budapest Royal School of Decorative Arts. In Paris he had a difficult life, occasionally exhibiting at the Salon d'Automne. He spent the war years as a volunteer in the French Foreign Legion and after the war worked for Jacques Doucet, designing carpets and working with enamels and silver. In 1923 he began sculpting, working in a figurative amalgam of African sculpture and Cubist interpretation.

The human figure was transformed by Gaston Lachaise. Born in Paris, the son of a master wood carver, he received a strict academic training at the Bernard Palissy School of Applied Arts and at the Ecole des Beaux-Arts. In about 1901 he met the woman who was to transform his life. A Canadian-American, some ten years older than himself, married with a son, she nevertheless enchanted him so completely that he followed her to the United States and waited for years until her son had grown up and she was prepared to marry him. His unwavering vision of her as Venus led him to sculpt her over and over again, transforming her natural shapes to enormous breasts, gigantic thighs, a tiny waist or else a huge, smoothly carved belly—the truly heroic woman.

While developing the theme of woman as universal subject, Lachaise also executed a number of stylised portrait heads, including those of the poets e.e. cummings and Marianne Moore, the photographer Alfred Stieglitz, the painters Georgia O'Keeffe and John Marin, the composer Edgar Varèse and the novelist Carl Van Vechten. Similarly fine portrait heads, though with a greater degree of stylisation, were made by Chana Orloff, whose sitters included the painters Romaine Brooks and Alexandre Iakovleff, the engraver Laboureur, Chagall's wife Ida and the art editor Lucien Vogel. Joseph Bernard varied his walking female nudes with occasional heads of great strength, while the Swedish sculptor Dagmar Dadie-Roberg produced some exquisite portraits and stylised figures.

Elie Nadelman's portrait sculptures varied from straightforward marble or bronze depictions to humorous, sharp observations in which he simplified features, sometimes to the point of caricature, and often painted portions of the bronze. Born in Warsaw, he studied there and in Munich before going to Paris in 1902. He exhibited at the Salon d'Automne from 1905, showing drawings in which he refined and simplified human outlines to nearly abstract geometricism. Leo Stein, Gertrude Stein's brother, took Picasso to Nadelman's studio in 1908 and Nadelman later asserted the importance of his influence on Picasso and the development of Cubism. His first one-man exhibition was held in Paris in 1909, but real success came to him at his first exhibition held in London in 1911 when Helena Rubinstein bought the entire exhibition, became his leading patron and helped him to emigrate to the United States in 1914. It was there that he was to develop his characteristic creations, carved and painted wood figures, primitive in inspiration but highly sophisticated in conception and execution—a couple dancing the tango, a piano player, an orchestra conductor, singers, dancers or circus performers.

Another artist who also frequently painted his sculpture was Lambert-Rucki. Born in Cracow in 1888, he later joined his old school mate Kisling in Paris, where he exhibited with Duchamp's 'Section d'Or' group. He fought in the First World War as a volunteer in the French Foreign Legion, returning to sculpture and painting in 1918. In sculpture his preferred medium was carved wood, though he occasionally modelled for bronze. Frequently carving totem-like Cubist 'heads' or figures, alternating with streamlined, stylised human figures, he treated the finished wood surface in a variety of ways—covering it in gold or silver leaf or with a mosaic of mirror-glass, painting it or lacquering it. He worked very closely with Jean Dunand, frequently designing sculpture, paintings and panels for lacquering. In the 30s he worked equally closely with Le Corbusier, Mallet-Stevens and Pingusson, executing a major relief sculpture for the Union des Artistes Modernes pavilion at the 1937 Exhibition, for which he also created a sculpture of tin cans and tennis balls connected with electric wires and light bulbs to form an electric robot for the Pavilion of Light.

In Britain, Eric Gill sought to unite his two basic drives, a vibrant faith which converted him to Roman Catholicism and led him to carve the Stations of the Cross in fourteen reliefs for Westminster Cathedral, and an equally active sexual drive which caused him to carve, draw and etch the most exquisite of couplings. Mixing simplification of features with a love for the sculptural treatment of the Middle Ages, in which he saw simple faith uncomplicated by interpretation, he frequently elongated and stretched his figures to dynamic shapes, occasionally painting or highlighting some of the features. Often referred to as the father of modern sculpture in Britain, Leon Underwood taught, painted and sculpted in voluntary obscurity for much of his life. He absorbed the teachings of all modern movements while reviling them for their soullessness, and alternated between massive, wrought sculpture and airy, light structures. He adapted the use of the Moebius strip to bronze, using its gentle continuous curve to catch, reflect and conceal light. He used this device in particular in his *The New Spirit* of 1932, a tribute to Faraday, the scientist who had experimented with electricity and electro-magnetism in the nineteenth century. Umberto Boccioni's great Futurist sculpture of 1913, *Unique Forms of Continuity in Space,* had shown in bronze a figure in movement using slow motion to retain the vision of where it had been simultaneously with where it was going in order to achieve pure form. Using a similar structure, Underwood produced a continuous ribbon of curling bronze slashed by hatchet-blade head and sexual organs to achieve what he called 'pure plastic rhythm'. The Scottish painter John Duncan Fergusson first essayed sculpture in 1908, encouraged by his friend Jo Davidson, the American sculptor who executed several well-known portraits, including that of Gertrude Stein. Though he was to execute only a handful of sculptures over the years, including stone and wood carvings and some bronzes, Fergusson managed to translate his painterly ideas of rhythm into a three-dimensional context through a modified form of Cubism.

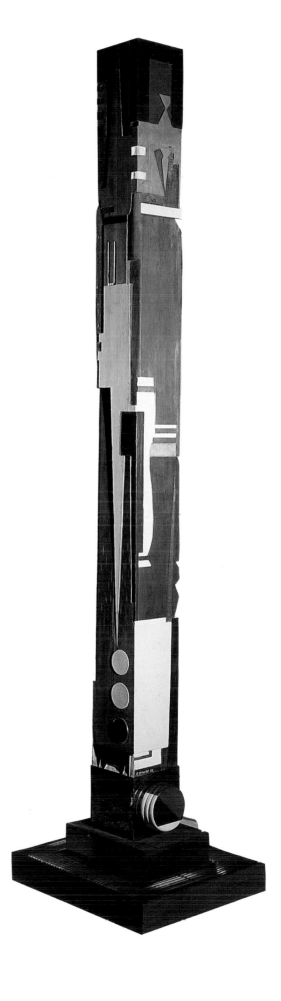

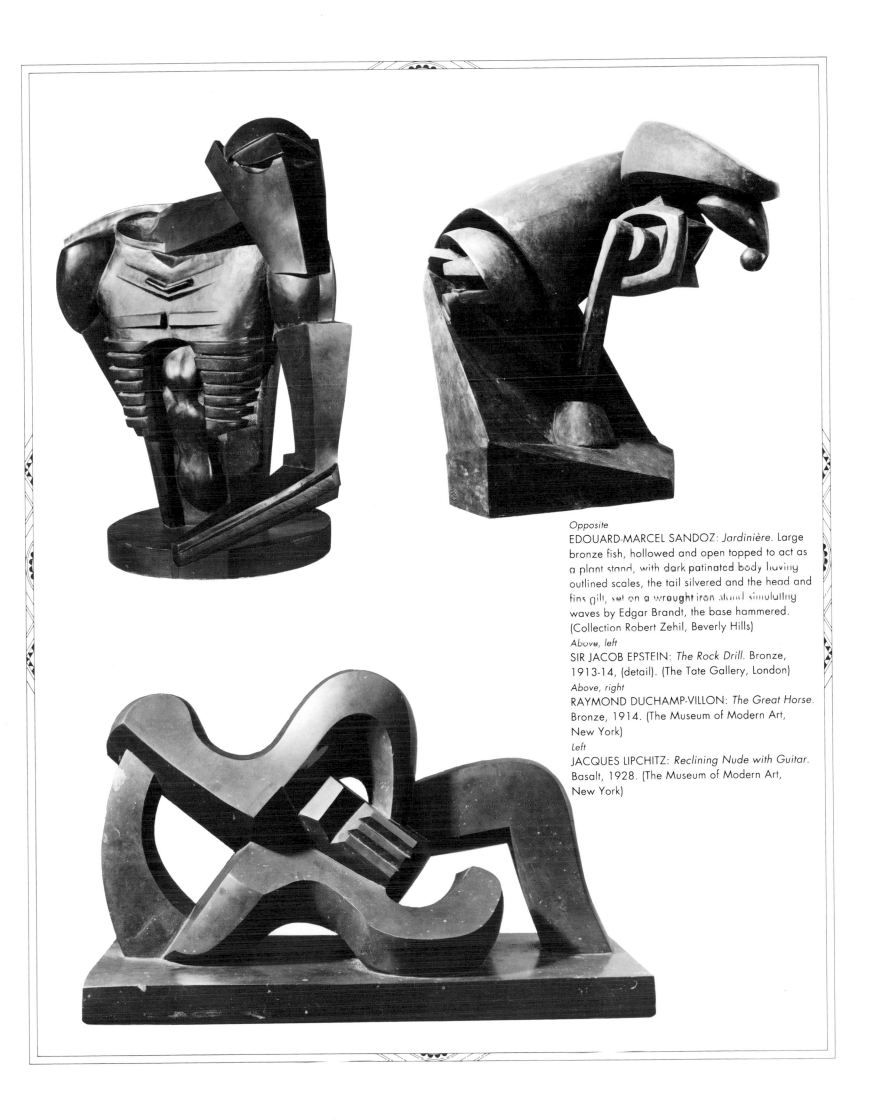

Opposite
EDOUARD-MARCEL SANDOZ: *Jardinière*. Large
bronze fish, hollowed and open topped to act as
a plant stand, with dark patinated body having
outlined scales, the tail silvered and the head and
fins gilt, set on a wrought iron stand simulating
waves by Edgar Brandt, the base hammered.
(Collection Robert Zehil, Beverly Hills)

Above, left
SIR JACOB EPSTEIN: *The Rock Drill*. Bronze,
1913-14, (detail). (The Tate Gallery, London)

Above, right
RAYMOND DUCHAMP-VILLON: *The Great Horse*.
Bronze, 1914. (The Museum of Modern Art,
New York)

Left
JACQUES LIPCHITZ: *Reclining Nude with Guitar*.
Basalt, 1928. (The Museum of Modern Art,
New York)

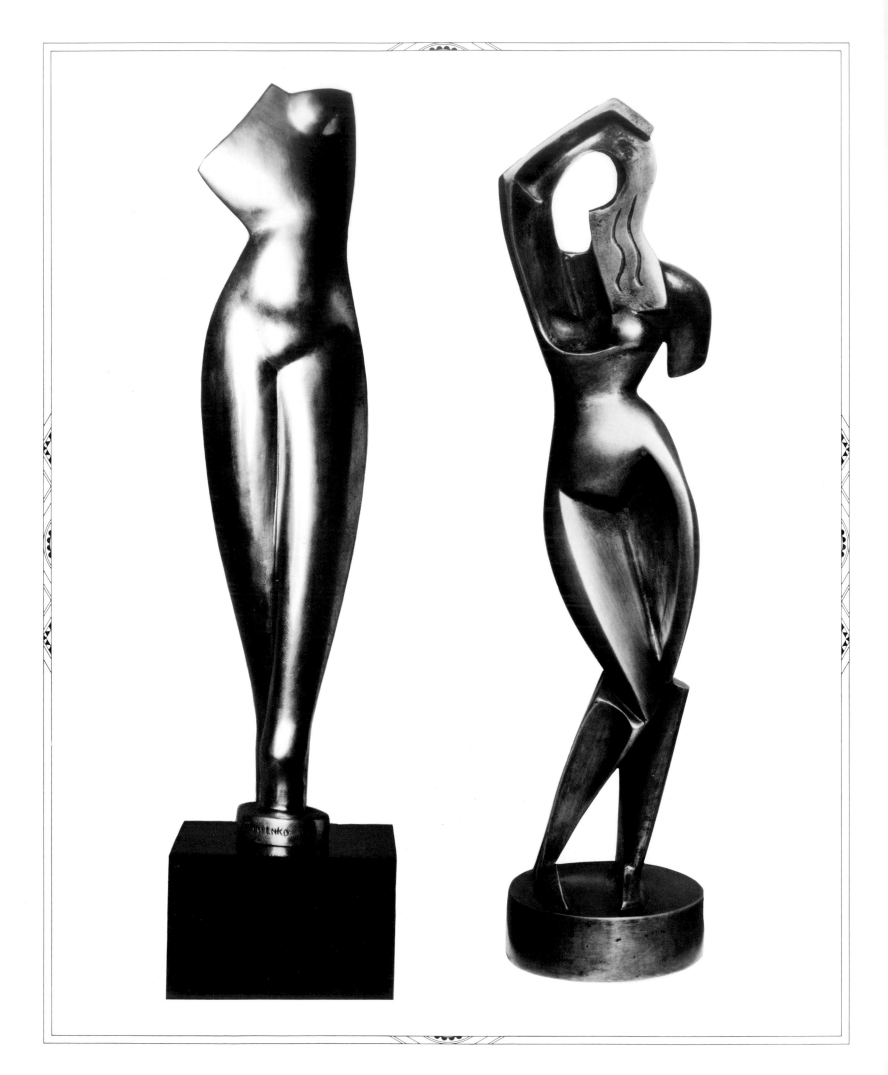

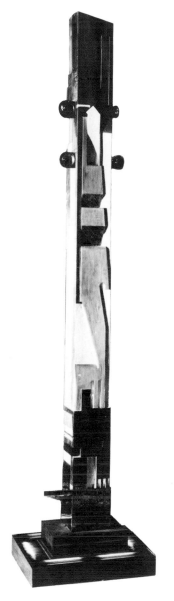

Opposite, left
ALEXANDER ARCHIPENKO: *Flat Torso.* Polished
bronze and nickel, 1914. (Collection Donald
Karshan, Paris. Photo: Sully Jaulmes)

Opposite, right
ALEXANDER ARCHIPENKO: *Woman Combing
her Hair.* Bronze. (The Tate Gallery, London)

Above, left
GUSTAVE MIKLOS: *Femme au Tambourin.*
Bronze, 1929. (Private Collection, Paris. Photo:
Sully Jaulmes)

Above, centre
GUSTAVE MIKLOS: *Column.* Polychrome and
silvered wood, 1923. (Private Collection, Paris.
Photo: Sully Jaulmes)

Above, right
GUSTAVE MIKLOS: *Seated Man.* Bronze. (Private
Collection, Paris. Photo: Sully Jaulmes)

Right
GUSTAVE MIKLOS: *Locomotive in Motion.*
Chrome-plated bronze. (Collection Alain
Lesieutre, Paris)

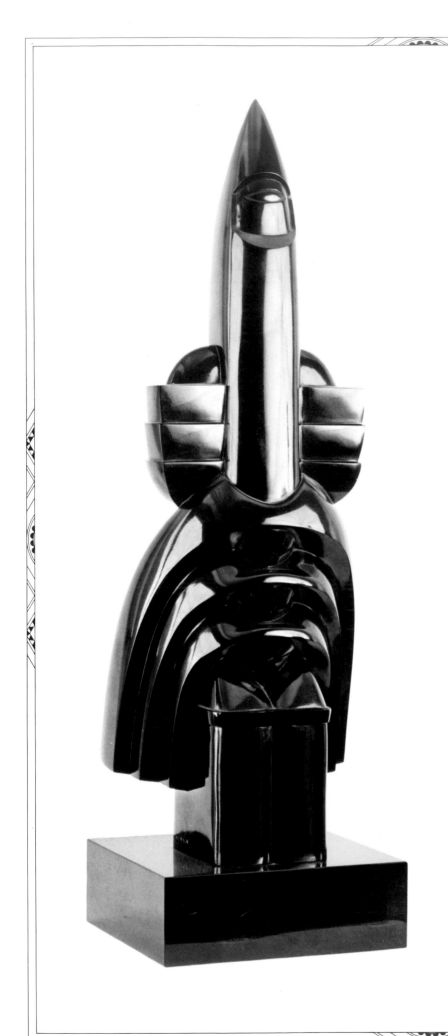

Opposite
ALEXANDRE KELETY: *Modern Medusa.* Bronze on black marble base. (Private Collection, Paris. Photo: Sully Jaulmes)

Left
JEAN LAMBERT-RUCKY: *Kneeling Figure.* Wood, lacquered and with eggshell by Dunand. (Collection Félix Marcilhac, Paris. Photo: Sully Jaulmes)
Above
JEAN LAMBERT-RUCKY: *Couple Kissing.* Engraved ebony. (Galerie Vallois, Paris)

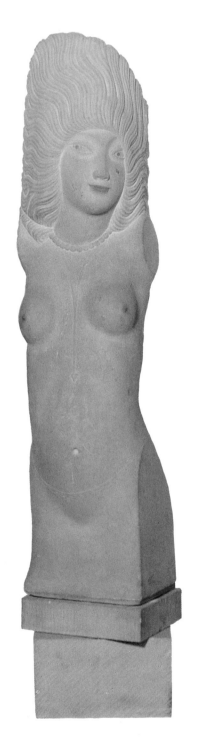

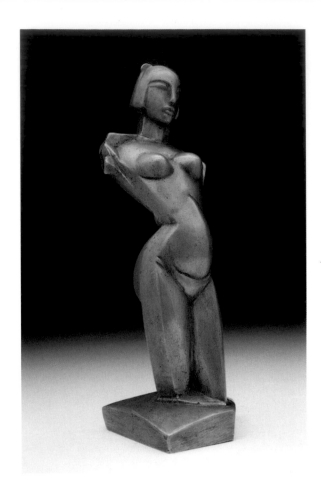

Above
ERIC GILL: *Headdress*. Beerstone, c. 1927.
(Collection John Scott, London)
Above, right
JOHN DUNCAN FERGUSSON: *The Patient Woman*. Brass, 1920. (Author's Collection)
Right
UMBERTO BOCCIONI: *Unique Forms of Continuity in Space*. Bronze, 1913. (Contemporary photograph)
Opposite
LEON UNDERWOOD: *The New Spirit*. Chased bronze, 1932. (Private Collection)

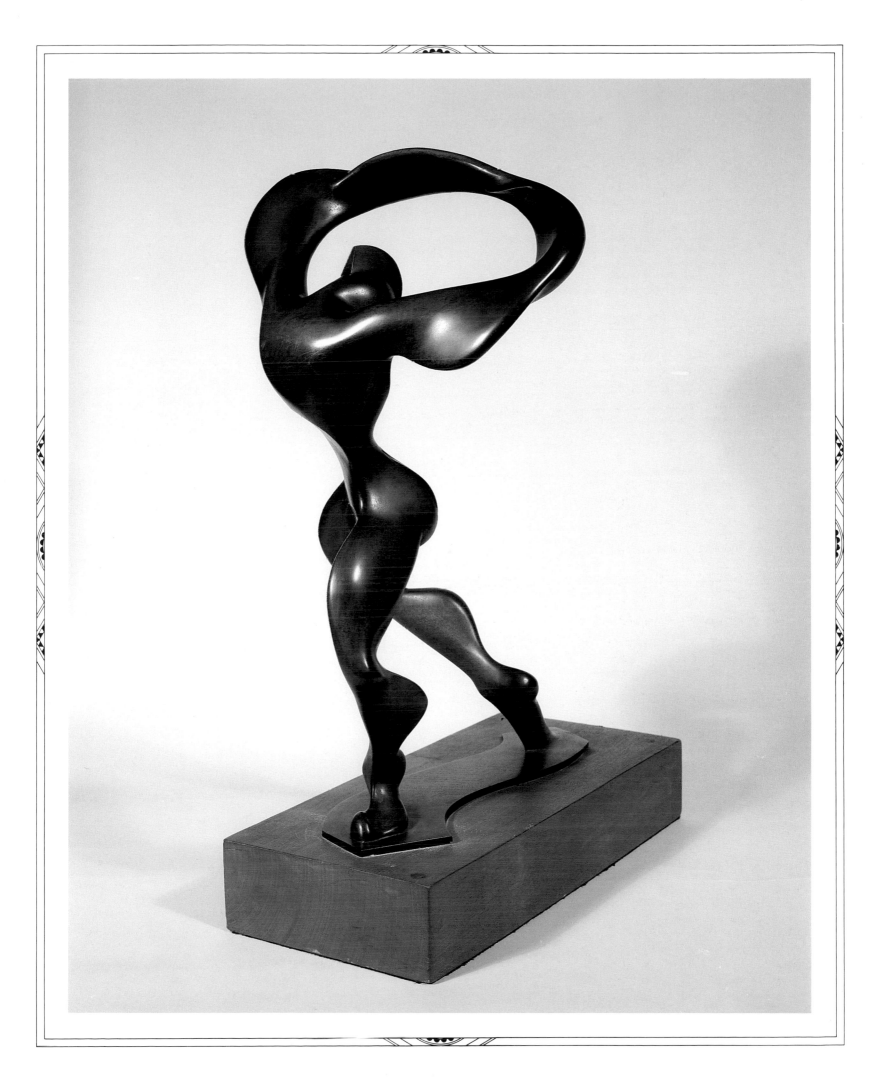

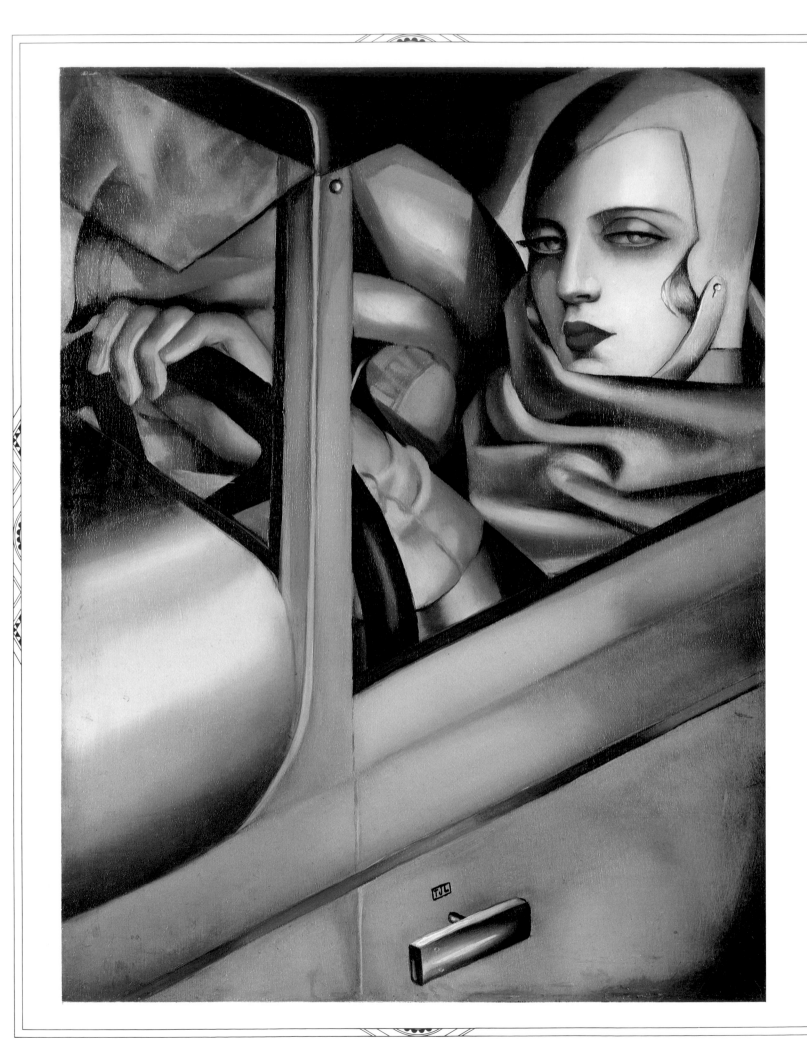

PAINTINGS, POSTERS, GRAPHICS AND BOOK ILLUSTRATION

The decorative arts had been under the tutelage and control of fine arts juries for so long in the Salons that even when set up as an autonomous group, their organisers found it difficult, if not impossible, to assign a direct role to painting. 'La decoration plane' or flat decoration, was taken to include tapestry, wallpapers, and 'decorative compositions', thus leaving it to each decorator to deal with painting as he saw fit. The organisers of the 1925 Exhibition gave no help (and only a little hindrance) in the choice of painters and paintings, and painting was not assigned a separate Exhibition Section.

Over the pre- and post-war years decorators had tended to include painters within their group. In some cases the painter and decorator had been brought together by personal friendship, in others by mutual admiration and in others still by family connections. In all cases the empathy between painter and decorator created

Above, left
GEORGES BARBIER: *Sous l'arbre.* Wood engraving for the preface by Paul Valéry of *Poèmes en prose* by Maurice de Guérin, 1928. (Private Collection, London)
Above
GEORGES BARBIER: *Les Bacchantes.* Wood engraving for *Poèmes en prose* by Maurice de Guérin, 1928. (Private Collection, London)
Opposite
TAMARA DE LEMPICKA: *Autoportrait.* Oil. (Private Collection, Paris. Photo: Sully Jaulmes)

Above
JEAN DUPAS: *Les Perruches.* Crayon drawing,
1925. (Collection Barry Humphries, Sydney.
Photo: Prudence Cuming Associates Ltd.)
Opposite, above, left
JEAN DUPAS: *Fleurs sous verre.* Oil, 1926.
(Collection Alain Lesieutre, Paris. Photo: Philippe
Doumic)
Opposite, above, right
ROBERT POUGHEON: *Amazone.* Oil. (Collection
Barry Humphries, Sydney)
Opposite, below, left
JEAN DESPUJOLS: *Vénus.* Oil, 1925. (Collection
Barry Humphries, Sydney)
Opposite, below, right
EMILE AUBRY: *La Voix de Pan.* Oil. (Contempo-
rary photograph)

unities in style, each consciously or unconsciously influencing the other. Thus, when decorators prepared an interior for a client, they frequently included paintings within their schemes. Certainly, paintings were always included in Salon and other exhibition set ups.

Then again, the decorator's client frequently had his own tastes in painting and the decorator could be required to design around a particular painting or collection. Several of the major patrons of the decorators were also great collectors of paintings, frequently of the then avant garde.

With hindsight, it is clear that some painters were particularly suited to fit into the Art Deco movement. The surprising thing is how diverse some of these artists were. Few were innovators. Most very capably adapted avant garde mannerisms and solutions to traditional problems, picked and chose certain traits from the styles of the past and the movements of the present, and succeeded in creating strong, recognisable images that are often the very epitome of the Art Deco style in all its diversity.

The City of Bordeaux was responsible for nurturing a whole group of these painters. Marginally the eldest, Jean Dupas, born in 1882, studied at both the Bordeaux and Paris Ecoles des Beaux-Arts. Exhibiting at the Paris Salons of the Société des Artistes Français from 1909, he was awarded a Medal 3rd Class in 1910, the same year he was awarded the Grand Prix de Rome. In Rome he studied at the Académie de France under Carolus Duran and then with Albert Besnard. He was later joined in Rome by two young men who had both won the Rome Grand Prix in 1914: Robert Eugène Pougheon, born in Paris in 1886 and a student of Charles Lameire and Jean-Paul Laurens; and Jean Despujols, also born in 1886 and a student of both the Bordeaux and Paris Ecoles des Beaux-Arts. Partly under Besnard's influence, they developed a neo-classic style of painting, though each developed in his own way. The human figure was treated in a volumetric fashion, attitudes were frequently heroic (as were some proportions) and the highly decorative detail, allied with often rich colours, made these artists ideal exponents of large, often allegorical frescoes. Dupas in particular tended to dehumanise his characters, turning them into pretty, sharp-featured but expressionless mannequins. Emile Aubry, born in Algeria in 1880 and a winner of both a Rome 2nd Grand Prix in 1905 and a 1st Grand Prix in 1907, painted very similar large compositions.

Dupas was awarded a Gold Medal at the 1922 Salon and exhibited thereafter Hors Concours. At the 1925 Exhibition he supplied large decorative compositions for several pavilions, most notably the large panel *Les Perruches* for Ruhlmann's Salon, and he was commissioned to execute large compositions on glass for the liner Ile de France in 1930, the Normandie in 1935 and the Liberté in 1949.

Four Bordeaux artists were commissioned to paint frescoes representing that area's commerce for the wine pavilion at the 1925 Exhibition. François Roganeau dealt with the products of the forest, Marius de Buzon with the port, Dupas with wine and Despujols with agriculture. The four pictures were again exhibited at the 1931 Colonial Exhibition in Paris and were then purchased by the Marquet Municipality to decorate the amphitheatre of the Municipal Theatre. The paintings by

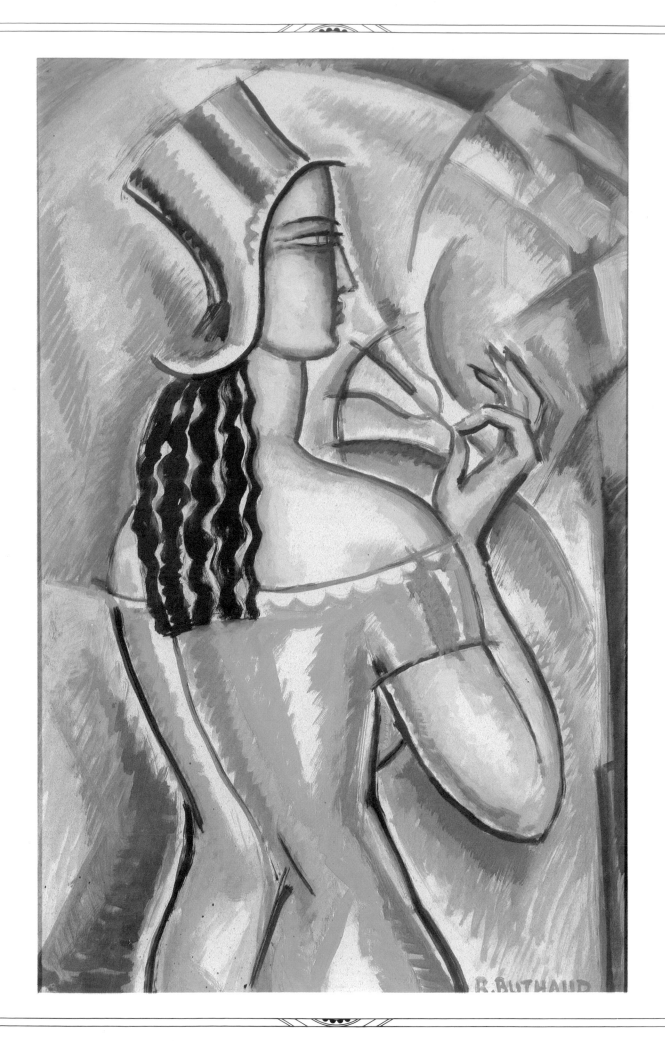

Dupas and Despujols, abounding with nude and semi-nude women, caused a storm of self-righteous attacks which they eventually weathered, and are now in the Aquitaine Museum.

René Buthaud, the ceramist, was another notable Bordeaux artist. Though many of his drawings and watercolours were studies for the decoration of his stoneware vases, it is clear that he was, basically, a painter. He produced some charming watercolours and drawings, several frescoes painted on glass, and treated his stoneware as a medium for painting, an extension of the traditional paper, wood and canvas surfaces. Another was Jean-Gabriel Domergue, a student at the Ecole des Beaux-Arts of Bordeaux and winner of the Rome Grand Prix in 1913. After a brief period as a landscape artist, Domergue developed into a celebrator of beautiful, chic women—painting portraits of celebrities and nudes, exaggerating certain features, creating a highly recognisable type of Parisian woman which was delicious in his early work though the images became stereotyped and mechanical towards the end of his life. At the 1925 Exhibition he painted four panels for the ceiling of the restaurant in the Bordeaux Tower.

Raphael Delorme studied at the Ecole des Beaux-Arts in Bordeaux under Gustave Lauriol and Pierre-Gustave Artus. The former was the author of a standard work on perspective, published at the turn of the century, and both teachers spent their time away from teaching as painter-decorators at the Bordeaux Grand Théâtre. Under their combined influence Delorme became a stage designer in Paris, specialising in effects of perspective. He would probably have remained at this task for the rest of his life had not a wealthy cousin, Madame Metalier, offered him the hospitality of her castle in Valesnes, in the Indre-et-Loire, provided he turned away from the theatre and began easel painting. He executed several frescoes for her and, indeed, devoted the rest of his working life to easel painting. Working in a neo-classic, frozen style similar to that of Dupas or Despujols, Delorme nevertheless injected a deadpan form of humour into his compositions, indulging in outrageous visual puns, combining his love of exercises in perspective with his experiences with the stage and circus. Detailed bits of architectural constructions are combined with mythological creations and well-fleshed, well-muscled women in odd, irrational conjunctions, some compositions being built up like a collage of disparate images snipped from a colour supplement. His paintings often build up an uneasy tension between subject and treatment which is more intense than anything in Dupas or Despujols. It should be said that although Delorme exhibited extensively in the Salon d'Automne, the Salon des Tuileries and the Salons of the Société Nationale des Beaux-Arts both at Tours and Bordeaux, he remained almost totally unsuccessful throughout his life, though proud of having sold a painting to the Maharajah of Kapurthala. His pictures only became sought after some time after his death in 1962.

Undoubtedly the most influential Bordeaux-born artist of the period was André Lhote. Born in 1885, he studied decorative sculpture at the Bordeaux Ecole des Beaux-Arts after a ten-year apprenticeship as a wood carver, yet was brought to painting by reading Delacroix's *Journal* and Baudelaire's *Aesthetic Curiosities*.

Above
JEAN GABRIEL DOMERGUE: *Madame de . . .*
Gouache, 1923. (Author's Collection)
Opposite
RENE BUTHAUD: *Femme tenant une fleur.*
Gouache, 1924. (Editions Graphiques Gallery, London)

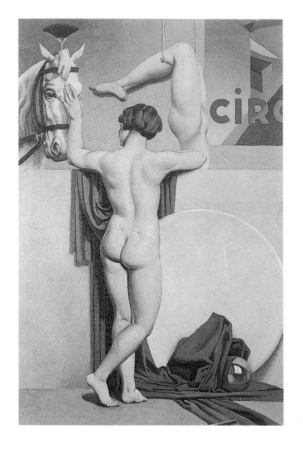

Completely self-taught as a painter, he submitted his first landscapes as early as 1904 to the Salon des Artistes Indépendants and was admitted to the Salon d'Automne two years later. His first one-man show was held in Paris in 1910 and he quickly made friends of his admirers, including Guillaume Apollinaire, André Gide, Maurice Denis and Charles Morice. He exhibited in all the early Cubist exhibitions, aligning himself with the 'Section d'Or' group of moderates, including Roger de la Fresnaye, Jacques Villon and Robert Delaunay. Lhote taught in various academies between 1918 and 1922, when he opened his own school in Paris in which he was to train a vast number of artists and from which he was to send out a constant stream of books, manifestoes, articles and artistic theories.

Essentially unwilling to reject the representational, Lhote combined the outward, physical reality, which he considered the emotive factor, with the spiritual factor, which he believed stemmed from the interpretation of this external reality. The result was a new figuration, reinterpreted from image to image, recognisable yet interpretative, in which the image is subjected to a degree of geometric analysis, partly disintegrated, then rebuilt using slabs of colour and shading. The treatment varied to accord with the subjects, which ranged from the febrile action of a football match to the quiet stillness of a sleeping bather, the gaiety of sailors on shore leave, or the vivid intelligence in a portrait. Inevitably with such a prolific artist, some of his paintings do not work, but at his best he produced some of the great visual masterpieces of twentieth-century French art, as well as a wealth of images on a lesser, though very enjoyable plane.

One of Lhote's students was to epitomise the very language of Art Deco. Born in Warsaw, the mysterious and beautiful Tamara de Lempicka arrived in Paris in about 1923 as a refugee from Soviet Russia. Brief studies with Maurice Denis were followed by a longer period with André Lhote and some attendance at the Grande Chaumière life class. On a trip to Milan she showed Count Emmanuele de Castelbarco some photographs of her work. He was enthusiastic enough to exhibit her work in his gallery, the Bottega di Poesia, in 1925. This was followed a year later by a show at the Galerie Colette Weill in Paris. In 1927 she won First Prize at the Exposition Internationale des Beaux-Arts in Bordeaux. After her divorce from Lempicki in 1928 she continued to receive international awards and was given her first American exhibition at the Carnegie Institute in Pittsburgh in 1930. In 1934 she married the Hungarian Baron Raoul Kuffner and they settled in Paris in a home designed by Robert Mallet-Stevens. Her studio in the house was designed by her sister, Adrienne Gorska, an architect who had trained with Mallet-Stevens. The Kuffners entertained Paris society at their home and mixed European aristocracy with a leavening of fashionable scientists, presentable ambassadors and such artists as Lhote, Kisling and Van Dongen. They moved to the United States in 1939, travelling throughout the country, and spent some of the war years in Beverly Hills, during which time she participated in various fund-raising efforts. They eventually settled in Texas.

Between 1924 and 1939 Tamara de Lempicka painted some one hundred extraordinary portraits and nudes, ultra-sophisticated conjunctions of people caught in a

Above
RAPHAEL DELORME: *La Répétition*. Oil. (Private Collection, Paris. Photo: Sully Jaulmes)
Opposite
RAPHAEL DELORME: *Cléopatre*. Oil. (Private Collection, Paris)
Overleaf, left
ANDRE LHOTE: *Deux jeunes femmes*. Pastel and gouache, 1929. (Editions Graphiques Gallery, London)
Overleaf, right
TAMARA DE LEMPICKA: *Nana de Herrera*. Oil. (Private Collection)

dynamic situation, contrasted with a multiplicity of angular planes, skyscrapers or stylised flowers. The Lhotian synthesis is there, the Cubist-inspired analysis, the strongly accented shadows that dramatically highlight expression, but the gleam of malice or challenge is purely hers, as is the highly charged sexuality that comes through in so many of the portraits, from the soft, 'bedroom' eyes she gave herself in the self portrait, the softness contrasted with the metallic rigidity of the car she is driving, to the almost anguished sensuality of the Spanish dancer, Nana de Herrera, a painting described by Giancarlo Marmori in his book on Lempicka as 'an electrifying allegory ot Hispanic wantonness.

Robert Delaunay and his wife Sonia Delaunay-Terk were closely connected with the creations of the Art Deco image. He began working in a studio specialising in stage setting at the age of seventeen and gradually evolved his own style in easel painting, influenced by the various post-Impressionist styles. Though using some of the mannerisms of Cubism and having a great influence on abstract painting, he remained largely figurative while experimenting with the effects of light, space and colour to achieve simultaneous contrasts. His wife applied these experiments to fabrics and embroidery as early as 1911, later expanding to open her own fashion house, for which she designed fashions, scarves, dresses, men's clothes, furs for Jacques Heim, decorative schemes for cars, interiors, etc. Both husband and wife designed for the Ballets Russes. At the 1925 Exhibition Robert Delaunay exhibited the huge painting *La Ville de Paris, La Femme et la Tour* in the Hall of the French Embassy designed by Mallet-Stevens. Paul Léon, director of the Beaux-Arts, ordered its removal, along with a decorative panel by Fernand Léger, on the grounds that these pictures clashed with the style of the Embassy. After loud and vociferous protests, both paintings were reinstated. Sonia Delaunay-Terk designed Jacques Heim's boutique on the Alexandre III Bridge and her designs were photographed everywhere. Though she was later to concentrate on painting, the influence of her fashions and clothes pervaded the theatre and the avant garde cinema.

Fernand Léger was one of the leaders of a type of Cubism set in opposition to Picasso, but his varied interests and experiments led him to Constructivism and then to a love for the machine and its product. He designed quirky costumes and sets for the Swedish Ballet and a Negro dance group and made avant garde films. He worked with Amédée Ozenfant and became friendly with Le Corbusier in 1920, the year the review *L'Esprit Nouveau* was founded. At the 1925 Exhibition Léger exhibited at the *L'Esprit Nouveau* pavilion in addition to the Embassy.

Born in Delfshaven, in the Netherlands, Kees Van Dongen first made his name with a special issue of *L'Assiette au Beurre* in 1901, in which he related the sad tale of the progress of a girl from kept woman to prostitution and poverty-stricken death, the illustrations drawn with broad brush strokes in a fin de siècle manner. He very quickly developed his own style, a delicate, yet powerful depiction of women, landscapes and more women. Using such striking colours that he was accused of confusing the make-up box with his paint palette, he exhibited with Matisse, Derain, Vlaminck, Othon Friesz and others at the famous Salon d'Automne in 1905 when the critic Louis Vauxcelles, struck by the contrast between a little classical bronze in a

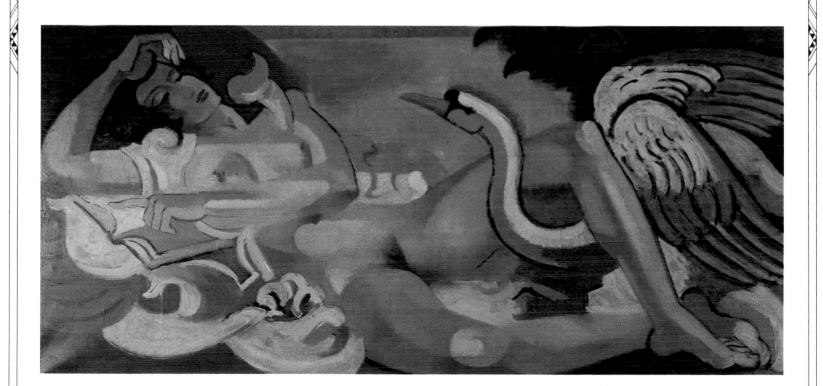

room ablaze with the raw colours of the paintings, exclaimed that it was 'Donatello among the wild beasts' (Donatello parmi les fauves) and a new movement was born. All the artists exhibiting were proud to be called Fauves, but within two years they had all begun to move in different directions. Van Dongen was never to lose his love of colour, which he controlled absolutely, and mastered extraordinary shades of grey as well as the most explosive reds.

Van Dongen soon emerged as the leading portraitist of the most beautiful, elegant and fashionable women in Paris, Deauville, Biarritz, Venice and the South of France. He painted them in all their finery, in bathing costumes, in underwear, or nude, bringing out the latent sexuality in all women, simplifying but never distorting, lavishing attention on the texture of silk, taffeta or muslin, sometimes stripping his models more by dressing than undressing them. Often careless of seeking a likeness, and disdaining psychological expression in favour of huge, brilliant, heavily made-up eyes and sensual, pouting lips, he found that women did their best to look like the portraits he had created. He illustrated several books, notably Victor Margueritte's *La Garçonne,* which defined the new 'modern' woman, and he produced an extraordinary series of lithographs of women's heads, some in colour, others in plain black or with only a touch of colour, in which he expressed the complete look of the women of the 20s.

Raoul Dufy pursued parallel careers as painter and designer. While it is clear that he first began designing fabrics in order to earn enough to enable him to paint, he soon realised that he not only had a talent for design, but a liking for it. Fabrics, tapestries, fashion designs, ceramics, complete ceramic gardens and painted mirrors alternated with woodcuts, book illustrations and colourful, faux-naif paintings.

Marie Laurencin's work was a highly individual conception. Her early training was at the very staid Académie Humbert, where she had gone to study porcelain painting, but Georges Braque, who was one of her fellow pupils, was struck by her independence of outlook and introduced her to the Bateau-Lavoir, a curious old building on the top of Montmartre where Picasso, Van Dongen and a number of young poets lived. It was 1905, and the young artists were arguing, on the verge of exploding their various ideas into Fauvism and Cubism. Marie Laurencin painted portraits of Picasso and his mistress Fernande Olivier and struck up a powerful romantic friendship with the poet Guillaume Apollinaire. These early paintings had a harder edge to them than her later work and she also produced some fine, strongly outlined etchings and lithographs. She was never attracted to either Cubism or Fauvism, preferring a personal and very feminine pastel palette, her clear outlines filled with wide bands of colour, choosing for her subjects endless processions of amazons, does and pretty young girls. She spent much time with her friends Jacques Villon, Duchamp-Villon, Léger, Metzinger and Gleizes, supplied paintings for the decoration of the Maison Cubiste at the 1912 Salon d'Automne and exhibited regularly at Léonce Rosenberg's gallery from 1913 to 1940. In 1924 she designed costumes and decor for the ballet *Les Biches* to Francis Poulenc's music for Diaghilev's Ballets Russes. She also worked closely with her brother-in-law, André Groult, supplying paintings for many of his interior designs, including the Chambre de Madame in the French Embassy pavilion at the 1925 Paris Exhibition. Groult frequently designed the frames for her paintings, gessoed and softly painted wooden mouldings, usually set with strips of mirror-glass.

Tsuguharu Foujita came to London in 1912 from Japan, where he had had considerable success as a painter, via Korea, where the emperor had commissioned his portrait from him, but the only work he could find in London was a temporary job drawing illustrations for a catalogue for Selfridges, the department store. The following year he moved to Paris, tempering the difficulties of his early years there with good wine, close friendships with fellow painters, poets and musicians, and the company of pretty girls. His first exhibition was in 1917 and he soon acquired an international reputation, his work combining traditional Japanese techniques with European subjects, Western tradition and his pick of contemporary experiments, overlaid with his own personal delicacy. He recieved major commissions as a decorator, including painting frescoes for the Japanese pavilion at the Paris Cité Universitaire and for the Cercle Interallié, and was a member of the jury at the 1925 Paris Exhibition. Foujita was an exceptionally fine graphic artist, producing series of black and white or delicately tinted etchings and lithographs of nudes, children and cats as well as designing a few posters and illustrating a number of books. Other Japanese artists working in Paris within the same tradition were Kiyoshi Hasegawa, primarily a graphic artist specialising in burin engravings, etching and woodcuts, though he also painted; and Miçao Kono, who established himself as a painter and engraver of pretty Parisian women.

A number of artists specialised in painting the human form in a slightly stylised way which situated it absolutely within the Art Deco mood. Moise Kisling came from Cracow, in Poland, developing in Paris a powerful recurring image of a pretty, sloe-eyed girl bathed in melancholy. His early work had been spiky and awkward, but in the years following the First World War, in which he fought in the French Foreign Legion and was wounded, he smoothed out his techniques, presenting a surface appearance of great charm and prettiness; though his models carry within them the knowledge of pain and suffering, he succeeds in bringing them just to the verge of sentimentality and hardly ever slips into it.

Clémentine-Hélène Dufau often sacrificed insight to decorative supremacy in her quiescent, sensual women, dressed or nude, and painted a number of allegorical murals, such as the four panels on the sciences at the Sorbonne University in Paris. She also illustrated a number of books and designed several posters. Bernard Boutet de Monvel, son of a well-known painter and illustrator, studied with Luc-Olivier Merson and Jean Dampt and painted landscapes and humorous subjects in addition to a number of fine, sombre studies of nudes and women suffering from spleen, that melancholy disease of the soul that had been so fashionable in the 1890s. Federico Beltran-Masses, born in Barcelona though he lived mainly in France, was only the third artist, after Rodin and John Singer Sargent, to be honoured with an exhibition in the Hall of Honour at Venice's International Exhibition in 1920, after which his portrait was admitted to the Uffizi Gallery in Florence. He was also named as organiser of the 1919 Hispano-French Exhibition in Saragossa

Above
VERA WILLOUGHBY: *The Lesbian Flute Player.*
Gouache and watercolour, 1927. (Private
Collection, London)
Opposite
KISLING: *Kiki au foulard bleu et chandail rouge.*
Oil, 1925. (Petit Palais, Geneva)

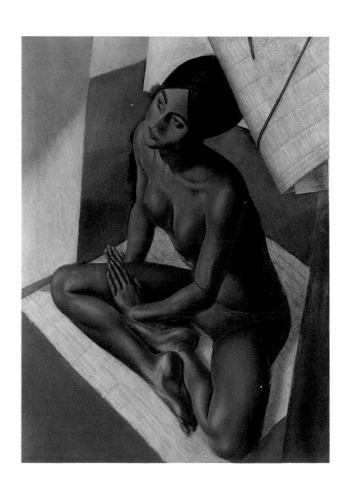

and the 1927 International Fine Arts Exhibition in Bordeaux. He became a fashionable portrait painter, painting not only the King of Spain and the Shah of Iran, but also Rudolph Valentino and Pola Negri; and used his considerable ability to paint a number of ambiguous, sexually charged subjects, such as *Ladies of the Sea* and *The Damned Maja*. Clement Serveau, famed primarily as a wood engraver and book illustrator, painted a number of portraits, frescoes and murals, some of which are reminiscent of those of Aubry or Dupas. Georges Manzana-Pissarro, son of Camille Pissarro, the great Impressionist painter, established his own reputation with a series of watercolours and prints of birds, animals and fish, heightened with gold and silver. He designed tapestries, experimented with enamelling on glass and painted several exotic portraits in addition to a number of densely composed pictures of flowers and trees. Sacha Zaliouk painted portraits of the demi-monde, his sharp eye using Cubist conventions to balance the figurative aspects. He also specialised in illustrations of fluffy girls for *La Vie Parisienne* and other girlie magazines. Paul Alex Deschmaker exhibited a number of powerful portraits of 20s women in the Salon des Tuileries and the Salon d'Automne.

Henri Matisse painted many broadly composed colourful frescoes and other large compositions on such subjects as 'The Dance'. For the Modern Art Museum of the City of Paris, one of the twin museums built for the 1937 Paris Exhibition, Matisse painted a lunette-shaped mural frieze. Charles Alexandre Picart le Doux, who first exhibited at the Salon des Indépendants in 1904 and was awarded the Grande Medaille d'Or at the 1937 Paris Exhibition, painted several ceiling frescoes for the liner Normandie, in addition to a number of other official commissions for town halls, schools and even police headquarters. Specialising in the painting of the nude figure, he even taught that subject at the Académie Colarossi and illustrated several books.

Animalier painters continued and revitalised the nineteenth-century tradition. Paul Jouve painted and etched his beloved animals all over the world. He had exhibited his first lions at the Salon of the Société Nationale des Beaux-Arts at the age of fifteen. At the age of eighteen he designed the ceramic animal frieze for the Binet Gate at the 1900 Paris Exhibition. A few years spent at the zoos of Antwerp, Hamburg and Algiers inspired him to illustrate Kipling's *Jungle Book,* a task which took several more years and thousands of sketches and finished drawings, which were cut on wood by F. L. Schmied. Jouve went on to illustrate many more books and produced an important body of animalier etchings, drawings, watercolours and paintings. Jacques Nam spent a lifetime portraying cats on paper, canvas and in lacquer, André Margat produced a wide range of beasts and Henri Deluermoz alternated between voluminous, small-scale book illustrations such as his own two-volume *Jungle Book,* and enormous decorative paintings in which the allegorical subjects were drawn from myths involving animals. Orovida Pissarro, daughter of Lucien and granddaughter of Camille, etched and painted an important body of animalier works, while Norbertine Bresslern-Roth produced many lively and decorative colour woodcuts of animals. Schmied himself was to devote his life to the

La femme a l'éventail
Picasso

BRUNELLESCHI

book, choosing the text, carrying out the illustrations, cutting them on wood, designing the lettering and the complete layout, printing it on his hand press, and designing and executing the binding, though he rang the changes by using illustrations by his friends and having his own illustrations transferred onto wood by his son, Théo.

Alexandre Iakovleff, born in St. Petersburg, studied at the Academy there before leaving Russia to travel for years through Japan, China and Mongolia. He exhibited some of his Far Eastern paintings and drawings in Shanghai in 1918, then in London and Paris in 1920, after which he settled in Paris. Traditional as a painter, he nevertheless absorbed enough of the atmosphere of his time to reflect a strong Art Deco flavour in much of his work, sometimes schematising a composition with smooth brushwork to give a painting on canvas the look of a lacquer panel. He accompanied the Citroën mission through Africa (the Croisière Noire) as its official painter, and later published a companion volume of paintings on the Far East, the Croisière Jaune. He painted a number of large decorative frescoes, including a series on 'The Joys of Life' for a Montmartre cafe.

In Germany the Neue Sachlichkeit group created images in a style that fitted perfectly into the Art Deco mood, while choosing subjects that were just too powerful, too acid or too bitter to have been painted by the Parisians. Christian Schad, in particular, has fixed on canvas some of the erotic perversity of Berlin between the wars. Jeanne Mammen painted and etched some very affecting feminine encounters; in Paris Romaine Brooks painted delicious portraits of her lover, Natalie Barney ('The Amazon'), Ida Rubinstein and the unforgettable image of Una, Lady Troubridge in tailored suit and short cropped hair, wearing a monocle and petting her two dachsunds. Most of these pictures are now at the National Collection of Fine Arts in Washington, D.C.

Much of the Art Deco style was developed by the illustrators who worked with the fashion industry. Paul Poiret, ever the innovator, was the first of the high fashion priests to create a catalogue illustrated by artists, rather than by the hacks of fashion illustration, though such Parisian furriers as the Maison Max were quick to seize on the idea. A publisher, Lucien Vogel, was to create the atmosphere in which those illustrators could work. The son of a painter, Vogel had had to give up architectural studies to work in a bookshop, but by 1906 had become art editor of the magazine Fémina. Over the years he was to launch L'Illustration des Modes, later to become Le Jardin des Modes; Vu, the first weekly magazine with photographic illustrations and which Henry R. Luce was to acknowledge as the inspiration for Life; and a daily newspaper, Le Petit Journal; as well as editing Art et Décoration for a time and being the art director of French Vogue. In 1912 he launched La Gazette du Bon Ton, a beautifully printed periodical which mixed prose from leading writers with illustrations coloured by the pochoir process.

The list of illustrators who worked for the Gazette includes George Barbier, Georges Lepape, Edouard Garcia Benito, Robert Bonfils, Pierre Brissaud, Umberto Brunelleschi, Robert Dammy, Erté, Valentine Gross (later Valentine Hugo), Edouard Halouze, Alberto Fabius Lorenzi, Charles Martin, André Marty, Marthe Romme,

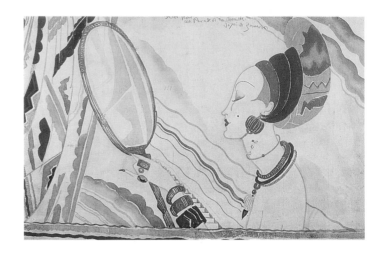

Above
JOSE DE ZAMORA: *La Parade de la beauté*.
Gouache. (Private Collection, London)
Left
JOSE ZINOVIEW: *Elegante*. Gouache. (Private
Collection, London)
Below, left
ENDRE: *La Folie bouquetière*. Watercolour and
gouache. (Private Collection, London)
Below, right
DOLLY TREE: *Robe excentrique*. Gouache and
watercolour. (Private Collection, London)

Above
ERTE: *Les Fleuves: Le Gange.* Gouache, c. 1923.
(Editions Graphiques Gallery, London)
Right
ERTE: *Le Coq d'or.* Gouache, 1926. (Editions
Graphiques Gallery, London)

Voici l'heure entre toutes si délicate,

Thayaht, Bernard Boutet de Monvel, José Zinoview and José de Zamora. All of these, plus such artists as Paul Iribe, Guy Arnoux, René Ranson and Etienne Drian divided their time between book illustrations, illustrations for fashion and other magazines and theatrical design. Other illustrators such as Endré, Dany, Michel Gyarmathy, Revolg, Dolly Tree, Freddy Wittop and Zig concentrated on designing for the stage and screen. Vogel's great innovation in terms of creative illustration and creative advertising was to connect his *Gazette* with a certain number of major dress designers and milliners and arrange for his team of artists to produce designs in pairs for each house, one drawing being of a design from the house, the second being an original design by the artist which the house could then make up if it wished. The *Gazette* survived until December 1925, and many fashion innovations began in its pages.

Erté, José de Zamora and Jeanine Aghion began their careers by working for Paul Poiret, the first two in his fashion house and Aghion as a designer in the Atelier Martine. Both Erté and Zamora went on to work extensively for the music hall and theatre, producing deliciously outrageous confections for showgirls to nearly wear. Erté, born Romain de Tirtoff in Russia, and forming his nom-de-plume from the French pronunciation of the initials RT, showed great acumen by retaining all his original drawings over the years. He was more careful in finishing his designs as drawings than many of his contemporaries, and if working drawings were to be used he would make a pristine finished example of the design. As a result, there is a far greater body of work by Erté than by any other of his contemporary illustrators, though in recent years most of it has gone into museums and major collections.

Like Erté, Georges Lepape and George Barbier executed much fashion illustration. Over several years Erté produced a vast number of covers for *Harper's Bazaar*, while Lepape carried out as many for *Vogue*. Erté and Barbier both designed sets and costumes for Hollywood films, Barbier designing the costumes for Rudolph Valentino's *Monsieur Beaucaire*. They also both designed costumes for the Folies Bergère and the Casino de Paris. Barbier was more involved than either of the other two with book illustration, and most of his drawings were reproduced in the colour pochoir process, though his finest illustrations were cut on wood by F. L. Schmied or one of his disciples.

A small group of women artists developed an exotic vein of erotic romance. Gerda Wegener, born in Denmark, studied at the Fine Arts Academy in Copenhagen before travelling extensively and settling in Paris in 1912. In France she painted a number of nudes, lovers of mixed and single sexes and picturesque locales. She also illustrated several books, including the *Fables* of La Fontaine and Casanova's *Une Aventure d'amour à Venise* and executed a number of cartoons of risqué humour for various French magazines, including *La Vie Parisienne* and *Fantasio*. Her husband, the Danish landscape painter Einar Wegener, had a sex change operation in 1930 and became a woman, taking the name of Lili Elbe. Vera Willoughby, though English, spent several years in France. In England, she illustrated a large number of books, including *The Memoirs of a Lady of Quality* and several volumes illustrating translations of Greek love poems and the *Odes* of

Above
FRANCOIS LOUIS SCHMIED: *Salammbô*. Colour woodcut. (Private Collection, London)
Opposite, above, left
GEORGES LEPAPE: *Les Coussins*, a gouache reproduced by the pochoir process from the first edition of *Modes et Manières d'Aujourd'hui*, 1912. (Private Collection, London)
Opposite, above, right
GEORGES LEPAPE: *Au Clair de la lune*. Pochoir plate from the *Gazette du Bon Ton*, 1913, depicting an evening gown by Paul Poiret. (Private Collection, London)
Opposite, below, left
GEORGE BARBIER: Pochoir illustration engraved on wood by F. L. Schmied from *Personnages de Comédie* by Albert Flament, Paris 1922. (Private Collection, London)
Opposite, below, right
GEORGE BARBIER: Pochoir illustration, one of twelve from the album *Nijinsky*, published in 1913 with introduction by Francis de Miomandre, depicting the dancer in the Ballets Russes's production of *Schéhérazade*. (Private Collection, London)

Horace. She wrote an impressionist account of travels through Greece, *A Vision of Greece*, in 1925, which she illustrated with sixteen watercolours, an exercise which led her to execute a series of paintings and gouaches on various Greek mythological figures. She also painted a number of scenes of harem life, teeming with fleshy delights. Dorothy Wheeler illustrated several books with precisely drawn watercolours of contrasting naked black and white women, frequently placed against exotic tapestries or Oriental surroundings. Dorothy Webster Hawksley, a pupil of Clausen, Solomon and Dicksee at the Royal Academy Schools, exhibited at both the Royal Academy and the Paris Salon, where she was awarded a Silver Medal in 1931. Infatuated with Japan and Japanese art, she executed a quantity of such highly romantic subjects as a samurai in full rig clasping his lady love to his bosom as they both jump off the cliff to their deaths below, or ethereal, white-clad beauties with distinctly Oriental features languishing in a precisely delineated garden.

Illustrators such as Edmund Dulac from France, Kay Nielsen from Denmark, Vernon Hill, Kettlewell and René Bull produced charming and occasionally unsettling images for books published in England and the United States. The purely linear style of illustration created by Aubrey Beardsley was pursued effectively by Alastair, the mysterious Baron Hans Henning Voigt, who created haunting images inspired by Poe, Choderlos de Laclos, the Abbé Prévost and Wilde, giving most of his female creations the tragic mask of the Marchesa Casati. John Austen's stylised characters, frequently drawn in ink on scraper-board, are deliberately treated two-dimensionally, the concentrated detail pointing the subject to pure decoration. Norman Lindsay, an Australian artist, produced some delightfully busy subjects of hoydenish minxes leering irresistibly from the pages on which they are drawn or etched. Beresford Egan, originally from South Africa, occasionally substituted vitriol for ink in his satirical drawings, calligraphically stripping away the pretensions he saw around him. He illustrated Baudelaire's *Fleurs du Mal* as well as contemporary poems and novels, some written by himself.

Among the many British artists strongly influenced by French art of the period, John Duncan Fergusson succeeded in retaining his individuality as a leading Scottish painter while absorbing the lessons of the experimentation that surrounded him. More conventionally orientated, the sisters Doris and Anna Zinkeisen, both born in Scotland, exhibited at the Royal Academy and the Paris Salon, both winning Silver Medals. Both painted portraits which reflect the look, makeup, clothing and surroundings of the 20s and 30s, and both designed sets and costumes.

A handful of English graphic artists produced etchings, drypoints or woodcuts in the Art Deco style, including Sir William Russel Flint, E. H. Lacy, William E. C. Morgan, John Buckland Wright, Lettice Sandford and Eric Gill. In France Paul Iribe had produced some fine-lined nudes and entertaining attacks on anything foreign or unfamiliar, from Scotch, vodka and cocktails to Modernism. Jean-Emile Laboureur used the Cubist line to produce sharp, spiky etchings of great presence, while Chas-Laborde illustrated volumes on London, Berlin and New York with etchings depicting the quirkiness of the inhabitants of each city with humour, tolerance and an unerring eye for the telling detail which he promptly buried in a bee-hive of activity.

AVEC LES FILLES DES ÉLÉMENTS OU DES MORTELS.
AELLO DESCENDAIT DE LA SCYTHIE, OU ELLE S'ÉTAIT
ÉLEVÉE JUSQU'AUX SOMMETS DES MONTS RIPHÉES, ET
SE RÉPANDAIT DANS LA GRÈCE, AGITANT DE TOUTES
PARTS LES MYSTÈRES ET PORTANT SES CLAMEURS SUR

Poster artists split into two basic camps. First came the illustrative artists, whose style was developed from the early posters of Chéret. Capiello had taken Chéret's favourite figure, the 'Chérette', and used the techniques of a single figure, but varied it by creating a different figure for each product, then associating the figure with the product. This was so successful that some of the brand images went on being used for a half a century. George Barbier and Jean-Gabriel Domergue used this same technique. So did Charles Gesmar, the very young artist who joined the Casino de Paris when he was barely seventeen years old. Attaching himself to Mistinguett, he·designed her costumes, including variations of her long feathered trains, elaborate sets and large colourful posters based on her face. After his death at the age of twenty-eight, several Casino de Paris designers produced posters for her, including Zig, who was also to execute posters for Josephine Baker, the startling black American singer and dancer who arrived in Paris in 1925 with the Revue Nègre and knocked them in the aisles for the next fifty years (give or take the war years, when she won the Croix de Guerre, the Légion d'Honneur and many other decorations). Very young and very innocent, she was persuaded to shed her clothes and appear on stage wearing only a string of bananas. Count Harry Kessler has written in his memoirs of his first seeing her at a private party in Berlin, where she was performing. The party was held at the house of Karl Vollmoeller, the successful playwright whose 'spectacle', *The Miracle*, staged by Max Reinhardt, was performed for years throughout Germany, Britain and the United States and was filmed on several occasions. Lady Diana Manners (who later wed Duff-Cooper, who became Lord Norwich), one of the great English society beauties, played the part of the Virgin Mary in this play for several years.

'At one o'clock,' wrote Kessler, 'a telephone call from Max Reinhardt. He was at Vollmoeller's and they wanted me to come over because Josephine Baker was there and the fun was starting. So I drove to Vollmoeller's harem on the Pariser Platz. Reinhardt and Huldschinsky were surrounded by half a dozen naked girls, Miss Baker was also naked except for a pink muslin apron, and the little Landshoff girl (a niece of Sammy Fischer) was dressed up as a boy in a dinner-jacket. Miss Baker was dancing a solo with brilliant artistic mimicry and purity of style, like an ancient Egyptian or other archaic figure performing an intricate series of movements without ever losing the basic pattern. This is how their dancers must have danced for Solomon and Tutankhamen. Apparently she does this for hours on end, without tiring and continually inventing new figures like a child, a happy child, at play. She never even gets hot, her skin remains fresh, cool, dry. A bewitching creature, but almost quite unerotic. Watching her inspires as little sexual excitement as does the sight of a beautiful beast of prey. The naked girls lay or skipped about among the four or five men in dinner-jackets. The Landshoff girl, really looking like a dazzlingly handsome boy, jazzed with Miss Baker to gramophone tunes.

'Vollmoeller had in his mind a ballet for her, a story about a cocotte, and was proposing to finish it this very night and put it in Reinhardt's hands. By this time Miss Baker and the Landshoff girl were lying in each other's arms, like a rosy pair of lovers, between us males who stood around. I said I would write a dumb show for

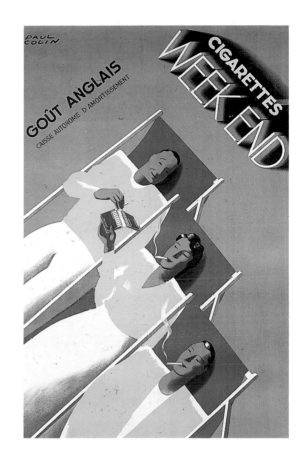

them on the theme of the Song of Solomon, with Miss Baker as the Shulamite and the Landshoff girl as Solomon or the Shulamite's young lover. Miss Baker would be dressed (or not dressed) on the lines of Oriental Antiquity while Solomon would be in dinner-jacket, the whole thing an entirely arbitrary fantasy of ancient and modern set to music, half jazz and half Oriental, to be composed perhaps by Richard Strauss.

'Reinhardt was enchanted with the idea, as was Vollmoeller. We fixed on the twenty-fourth of this month for dinner at my apartment to discuss the matter, the two of them and the Landshoff girl, Miss Baker coming later. Vollmoeller asked me to invite Harden too. It was past four when I left.'

Though this particular project never materialised, Josephine Baker both gave pleasure and caused scandal throughout the world and was drawn, painted and photographed in every conceivable style. Her favourite poster artist, who also painted her a number of times, was Paul Colin, who had originally made his reputation as the poster artist for the Théâtre des Champs-Elysées. He caricatured her, lovingly depicting the graceful, gangling arms, exaggerating the pouting lips, the gleaming teeth, the sparkling eyes and the patent-leather short hair.

Marcel Vertès was a Hungarian artist who, helped by Alexander Korda, went to Vienna, where he became one of the leading poster artists there. Armed with this reputation, he arrived in Paris and was utterly ignored for years. Shortly after his arrival he published two volumes of lithographs, *Maisons*, which dealt with the houses of prostitution and their inmates and visitors in a humorous, sly way and *Dancing*, a set of twelve colour lithographs on Parisian night life. Though unsuccessful when they were first published, both sets eventually became greatly prized by collectors, and were followed by several other sets, such as *La Journée de Madame*. All tend to deal with the world on the fringes of respectability, generally in a delicious, frequently witty manner. He produced a few posters in France. Vertès eventually settled in the United States in the 40s and painted murals for shops and restaurants as well as for private homes, including that of Gypsy Rose Lee.

One aspect of the Art Deco image was that of the pretty girl in the appropriate setting: the garçonne, the chic, sleek girl with the chic, sleek greyhounds straining at the leash, symbolising speed and streamlining; the pert girl reclining half-undressed as she daringly smokes a cigarette; the 30s sophisticate with her dyed platinum hair and figure-hugging dress. A group of artists soon exploited this vein through coloured etchings and aquatints often produced in quite large editions. William Ablett, Maurice Millière, Kaby and Miçao Kono all contributed, but the most prolific and most famous of the group was Louis Icart. Finding ever new variations on his themes, he produced a vast quantity of dynamic, often very attractive images which were so popular that a Louis Icart Society was formed in the United States to distribute his graphics. He was, sadly, a very poor artist when away from the discipline of graphic techniques, but he illustrated several books with charming etchings.

A completely different style of poster work from that of Domergue, Gesmar, Vertès or Zig was exemplified by Cassandre. Born Adolphe Jean-Marie Mouron in

Above
MIÇAO KONO: *Le Loup.* Oil. (Private Collection, London)
Opposite, above
LOUIS ICART: *Les Hortensias.* Colour etching and aquatint, 1937. (Editions Graphiques Gallery, London)
Opposite, below
LOUIS ICART: *Vitesse.* Colour etching and aquatint. (Editions Graphiques Gallery, London)

CHEMIN DE FER DU NORD
A.M.CASSANDRE 27
NORD
EXPRESS
HACHARD & Cie PARIS
SOUTHERN RAILWAY = CHEMINS DE FER BELGES
DEUTSCHE REICHSBAHN GES. = POLSKIE KOLEJE PANSTWOWE
LONDRES BRUXELLES
PARIS
LIEGE
BERLIN
RIGA
VARSOVIE
COMPAGNIE DES WAGONS - LITS

the Ukraine of French parents, Mouron used the pseudonym Cassandre (the name of Troy's prophet of doom), usually with his own initials, A.M. His first poster was executed in 1924, but within a year he had created the amazing poster for the newspaper *L'Intransigeant,* the newsvendor's face a mere outline, the very title simplified to its popular contraction, 'L'INTRANS'. This won him the Grand Prix for posters at the 1925 Paris Exhibition. The following year Cassandre met Maurice A. Moyrand and the two of them set up a new and highly adventurous advertising agency which enabled Cassandre to develop his themes and ideas. 'The poster demands complete renunciation from its painter. He cannot express himself in it,' he wrote. 'The poster is only a means, a means of communicating between tradesman and public, something like the telegraph. The poster artist plays the part of the telegraphist: he does not emit messages, he transmits them. One does not ask him for his advice, one merely asks him to establish clear, powerful and precise communication.'

Nevertheless, his pure and simplified images were frequently sufficiently inspiring to bring Blaise Cendrars, the French poet and novelist, to write that 'here advertising approaches poetry.'

In 1930, Moyrand brought Charles Loupot into the Alliance Graphique. Loupot's first posters, executed in 1918, were of the romantic type favoured by the German and Swiss designers of the day. He had studied at the Ecole des Beaux-Arts of Lyon before the war. Wounded in the war, he had joined his parents in Switzerland after his demobilisation, and it was there that he studied poster technique and worked for several years. Some of his posters from this period are sumptuous in the richness of colour, and his growing reputation led to his being summoned to Paris by the printer Devambez in 1923. Soon after his arrival he began to work for the *Gazette du Bon Ton* and *Fémina,* but the two posters he produced that same year for the Voisin car showed the direction he had come and the direction he was about to follow. The first showed the car standing four-square in the middle of a lush forest. The second, almost a blank sheet, had a schematic, aerodynamic car about to take off into space from the surface of the barely-sketched curve of the globe, the name VOISIN backed by a winged scarab.

Loupot supplied one of the three posters for the 1925 Paris Exhibition, the others being supplied by Bonfils and Girard. The Damour brothers set up an advertising agency called Les Belles Affiches for him, putting in a man called Aubespin as commercial manager. Loupot was a perfectionist who kept constantly reworking his projects, but Aubespin kept him at it by a constant stream of commissions which he would take away from Loupot as soon as executed, before he could have second thoughts.

The years of the Alliance Graphique ended in 1934 when Moyrand died, but during this brief collaboration Moyrand frequently got both Loupot and Cassandre to produce projects for the same poster, giving the client the choice. After Moyrand's death Cassandre produced only occasional posters, and designed type faces, fashion illustrations and theatre designs. Loupot, however, remained a leading poster artist until his death.

Above
CHARLES LOUPOT: *La Femme au vase.* Watercolour, 1924. (Contemporary photograph)
Opposite
CASSANDRE: *Nord Express.* Poster, 1927. (Editions Graphiques Gallery, London)

BOOKBINDING

The final years of the nineteenth century saw a renewal of fine bookbinding in France, at a time when binders concentrated solely on traditional designs and techniques. They had weathered the brief fashion for romantic bindings and were clothing books in fine morocco encrusted with gold tooling in traditional patterns, the binding generally sewn as tightly as possible, making it extremely difficult to open. This difficulty was, however, irrelevant to the bibliophile, since a fine art binding was not expected to go over a book to be opened, much less read.

Much of the change was due to one farsighted binder who was to dominate French bookbinding until his death in 1925. Marius-Michel, born in 1846, was the son of a bookbinder with an acknowledged reputation as a finisher. After a long apprenticeship, studies as an artist, and considerable travel, he joined his father in 1876. Two years later he was awarded a first medal at the Paris International Exhibition.

Despite this early success, Marius-Michel found great difficulty in persuading the wealthy bibliophiles to have their books bound by him. The taste was still to copies of earlier ornament, while he was developing a floral ornamentation based on researches that paralleled those of Eugène Grasset and Emile Gallé, and led him to create some of the first bindings with Art Nouveau designs. His stubbornness and refusal to compromise delayed, but could not halt, fame and success, which followed within ten years of his starting work. His innovative designs for floral gold tooling were soon followed by his revival of incised and embossed leather panels inset on the upper cover, sometimes reproducing one of the book's illustrations. He often commissioned the book's illustrator, or another artist, to produce an original incised, cut, inked and coloured, embossed or blind-embossed drawing, and established artists such as Steinlein, Louis Legrand, Tony Minartz and Alexandre Lepère produced incised panels. As his reputation grew, so did his influence, and his styles were soon copied and adapted, Marius-Michel himself often producing some extraordinary tours de force, such as the incised bindings for twenty-four copies of Grasset's book *Les Quatre fils Aymon* which he exhibited at the 1894 Paris Salon. He also wrote several books on the history of bookbinding and its contemporary state.

There were, of course, many other important bookbinders at the turn of the century producing new and creative designs, including Georges Canapé; Paul-Romain Raparlier; Léon Gruel; Petrus Ruban, who produced some of the most attractive and original decorations; and Charles Meunier, who specialised in decorating spines and was the first binder to turn publisher, publishing both books and magazines. At Nancy, René Wiener executed bindings designed by several of that

Above
PIERRE LEGRAIN: Red Morocco binding inlaid with polychrome calf, morocco and polished metal, inspired by the American and British flags, cocktail shakers and glasses, the title set in Palladium letters to simulate straws, gilt tooling, for *Petits et grands verres* by Nina Toye and A. H. Adair. (Courtesy Guy Loudmer, Paris)
Opposite
LEOPOLDO METLICOVITZ: White calf binding, gold and silver tooling, inlaid with a gouache and watercolour, for the score of Giacomo Puccini's *Turandot*, executed by G. Ricordi & Co. in Milan, 1926. (Author's Collection)

city's Art Nouveau artists, particularly Victor Prouvé. Yet, even as these binders were imposing themselves and collecting faithful bibliophiles, others were moving away from these styles and developing new ones.

One of the most interesting of the new binders was René Kieffer. Born in 1875, he was among the first group of graduates from the Estienne Technical College in Paris, where he had studied finishing. After a few years of acquiring experience with various bookbinders he joined the firm of Chambolle-Duru, which specialised in traditional gilt decoration. There young Kieffer was only occasionally allowed to work outside the house style, but in 1903, at the age of twenty-eight, he set up on his own, firmly convinced he was going to be an innovator. His friend Charles Jouas, an artist and book illustrator, introduced him to Henri Béraldi, a leading critic, collector and bibliophile, who asked him, 'Well, young bookbinder, are you going to work in the style of Marius-Michel or in that of Mercier?' The firm reply was, 'I shall work in the Kieffer style.'

Kieffer soon produced designs that matched the contents of the books he bound. He developed the practise of designing a motif, sometimes inspired by a book illustration, sometimes separately drawn by an artist, which was impressed and gilt onto the otherwise plain morocco binding. These motifs could be used on other bindings, either different copies of the same book or other titles, variations in the finished look being provided by the use of different coloured leathers. This enabled Kieffer to drastically reduce the price of bookbinding, since each individual book did not need to be separately designed and new tooling devised. He became an editor and bookseller, publishing many new books, as well as dealing in new and second hand ones, many of which he would bind before selling. Another speciality of his was to have the books he bound extra-illustrated, either by the original illustrator or by another. The first few years were difficult ones, but the 1911 Salon of the Société Nationale des Beaux-Arts saw his exhibits so widely admired that he was henceforth firmly launched. His son Michel, born in 1916, became his assistant in 1935.

The most influential bookbinder of the 20s was Pierre Legrain, who was catapulted into the craft independently of his will. At the outbreak of war in 1914 he attempted to join the army, but was turned down because of poor health. He did, however, manage to enlist briefly with a Zouave regiment and was sent to work on the shoring up of the sandpits at Valenton. Several transfers followed, from guarding highways to paperwork, before he was finally discharged in 1916. He found himself in broken health with the new responsibilities of a wife who also had a young son. In the years before the war he had built and painted stage scenery, designed dresses for Paquin, jewellery for Linzeler and furniture for Iribe. While working for Iribe he had met Jacques Doucet several times, and so now approached the grand couturier for help. Doucet had been forming a formidable collection of fine editions and manuscripts of novels and poetry by all the leading contemporary French writers. He wanted new and original bindings for these, but found the leading binders too traditional. He instructed Legrain to design bindings for him. Legrain's total ignorance of the craft seemed a positive advantage to

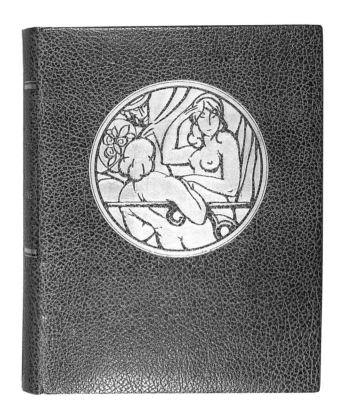

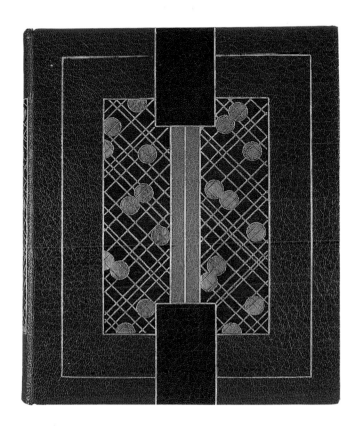

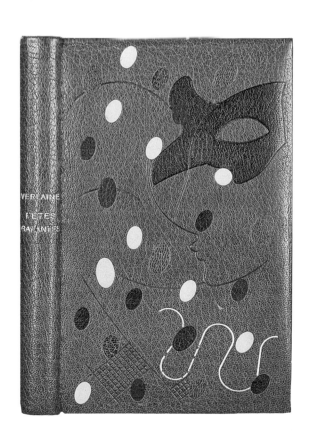

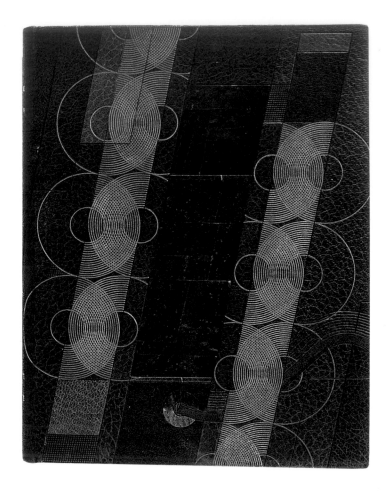

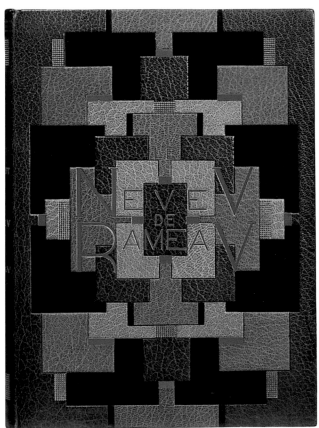

Doucet and Legrain's original doubts were quickly overcome by the prospect of steady employment at a reasonable, though not over-generous wage.

Legrain's first essay disappointed Doucet, who found it too timid. The couturier introduced him to the professional bookbinders of the day—Germaine Schroeder, René Kieffer, Canapé, Trinckvel, Noulhac—and Legrain began to design with increasing confidence and freedom, limited only by the availability of materials. The bindings themselves were executed by the various professional binders who, while not over-enthusiastic at the prospect, were unwilling to break with one of their best customers. French bookbinding had traditionally been divided into two separate streams, the forwarders or *relieurs* who executed the body of the binding, and the finishers or *doreurs* (gilders) who decorated it. Indeed, they had been members of separate guilds since the early seventeenth century. There was thus little difficulty in accepting an outside designer. In the space of two years Legrain designed 365 bindings for Doucet, many of which were still being executed when he left shortly after the Armistice.

Legrain used every variety of morocco and calf that was available for his designs, encrusting them with marquetry of various leathers, but also using inlays and onlays of various woods, ivory, mother-of-pearl, snakeskin, crocodile skin and shagreen, made from the skin of sharks or ray. The upper cover, and frequently the lower, was used pictorially, rather than emblematically. His earlier designs used motifs inspired by those Iribe had used on his furniture, but he soon replaced these with abstract geometric patterns executed with compass, ruler and T-square (or set square). These were executed in gold and silver, though he also introduced the use of other metals, such as platinum and palladium. He had various papers specially treated, sometimes coloured at random by treating them like batik, for use in large bindings for periodicals. He made increasing use of the book's title and author's name as the principal decoration, devising new lettering or curious ways of assembling the letters to obtain his decorative effects. Doucet never interfered at the design stage, though he felt free to criticise after the binding was executed. The two obstinate men quarrelled frequently, but retained their admiration for each other. Doucet's personal contribution to the bindings was a vast quantity of fabric remnants from his couture house to use as linings instead of the marbled papers that were in short supply.

Between 1919 and 1923 Legrain, who had now set up on his own as a designer, worked very closely with René Kieffer, to whom he was to write: 'At the beginning of my efforts you alone understood what I was trying to do, and placed at the service of my decorative aspirations the weight of your talent and your great fame.' He exhibited at the Salons of the Société des Artistes Décorateurs, his 1919 display bringing him several new and important clients, including Mrs. Florence Blumenthal, an American living in Paris, who commissioned both bookbindings and furniture. He was also awarded a Blumenthal Foundation prize for his bindings.

In 1923 Legrain was offered his own workshop by Briant et Robert, interior decorators. Enormously excited by the prospect of being able to have his own designs carried out by his own men, Legrain broke gently with Kieffer and hired a

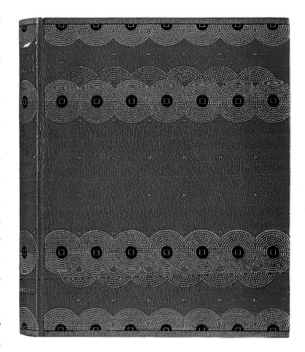

Above
PIERRE LEGRAIN: Blue morocco binding with inlaid bands of green and beige morocco discs with black centres, gold and platinum tooling and grey morocco borders at head and foot, for *Sagesse* by Paul Verlaine. (Contemporary photograph)
Opposite, above, left
PIERRE LEGRAIN: Blue morocco binding with inlays and gold tooling, for *La Canne de Jaspe* by Henri de Régnier. (Contemporary photograph)
Opposite, above, right
PIERRE LEGRAIN: Red morocco panels inlaid into a gold-tooled black morocco binding onlaid with 28 black morocco pastilles with the title in gilt, for *Chansons pour elle* by Paul Verlaine. (Contemporary photograph)
Opposite, below, left
PIERRE LEGRAIN: Green morocco binding with onlaid morocco mosaic in several colours, with gilt tooling, for *Le Neveu de Rameau* by Denis Diderot. (Contemporary photograph)
Opposite, below, right
PIERRE LEGRAIN: Green morocco binding with onlaid morocco mosaic in several colours with gilt tooling, for *Daphné* by Alfred de Vigny. (Contemporary photograph)

number of experienced craftsmen. His backers, however, were in some financial difficulties and the arrangement did not last long. A year later he moved to the rue d'Argenteuil and in 1925 he moved again to a large workshop in the avenue Percier. In 1926 he moved closer still to his home in the rue du Val-de-Grace, this time to the square of the same name. Each move found him more the master of the techniques used in the craft, more willing to extend their possibilities. When, in 1925, Doucet decided to remodel his home and studio yet again, he turned to Legrain.

These were the years of feverish hard work for Legrain. He designed and executed in his workshop bindings, furniture, and what he called 'ancillary works' (travaux annexes). These consisted of plinths, columns, bases, screens, frames, blotters, desk sets, compacts and panels for wall or furniture cladding, which were treated almost like books, clad in morocco or calf leather, frequently gilt. He designed book and magazine covers and was prepared to tackle any design problem that was brought to him. In 1928 he began to plan the creation of all aspects of book production. He wanted to publish books, for which he would manufacture the paper, design and illustrate the contents, and bind the finished product. He was never to carry out those plans as he died in July 1929 in his fortieth year. He had, in his brief career, designed over 1,200 bindings. A further seventy-five bindings were executed to his designs in his workshops after his death. His stepson, Jacques Anthoine-Legrain, took over the bookbindery and himself became one of the leading French designer bookbinders.

Legrain's new style of binding was greatly admired by the young craftsmen of the 20s and he found himself with both disciples and imitators. The most interesting of his disciples was Rose Adler. She was a student at the School of Decorative Arts until 1925 while simultaneously taking private lessons from Noulhac, a fine professional bookbinder. Jacques Doucet saw some of her work at a students' exhibition held at the Pavilion de Marsan (now the Musée des Arts Décoratifs) in 1923, bought three of her bindings and commissioned more. She was to work for him until his death in 1929 and went on binding books for the Jacques Doucet Literary Foundation after that. She met Legrain through Doucet and worked very much in his style, retaining his simplicity of design, total freedom in the use of non-figurative decoration and a similar use of unconventional materials. If anything, her designs are even more austere than his, while the materials used are frequently sumptuous. As her style developed in later years she essayed some figurative designs and later still began to adopt ever more unusual materials, including cork, wood and suede.

The 1925 Exhibition was a triumph for the Legrain style: most of the student works, as well as several professional works, were clearly derived from his bindings. Legrain was furious, not flattered, and circulated a letter of complaint to a number of artists and art critics. 'TO COPY IS TO ROB,' he wrote. 'For several years I have been the victim of open thefts. Every day a spontaneous generation of young bookbinders pillage my works.

'The School of the Union Centrale des Arts Décoratifs, sanctioning this method of operations, has included plagiarism in its curriculum. The exhibition on the first floor of the Grand Palais is the most signal proof of this. I hereby state that the works that make up this exhibition exist only as a result of my previous work.

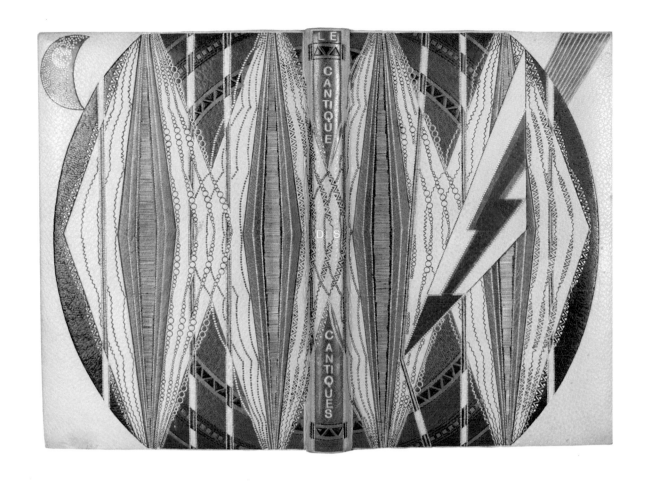

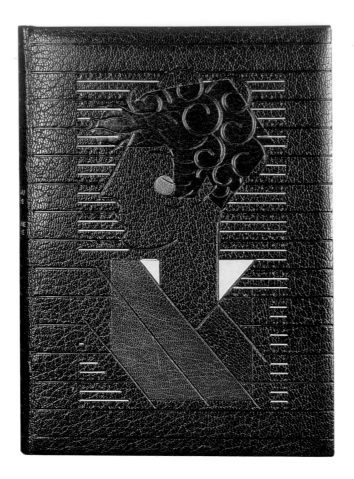

Above, left
ROBERT BONFILS: Dark blue pigskin with black calf onlay and blue, white and brown morocco inlays, gilt and blind tooling, for *La Campagne romaine* by René de Chateaubriand. (Collection Félix Marcilhac, Paris. Photo: Sully Jaulmes)

Above, right
ROBERT BONFILS: White morocco binding with inlaid morocco in various colours and gilt tooling, for *Eugénie Grandet* by Honoré de Balzac. (Collection Félix Marcilhac, Paris. Photo: Sully Jaulmes)

Left
FRANCOIS-LOUIS SCHMIED: Morocco binding set with a polychrome lacquer panel by Jean Dunand for *Ruth et Boaz*, the Biblical tale illustrated with wood engravings and published by F. L. Schmied in 1930. (Virginia Museum of Fine Arts, Gift of Sydney and Frances Lewis)

Opposite
ROBERT BONFILS: Red morocco binding with large inlaid design and gilt tooling, for *Manon Lescaut* by Abbé A. F. Prevost, executed in 1931 for Major J. R. Abbey. (Author's Collection. Photo: Rodney Todd-White)

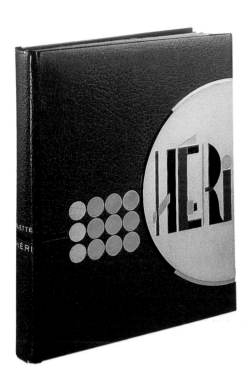

'I am decided to defend myself, and this cause goes beyond me, for it concerns all creative artists, to whom I now address myself. May I count on your sympathy, and lean on the authority of your name in the battle I must wage to defend my rights against a moral prejudice while waiting for it to become material?'

The replies were, somewhat to his surprise, rather mixed. While most were sympathetic, few agreed with his intention of fighting plagiarism. 'Is that not the consecration of success?' René Lalique wrote in reply. 'Throughout my years of labour I have been the victim of the same procedures, and was just as indignant.' André Mare wrote: 'When an artist creates works such that his contemporaries and the students at the Schools are inspired by them and seek to do similar work, I believe he has no reason to complain if he is imitated and that nothing could be more flattering for him. There is here no moral prejudice and not much chance of material prejudice.'

The jury of the Bookbinding Section at the 1925 Exhibition, led by its vice president, René Kieffer, kept strictly to the letter of Article 4 of the Regulations, which admitted only works of 'new inspiration and true originality.' To the fury of many critics, collectors and dealers, many binders whose fame had first been achieved around the turn of the century or who worked in the more traditional styles, were rigidly excluded. Marius-Michel was one of those excluded, though he did not live to visit the exhibition, dying in 1925 at the age of seventy-nine. His closest disciple was Georges Cretté, who had first come to work for him in 1911, soon becoming the best of his workers. Cretté was, however, called up to do his military service. Shortly thereafter war broke out and he was captured by the Germans. Cretté was finally liberated after the Armistice and returned to Marius-Michel in 1919. He was soon running the workshop and on January 1st, 1923 Marius-Michel took him as a partner, handing over the business to him on April 1st, 1925 shortly before his death.

Cretté, who was to sign all his bindings until 1930 'Cretté, successor of Marius-Michel,' was one of the revelations of the 1925 Exhibition. Eschewing both Art Nouveau stylisation and Legrain-style abstraction, he produced elaborately gilt bindings, frequently decorated with conventionalised flowers, leaves or fruit similar to the patterns used on furniture or pressed glass. Using the finest moroccos, and with impeccable techniques, he succeeded in weaning his firm's customers away from the decorations they had been used to from Marius-Michel. He was awarded a Grand Prix at the 1937 Paris Exhibition.

Robert Bonfils was one of the great independent designer bookbinders. He, Pierre Legrain and Robert Delauney became firm friends in 1904 when all three were students at the Germain Pilon School of Applied Arts in Paris: he was then eighteen years old. He entered Cormon's studio at the Ecole Nationale des Beaux-Arts in 1906, exhibited his pictures for the first time at the 1909 Salon d'Automne, and saw the publication of his first illustrated book in 1913. In 1919 he began teaching Decorative Composition and the History of Art and the Book at the College Estienne. He could never resist trying new techniques and essayed all graphic forms, though his preferred one was the woodcut. He also designed costumes and decor

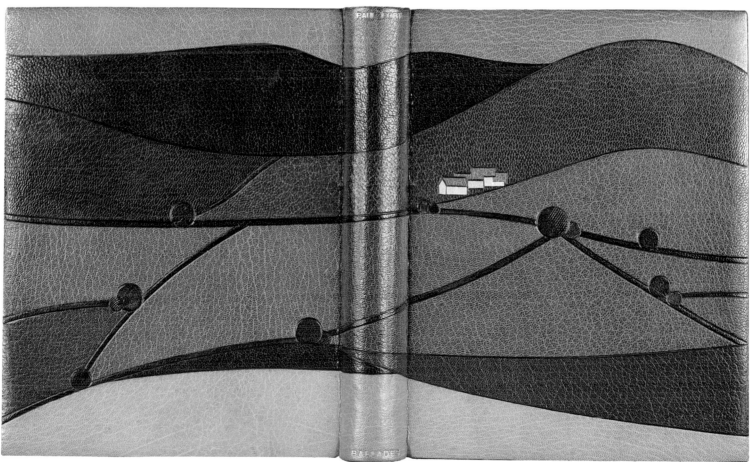

for the stage, fabrics, tapestries and ceramics. Inevitably, he began to design bookbindings, his first in 1923.

Most of the bindings Bonfils designed have a figurative base on at least the upper cover. Sometimes using one of the book's illustrations as starting point; sometimes using one of his recurrent motifs (which he used in everything, from ceramics to books) such as a guitar or a mask; sometimes using the book's title, subject or theme as starting point, he would elaborate a human outline, a girl's head, a boat, a landscape, which he would interpret in bookbinding terms as a mosaic, using onlays or inlays, with gilding or blind tooling. Even when designing an apparently abstract pattern, a Bonfils binding design is recognisably different from a binding by anybody else.

Bonfils was, needless to say, not just a designer, but also an executor, exploring all the techniques himself with André Jeanne, a professional binder who had worked for Marius-Michel, Pierre Legrain and Jeanne Langrand before setting up on his own in 1929. Jeanne executed designs for Rose Adler, Georges Cretté, Madeleine Gras, Paul Bonet, Henri Creuzevault and Bonfils himself. Bonfils exhibited his bindings at the 1925 and 1937 Exhibitions, as well as at the 1938 San Francisco Exposition, the 1939 New York World's Fair and the 1957 Brussels Exhibition. He also wrote a number of instructional articles and books and lectured extensively on the art of the book and bookbinding. He was one of the founder members of the Société de la Reliure Originale (Society of Original Binders) in 1946 and participated in their various exhibitions in France and elsewhere.

Louis Creuzevault, as a professional bookbinder, had taken over the Dodé workshop in 1904, and there executed run-of-the-mill bindings for ten years until the outbreak of war. He returned to his atelier in 1920, determined to confine himself to art bookbinding. He soon began to create a series of original designs, some in mosaics, others gilt, using broad symmetrical composition of flowers, leaves or abstract patterns. Some of the most interesting consisted of three-dimensional alternations of leather sections of different colours or of the same colour with different surfaces achieved by a form of discolouration. His spines were either smooth or with thick cording, sometimes as much as an inch thick. He was joined in the 1920s by his son Henri and the two worked closely until 1937, when the son took over the firm. Henri Creuzevault was also a founder member of the Société de la Reliure Originale and opened an art gallery. He abandoned bookbinding in 1957 to concentrate on his gallery.

Some of the most colourful designs of the period were designed by Francois Louis Schmied. This great Swiss illustrator had become totally involved in every aspect of book creation. He undertook to illustrate books, turn other people's illustrations into the most exquisitely executed wood engravings, design the dummy, create the lettering, design the type, and print the whole volume on his private presses. He was also, of course, prepared to publish the work.

Schmied's bindings vary from relatively sober, chic designs involving coloured inlays and gilding to wild, extravagant riots of colour and pattern. Using mostly figurative motifs, the design frequently incorporated lacquer panels which were

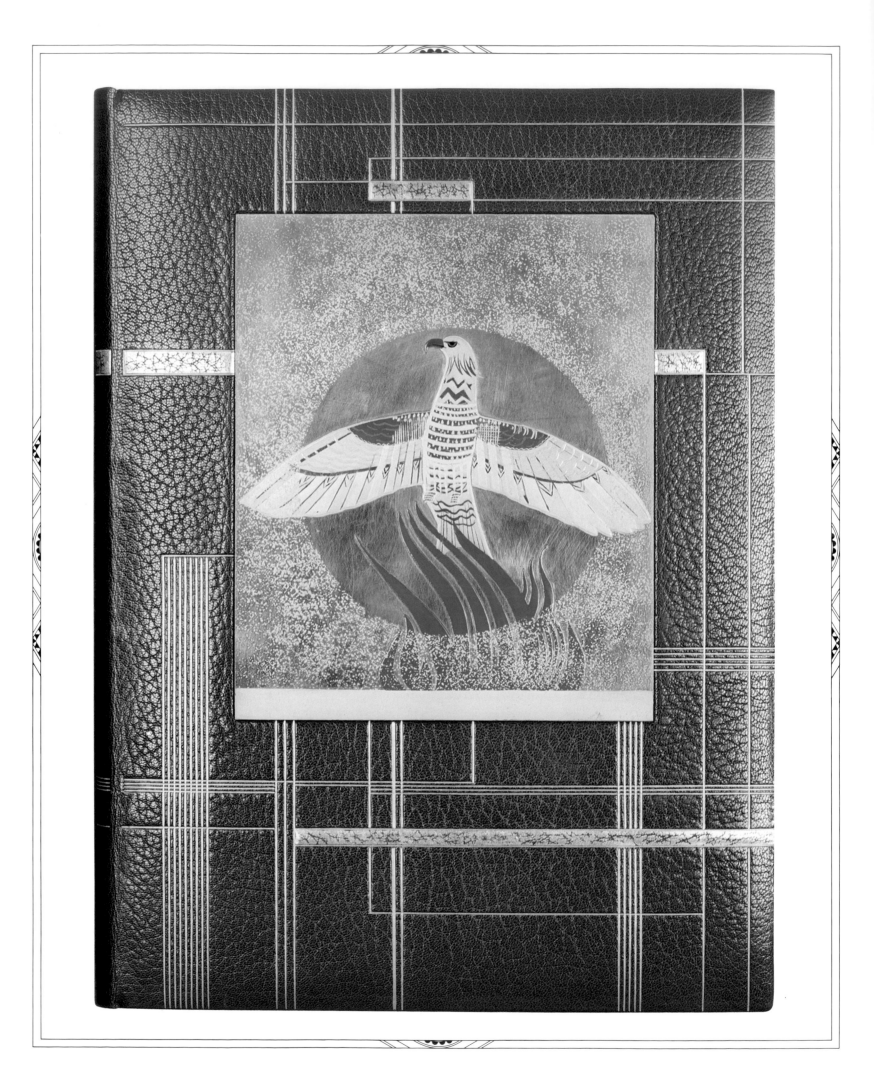

executed by himself or by Jean Dunand or Jean Goulden. He also frequently replaced paper or fabric linings and endpapers with leather ones, which were then treated as additional surfaces in which inlays, onlays and gilding could be wrought, often in complex designs. Most of his designs were executed by such professional binders as Cretté, Creuzevault and Mme Marot-Rodde, who was awarded a Silver Medal for bookbinding at the 1925 Exhibition. He also collaborated with Rose Adler, who designed some bindings for books illustrated by Schmied, and for which he executed lacquered panels which she incorporated into the covers. Schmied set up his own binding workshop in about 1930, but continued to have most of his designs executed by others. He painted a number of parchment bindings, as did his son, Theo Schmied.

The 1925 Exhibition proved a showcase for several women bookbinders. Some were amateurs, others were members of the Bookbinding Workshop set up by the Ladies' Committee of the Union Centrale des Arts Décoratifs, a few were professional binders. Jeanne Legrand, a disciple of Legrain's, showed a number of distinguished bindings in morocco, some with simple gilt decorations, others with a degree of fantasy in the composition. Mlle de Félice showed a wide range, from inlaid morocco to painted vellum, and some books bound in decorated fabrics; Marie Brisson exhibited painted and embroidered silk bindings; and Germaine Schroeder, Louise Germain and Suzanne Roussy also showed their work.

Since artistic bookbinding had become an essentially personal occupation, more women were able to approach the craft, both as designers and executants, avoiding the powerful anti-feminine bias shown by other craft guilds and unions. One woman designer, Laure Albin Guillot, introduced photography into bookbinding. Some of her photographs, printed on a variety of surfaces, were inlaid into the upper and sometimes the lower cover of the binding; others were printed on special papers for use as endpapers. While some of her subjects were figurative, she specialised in microphotography, the enlargement of plankton and other micro-organisms forming curious, abstract and fantastic designs. She often worked with such binders as Rose Adler and René Kieffer.

André Mare had been Doucet's first choice to design the bindings for his collection but was not available as he was in the army. As a binder he was not greatly original: virtually all his bindings are simple, well-executed vellum ones. Their interest resides in the decoration; he painted each with striking figurative designs in gouache on the upper and lower covers, often on the spine and sometimes also on the vellum linings.

New bookbinders and designers emerged after the 1925 Exhibition. These included Claude Stahly, who set up her atelier in 1934; Germaine de Coster, a graduate of the Ecole National Superieure des Arts Décoratifs, who became a well-known book designer and etcher and joined with Helene Dumas, who became professor at the Ecole des Arts Appliqués in 1934, the former designing the bindings, the latter executing them; and Paul Bonet.

Born in Paris of Belgian parents in 1889, the same year as Pierre Legrain, Bonet left school at the age of fourteen to become an apprentice electrician. When his

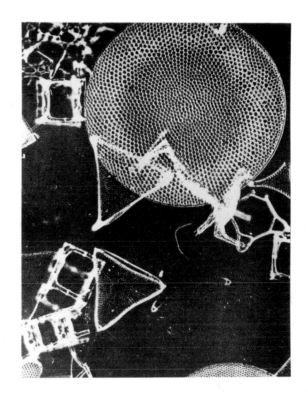

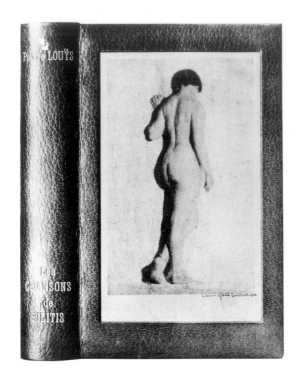

mother opened a milliners he went to work for her. His wish to become a painter was thwarted by his father, who wanted him to follow a trade which would enable him to earn money. In 1909 Bonet went to work as a fashion designer. In 1910 he took out French citizenship and went to do his military service. When war broke out he was mobilised, but was soon wounded. Discharged from the army in 1915 after long hospitalisation, he returned to his career as fashion designer, a career he was to maintain until 1938. Dissatisfied with the bindings executed on some of his books by a local binder, he decided to try for himself. The exhibition of Legrain's bindings had dazzled him. Paradoxically, this decided him to attempt to create a style utterly different from Legrain's. His first bindings were exhibited in the various Paris Salons in 1925 and 1926, but though his ideas were attractive, the execution was as yet imperfect. His luck turned at the 1926 Salon d'Automne, when a bibliophile, R. Marty, admired his designs and commissioned him to design some bindings for his collection. Bonet acquired a few more clients over the years, but binding was to remain a spare time occupation for him for the next four years, during which he became technically proficient at executing his ideas.

Fame came to Bonet in 1930, when the Marty collection was auctioned off, and his fifty-two bindings for it fetched unexpectedly high prices. From then on he was able to devote all his time to bookbinding and give up his other occupations. He was, however, never to open an atelier of his own, preferring to work with a number of master binders, engravers, gilders, jewellers and sculptors whose mastery of their various trades and techniques was perfection itself.

During an exhibition of his designs in a Brussels bookshop in 1931, Bonet met a Belgian bibliophile, René Graffé, who commissioned him to bind his collection of Surrealist books and manuscripts. Bonet plunged himself into these books, which fascinated him both in text and illustration and inspired him to create entirely new kinds of bindings, including metallic ones, bindings with a pierced design through which could be seen a further design on the endpapers, and the use of such materials as ivory, gold and lapis-lazuli. He loved creating variations on a design, and frequently bound several copies of a particular book: one of his favourites was *Calligrammes* by Guillaume Apollinaire, for which he designed over thirty bindings over the years. Another innovation of his was the creation of a spine design for a set of books, spreading the title or author's name as well as a continuous design over the complete set. He frequently did this for half-bindings. The extreme freedom of design Bonet soon adopted has made him the standard-bearer of contemporary binding design.

France, in the interwar years, seems to have been the only country to create the climate in which a number of bookbinders worked in the Art Deco style. Bookbinders elsewhere worked within traditional guidelines, devoting their ingenuity to creating variations on older designs and their experience to achieving the highest degree of competence. Italy saw the occasional essay in the Art Deco style; the white calf bindings with silver and gold tooling and painted inset by Leopoldo Metlicovitz executed for the 120 copies of Puccini's *Turandot* score, bound just nine days before the opera's première on April 16th, 1926 are a striking example of the

influence of the previous year's Paris Exhibition. In Denmark Anker Kyster devised some free tooling on otherwise plain skins. In England Charles Ricketts devised an interesting geometric pattern of gilt tooling for the 1929 edition of his book *Beyond the Threshold* while it was left to Sybil Pye almost alone to design Cubist inlays and advanced patterns on her bindings. Perhaps the greatest English patron of bookbinders was Major J. R. Abbey, who commissioned modern bindings of advanced design from the French bookbinders in the interwar years, the English binders producing non-traditional designs only after the Second World War.

Above, left
PAUL BONET: Green morocco binding with morocco inlays and onlays in various colours, and gilt and blind tooling, for *Rhumbs* by Paul Valéry. (Private Collection, Paris)
Above
MME MAROT-RODDE: Grey morocco binding inlaid with pink and red abstract flowers, gilt and platinum tooling, for *Poèmes* by Maurice Donnay. (Contemporary photograph)
Left
MAX PONSEQUE: Dark blue morocco binding with polychrome morocco onlays depicting flowers in a vase, and gilt tooling, for *Mitsou* by Collette. (Collection Félix Marcilhac, Paris. Photo: Sully Jaulmes)
Opposite
PAUL BONET: Green morocco binding cut in wide horizontal strips connected by the title, the author's name and the illustrator's name made up of nickel-plated, black-lacquered and partly enamelled letters, invisibly hinged over narrow striped panels of white, yellow, pale green and dark green morocco over a red ground, with Palladium lettering on the spine, for *Calligrammes* by Guillaume Apollinaire, illustrated by Giorgio de Chirico, executed in 1932. (Courtesy Guy Loudmer, Paris)

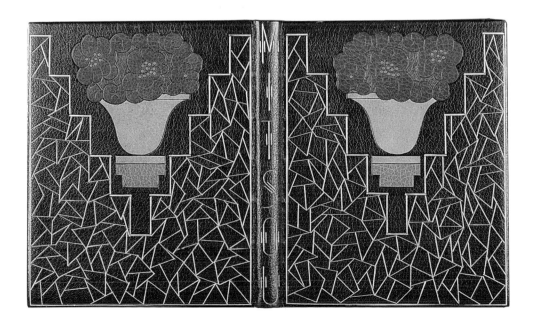

GLASS

The death of Emile Gallé in 1904 ended a great era of experimentation and achievement in art glass, though Art Nouveau floralism in coloured opaque cameo glass was to survive in industrial form for another thirty years. Indeed, the Gallé firm exhibited its cameo glass at the 1925 Paris Exhibition, and it was to end production only in 1933, when the world-wide Depression forced it to close down. Nor was Gallé the only firm to produce such glass for so long. In Bohemia, Loetz, Carl Goldberg, Graf Harrach, Kralik, Weiss and Solomon Reich produced a quantity of cameo glass of the quality of late industrial Gallé, as did a number of French firms. The creative impetus had gone out of this style and into other styles, but the great buying public had apparently not noticed. Iridescent art glass also ran parallel in time. Tiffany glass went on being made until 1928, Steuben Aurene until 1933.

Two main strands were to appear in artistic succession to Art Nouveau glass in France. One, pioneered by René Lalique, was in the direction of moulded glass capable of being produced in quantity; the other, developed by Maurice Marinot, involved great effort in creating the single pot.

At the turn of the century René Lalique was acknowledged as the greatest Art Nouveau jeweller. He was also a sculptor, silversmith and goldsmith. Glass interested him, and as early as 1902 he rented a small glass workshop at Clairfontaine, and employed four glassworkers. While small glass items were produced there to be used as part of some of the jewellery he designed, he was more interested in the sculptural use of glass. He designed both figures and vases to be made in the cire-perdue (lost wax) casting method, as used for bronze. In 1903 he designed a huge glass door for his house, which was cast at the Saint Gobain glassworks. Four years later his friend François Coty commissioned him to design some labels for his perfume bottles. Lalique designed the labels, then went on to design the bottles,

Above
RENE LALIQUE: *Grande nue, socle lierre.* Tall statuette moulded in greyish-brown glass on wooden base carved in the Chinese style. Model 836, 1919. (Author's Collection)
Opposite
RENE LALIQUE: *Amphytrite.* Green glass scent bottle, Four d'Orsay, c. 1919. (Cobra, London)

Above
RENE LALIQUE: *Victoire.* Moulded glass car mascot. Model 1147, 1928. (Gallery 1925, London)
Left
RENE LALIQUE: *Grande Libellule.* Moulded glass car mascot. Model 1145, 1928. (Editions Graphiques Gallery, London)
Opposite
RENE LALIQUE: *Tête de paon.* Moulded blue glass car mascot. Model 1140, 1928. (Gallery 1925, London)

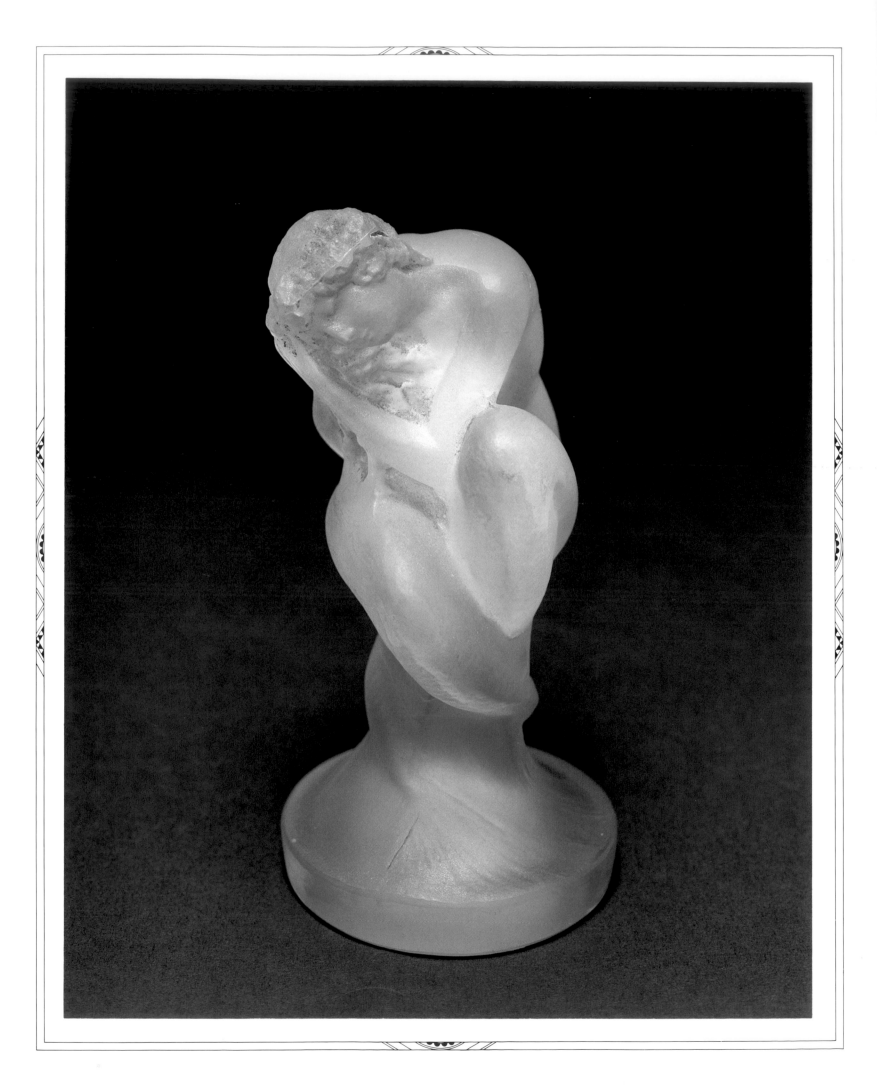

Opposite
RENE LALIQUE: *Sirène*. Opalescent
glass figurine. Model 831, 1920.
(Editions Graphiques Gallery, London)
Above, left
RENE LALIQUE: *Archers*. Amber glass
vase moulded with eagles and hunters.
Model 893, c. 1921. (Editions
Graphiques Gallery, London)
Above, right
RENE LALIQUE: *Malesherbes*. Green
glass vase moulded with stylised leaves.
Model 1014, 1927. (Editions
Graphiques Gallery, London)
Right
RENE LALIQUE: *Narcisse*. Scent bottle
moulded with Bacchanalian dancers,
c. 1922. (Cobra, London)

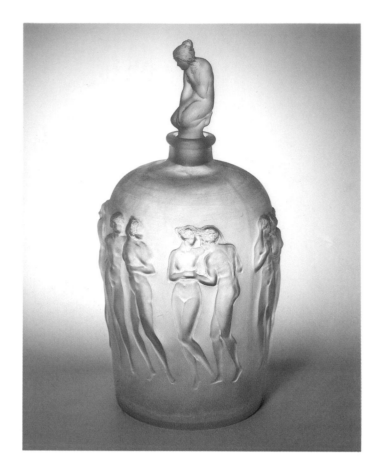

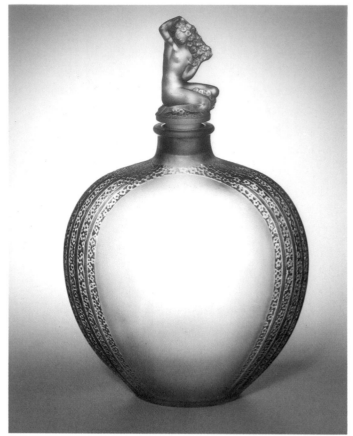

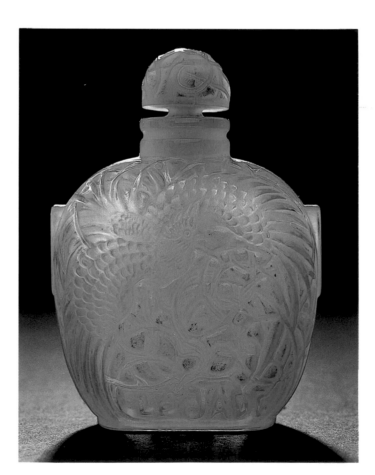

which were made at the Legras et Cie glassworks. The following year Lalique took over the Combs-la-Ville glassworks at Combs (Seine-et-Marne), but it was not until the Armistice of 1918 that Lalique, then aged fifty-eight, resolved to start a new career. He purchased a large glassworks at Wingen-sur-Moder (Bas-Rhin) in the area restored to France by the defeat of the Central Powers, and quickly adopted the latest available industrial techniques to produce a wide range of decorative and useful glass. Made by blowing the glass into moulds or cast in a stamping press, Lalique glass was made from demi-cristal, softer and more malleable than lead crystal, though certainly not as pure or sparkling.

Design was of supreme importance to Lalique, who treated glass as a sculptor, not as a glassworker. He, or one of his small group of sculptor-designers, would produce wax models of statuettes, vases, bowls, lamps and ornaments which were then used to make the moulds from which glass was cast. Coloured glass was used relatively sparingly, and included very pale amethyst, tan and grey tints as well as several shades of green, brown, blue, red, amber, yellow and black. Opalescent glass was frequently used; clear glass often had part or the whole of the outer surface stained a different colour with washes which lodged in the interstices while the protruding sections were wiped clean. Some glass panels with intaglio designs had the details finished with some wheel-carving, while all vessels were carefully polished and finished. A few curious vases were moulded with concave reserves into which were inserted small panels of moulded glass, usually in a colour different from that of the body, while a few others had metal mounts.

Lalique received a number of public commissions, and supplied decorative glass panels, lights, illuminated ceilings and other accessories for the transatlantic liners Paris in 1920, Ile de France in 1927 and Normandie in 1935, as well as for some of the luxurious carriages on certain French railways. He designed and erected a number of public fountains throughout Paris and elsewhere, in addition to a number of indoor ones, and supplied fittings for restaurants, cinemas, hotels and other public buildings. In 1932 he completely decorated the interior of St. Matthew's church in Jersey with glass panels moulded with madonna lilies in high relief, a glass altar and a huge glass crucifix.

The 1925 Paris Exhibition was a triumph for Lalique, whose works could be seen throughout the grounds. He had his own pavilion, of course, designed by himself with the technical collaboration of the architect Marc Ducluzand. Vases, bowls, light fittings, wall and floor tiles, fountains and ornaments were on display there, the central dining room having a huge sycamore pedestal table inset with illuminated glass panels, the table set with a full range of glass tableware and candelabra. He designed another dining room for the Sèvres pavilion, for which he supplied not only the table and its setting, but also an entire illuminated ceiling set with moulded opal glass panels. In the Cours des Métier was a monumental fountain by him, a tall slender glass column set on a star-shaped base, water jets shooting out and down from the nozzles placed all round and up its stem. It was at its most effective at night, when lit up. Lalique also supplied the moulded stylised glass fountains for the column tops of the monumental gate, the glass

Above
RENE LALIQUE: *Bellecour*. Clear glass vase with four applied sparrows in moulded, patinated glass. Model 993, 1927. (Editions Graphiques Gallery, London)
Opposite, above, left
RENE LALIQUE: *Vase douze figurines avec bouchon figurine*. Frosted glass bottle moulded in high relief, with kneeling nude stopper. Model 914, 1920. (Editions Graphiques Gallery, London)
Opposite, above, right
RENE LALIQUE: *Myosotis bouchon figurine*. Tinted glass bottle, kneeling nude stopper. Model 611, 1928. (Editions Graphiques Gallery, London)
Opposite, below, left
RENE LALIQUE: *Le Jade*. Opaque green glass scent bottle for Roger & Gallet, c. 1920. (Cobra, London)
Opposite, below, right
RENE LALIQUE: *Bague Serpents*. Glass lamp, the central ring moulded with a frieze of snakes. Model 2151, 1913. (Editions Graphiques Gallery, London)
Overleaf, left
RENE LALIQUE: *Oiseau de feu*. Fan-shaped glass plaque intaglio moulded with a firebird on bronze base with butterflies. Model 111, 1922. (Editions Graphiques Gallery, London).
Overleaf, right
RENE LALIQUE: *Suzanne*. Figure moulded in amber glass on illuminated bronze base. Model 833, 1925. (Editions Graphiques Gallery, London)

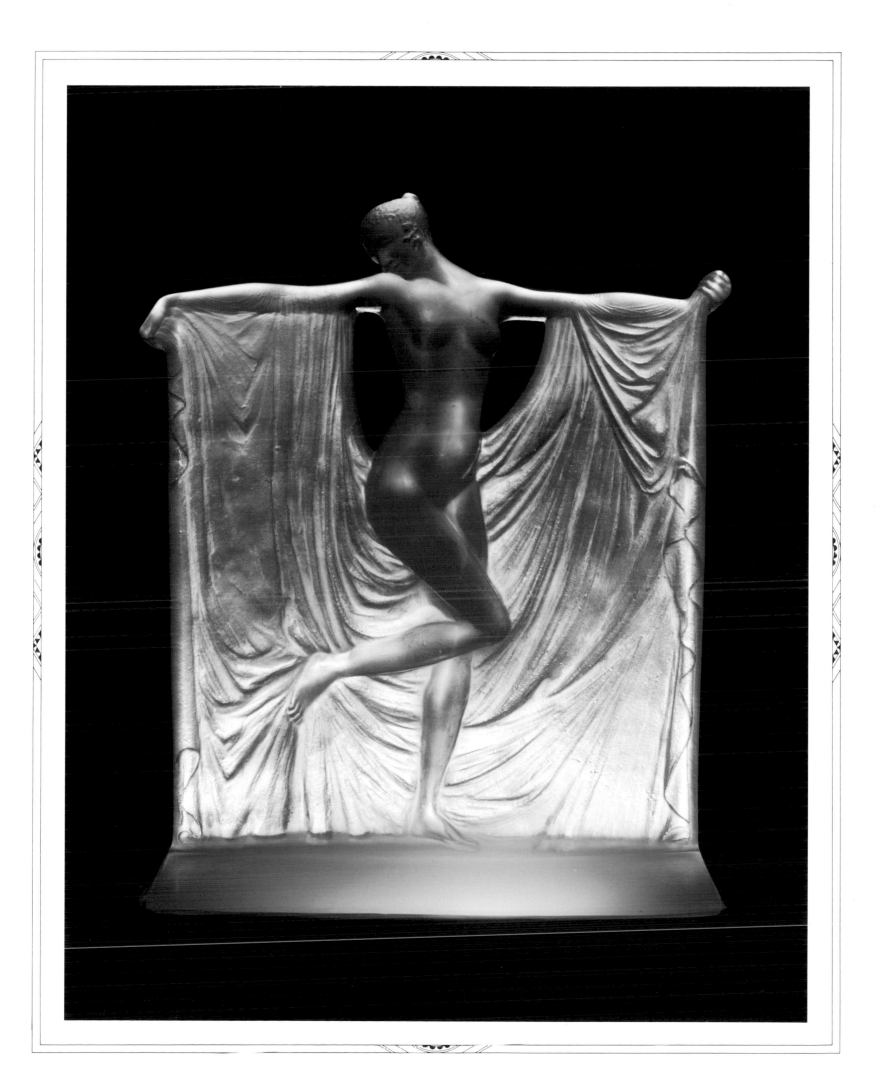

pebbles for the dome of the Primavera pavilion, and his tiles, lamps, light fittings and panels were to be found in many other locations.

An equally large range of glass items was manufactured by Marius-Ernest Sabino, who established himself shortly after the Armistice. In 1925 he exhibited at the International Exhibition as well as at the Salon d'Automne and the Salon des Artistes Décorateurs, his stand at the latter being designed by Henri Rapin. Electroliers, standard and table lamps and wall fittings were produced in a wide range of moulded models, some of them very large, with elaborate bronze, brass, wrought-iron or silvered metal fittings made in his own workshop. Other large items included illuminated glass tables, fountains and urns, though his vases and figurines were probably the most attractive part of his production. The figurines included nudes, animals, shepherds, fish, an idol, heads and busts, many of them in a brilliant opalescent glass which turned from milky white to blue and amber, depending on the light. Sabino's opalescence was less subtle, but more colourful than Lalique's.

The vases and bowls executed by Sabino were frequently moulded with friezes of animals, nudes or busts of women with fruit or flowers, or geometric patterns. They were occasionally produced in coloured glass, but were usually either of opalescent glass or clear glass with the pattern outlined in surface paint or enamel in black or bright colours.

An opalescence as bright as Sabino's, but of a paler blue tint, was used by the firm of Etling to produce figurines of nudes, birds, fish, animals and ships. The firm edited bronze and ivory figures, bronzes and ceramics as well as glass. Among the sculptors who designed figures and vases for Etling were Geneviève Granger, Lucille Sévin, Georges Béal, Jean-Théodore Delabasse and Geza Thiez. The moulded vases, which tended to mock-naive treatment when figurative, were frequently of a greyish glass with alternate polished and mat sections. Some of the figurines were fitted with illuminated bases.

Press-moulded glass panels in continuous rows at room-ceiling height, or up walls and across ceilings fitted with electric bulbs to provide indirect lighting schemes, were devised by Genet & Michon, a firm set up by two engineers after the Armistice. Light was diffused and glare reduced by rendering the glass panels slightly opaque by treatment with hydrofluoric acid on the surface, the direction of the light being broken up by moulding, engraving and etching the glass. They produced a number of schemes for public buildings, their most spectacular being the lighting system for the Hotel Splendid at Dax. They also produced a limited range of pressed-glass vases and table lamps.

Albert Simonet, the head of Simonet Frères, which had been established since the middle of the nineteenth century as a leading bronze manufacturer, shifted the firm in 1919 towards the production of pressed-glass lamps with bronze fittings. He took in the sculptor Henri Dieupart as co-designer, and the two of them designed and manufactured a wide range of floor, ceiling, table and wall lights which frequently combined elaborate bronze mounts with glass globes, panels or sections moulded in floral, bird or abstract patterns. The glass was frosted, tinted or

Above
EDMOND ETLING: Opalescent glass vase moulded with parallel lines and two nudes designed by Mme Lucille Sévin. (Editions Graphiques Gallery)
Opposite, above
MARIUS SABINO: Moulded glass plaque, c. 1925. (Private Collection, London)
Opposite, below
MARIUS SABINO: Opalescent glass fish, c. 1925. (Editions Graphiques Gallery, London)

opalescent, sometimes with added colour washes on the surface. Some of the patterns were used in vases, occasionally made in richly coloured glass.

Original moulded glass vases and other vessels were made by Pierre d'Avesn, a former Daum worker; André Hunebelle, who was later to become a feature film director, and the ceramist Cazaux in collaboration with Guéron, though each devised completely different designs, mostly bird or animal friezes for d'Avesn, moulded abstract designs for Hunebelle and sculptural human figurations for Cazaux. Original opalescent glass was also made by such firms as Verlys and Vernot. Derivative moulded glass was produced in quantity in France, Bohemia, England, Italy and the United States.

Paul Poiret was one of the first to adapt the old techniques of enamelling on glass to the new, bright designs produced by the girls in his Atelier Martine. Brightly coloured enamelled glass became enormously popular after the war, and was used on vases, bowls, decanter sets, light fittings, scent bottles, boxes and jewellery.

Marcel Goupy had studied architecture, interior decoration and sculpture at the National School of Decorative Arts in Paris before training as a silversmith and jeweller in addition to studying painting. When he joined the firm of Geo. Rouard in 1909, the world of ceramics was opened to him, for Rouard already represented such great porcelain and pottery manufacturers as Wedgwood, Nymphenburg and Bing & Grondahl. After the Armistice, Goupy rejoined Rouard as artistic director, bringing with him a young war veteran, August Heiligenstein, who had had a thorough grounding as a glassworker at the Legros firm since the age of eleven and a half, as well as subsequent training and employment as a glass gilder, ceramics decorator, glass decorator at Baccarat and commercial poster designer and painter. Goupy designed a wide range of vases, decanters, boxes, bowls, carafes and jugs, the enamelled decoration being executed by Heiligenstein. All these were signed with Goupy's name.

In 1923 Heiligenstein left Rouard's employment, married the ceramist Odette Chatrousse, and began to exhibit at the Salon des Artistes Français as well as at Rouard's, under his own name. One of his first patrons was Mrs. Florence Blumenthal, who was then having her Paris apartment redesigned by Léon Bakst. Heiligenstein executed bottles, jars and boxes enamelled after designs by Bakst for her, though he was to continue to supply her with enamelled glass for some eight years. After 1926 Heiligenstein stopped exhibiting at Rouard's and moved to the Edgar Brandt Gallery, executing increasingly complex enamelled and gilt vessels, often decorated with subjects from Greek mythology, stylised waves or clouds, or repeating geometric patterns.

Goupy continued to design enamelled glass vessels, supervising both the blowing and the decorating, frequently having them enamelled both inside and out, leaving clear reserves on the outside surface through which could be seen the inner enamelling. He also designed sets of tableware in porcelain (executed at the Théodore Haviland works at Limoges) and glass in which continuity was achieved by using a particular motif on both, though he used great ingenuity in transforming the motif as used on glass or porcelain, for instance putting concentric circles on the porcelain which he would then turn on their sides to produce an undulating pattern on the

Above
DAUM: Internally decorated glass vase applied with black and red glass berries and leaves on stalks. (Private Collection, London)
Opposite
ETLING: Opalescent glass figurine of a cloaked nude, c. 1925, 20.5 cms. (Editions Graphiques Gallery, London)

glass. He was vice-president of the jury in Class 33 (Glass) at the 1925 Exhibition.

Jean Luce also designed matched sets of tableware in glass and porcelain, using the same stylised motifs on each item. He had worked in his father's shop, retailing tableware, until the age of twenty-eight and opened his own shop in 1931, when he was thirty-six. He designed a quantity of enamelled glass, mostly with stylised floral designs, later designing etched and engraved vessels in abstract patterns contrasting mat and polished sections, as well as very striking thick-walled vessels of mirrored glass with acid-etched geometric patterns. He was a member of the Glass Section jury at both the 1925 and 1937 Paris Exhibitions.

Louis Vuitton, who had produced and retailed a wide range of such luxury goods as matched luggage and cases fitted for every conceivable purpose, also produced a number of crystal bottles, boxes and jars, often with silver and carved wood or ivory stoppers. Some were moulded or intaglio-cut with geometric patterns, while others were enamelled in abstract floral and scenic patterns by such designers as Suzanne Auzaneau and André Ballet. Mme Cless-Brothier designed sets enamelled with dancers from Diaghilev's Ballets Russes. Floral and abstract enamelled designs by Georges Chevalier and André Ballet were executed at the Cristalleries de Baccarat. Enamelled vessels were also executed in the workshops of such retail shops as Delvaux in the rue Royale in Paris and such glassworking firms as that of André Delatte, who had set up at Nancy in 1921, while a number are found signed 'Quenvit', 'H. Laroyer', 'Maxonade' and still others unsigned. The Gallé glassworks produced a number of enamelled vases and boxes for 'La Marquise de Sevigné', a chain of chocolate and pastry shops in Paris.

Maurice Marinot's first essays in glass consisted of enamelled vases, bottles and plates. Born at Troyes in 1882, he had early developed a passion for art which his family, who manufactured cotton bonnets, had allowed him to indulge by going to Paris to study at the Ecole des Beaux-Arts. An unruly student, he refused to conform to the techniques of his master, Cormon, a painter of prehistoric scenes, and ended up attending only those life classes when Cormon was not present. In 1905 he returned to Troyes, where he was to spend the rest of his life. Shortly before leaving Paris, however, he submitted a painting to the 1905 Salon d'Automne which was hung there in the same room as similar paintings by Matisse, Derain, Valtat, Manguin, Van Dongen, Marquet and Vlaminck. The group was dubbed 'Fauves', wild beasts, and critical and public attacks and insults ensured their notoriety. Marinot was to continue to exhibit regularly with them and separately at the Salon d'Automne and the Salon des Indépendants until 1913.

In 1911 Marinot visited the small glassworks run by his friends the brothers Eugène and Gabriel Viard at Bar-sur-Seine. It was love at first sight and he conceived 'a violent desire for the new game.' The Viard brothers gave him all help possible. He was given the rudiments of knowledge by a senior glassblower and a bench was assigned to him, to which he would come for daily practice at lunchtime, when the workers were away. In the meantime he designed shapes which were executed at the works, and he enamelled them himself, which meant learning both the craft and the chemistry of enamelling. Stylised fruit, plant and flower shapes, abstract pat-

terns and human figures were conceived through his painter's eyes, contrasting clear, tinted or speckled glass with rich enamelled colours. He exhibited these at the Salon des Indépendants and the Salon d'Automne from 1911, frequently in the room settings prepared by his friend André Mare.

Marinot soon learned to blow his own vessels. Though his work was interrupted when he was mobilised in 1914, he returned to his bench in 1919, experimenting with translucent rather than opaque enamels. In 1922, however, he began to create a new range of thick-walled vessels, the decoration trapped within the glass layers, bubbled, streaked or crackled, the outer surface smooth, and made in the shape of vases or bottles with tiny globular stoppers. Within a year of starting on this new technique he had abandoned enamelling and begun experimenting with sculptural forms.

Taking the thick-walled vessels as a starting point, he would deep-etch the surface into geometric patterns by covering portions of it with bitumen and soaking the exposed portions in baths of hydrofluoric acid. The extraordinarily deep bite he required sometimes needed as many as thirty acid baths. Finishing touches were occasionally given by wheel-carving, while he used the wheel largely to give the final polishing. Later still, from about 1927, he alternated what would be called direct carving of his glass with modelling of its shape in the kiln. 'For each piece,' he wrote, 'it is the struggle between breath acting on the inside, and the pressure, the demands of the tools applied to the outside, these two forces acting alternately. The different rhythms by the two pressures contradict each other, cross each other, inflate to form a coherent organic whole.'

In 1913 Adrien Hébrard, of the family of bronze founders, became Marinot's agent, and gave him the first of many exhibitions in his gallery in the rue Royale in Paris. At the 1925 Exhibition Marinot's glass was on view at the Ambassade Francaise Gallery, in the Süe et Mare Museum of Contemporary Art, and in Hébrard's shop on the Alexandre III Bridge. Marinot himself was vice-president of the admissions jury and a member of the awards jury. Between then and 1937, when the Viard glassworks closed down and he was forced to abandon glassmaking, his reputation continued to grow among those privileged to see his comparatively small output. Much of the work in his possession was destroyed during the bombing of Troyes in 1944; most of the glass which survived has been donated by his daughter to museums throughout the world. In an article in *L'Amour de l'Art* in September 1920 Marinot crystallised his beliefs: 'To draw a few lines, or to place a few stains on glass is not to be a glassmaker, for there is not true knowledge of the substance outside of a deep knowledge of the craft.

'To be a glassmaker is to blow the transparent substance beside blinding furnaces, using the breath of one's lips and the tools of one's art, to work in roasting heat and smoke, eyes full of tears, hands sooty and burned. It is to draw up simple lines within the molten matter through a rhythm conjugated with the very life of the glass in order to find, a little later, within the brilliant immobility of glassware, the life of human breath which will bring out the living designs.

'Those designs will then have worth in proportion to the respect, or rather the

Above
RENE LALIQUE: *Luxembourg*, moulded glass vase. Model 1018, 1929. (Collection Robert Zehil, Beverly Hills)
Opposite, above
DAUM: Internally bubbled vase with applied rings and blobs, c. 1925. (Private Collection, London)
Opposite, below, left
DAUM: Deeply etched, thick-walled green glass vase, part polished. (Collection Robert Zehil, Beverly Hills)
Opposite, below, right
DAUM: Deeply etched vase, part polished. (Private Collection, London)

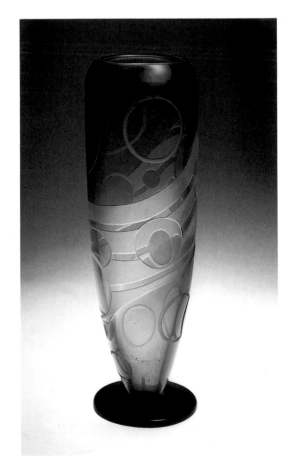

sharpening of the two most significant qualities of glass: transparence and brightness.'

Marinot directly influenced two artists: Henri Navarre and André Thuret. Navarre had been a successful sculptor when he first discovered Marinot's work, and began his first essays in glass in 1924. He produced much furnace-worked glass, internally decorated, some leaded glass windows and panels, and a number of sculptures where the details were modelled with hydrofluoric acid, including a large figure of Christ for the chapel in the liner Ile de France in 1927. Thuret was an engineer, a professional glass technician specialising in industrial glass. He fell under the spell of Marinot's glass at the same time as his friend Navarre, and began his own experiments in 1924, developing vases and stoppered bottles in internally decorated glass framed in undulating clear or tinted glass colours or wings. Other individual glass-workers were affected by Marinot. Georges Dumoulin, for one, had been awarded bronze, silver and gold medals for his glass at the various Salons of the Société des Artistes Français before he attempted some Marinot-style internal decoration, but he retained his own technique of using swirls of serpentine glass spiralling around the outside of his vessels with frequent glass trailings and applied pastilles.

Marinot's influence extended to the great glass factories. Daum, in particular, produced a range of thick-walled, chunky, heavy, frequently large vases in clear, tinted or coloured glass deeply acid-etched in geometric patterns, the backgrounds roughly finished to contrast with the polished sections in relief. In the 1930s Daum adapted this technique to thinner-walled vessels with simplified and more shallow-etched decoration, both geometric and stylised. They also produced a range of coloured glass vessels of smooth, symmetrical shapes with internally coloured patches of colour, or shredded silver, gold or platinum leaves, or swirls of coloured metallic oxides. Some of these were opaque, others transparent, while a few were blown into wrought-iron armatures by Majorelle or Edgar Brandt.

Such reticulated glass was executed by other firms and designers, including a range of curious stylised animals by Chapelle using Muller Frères glass. Opaque coloured glass vessels were made by Muller, Schneider, Degué and Legras, who also produced some vessels with acid-etched geometric designs. Schneider, in particular, produced a number of etched vases clearly influenced by Marinot, but in much lighter glass with shallower biting. Schneider also produced a range of cameo-glass vases, pitchers, bowls and light fittings using stylised floral, plant, animal and insect designs, which were normally signed 'Le Verre Français', or Charder (short for CHARles SchneiDER). Muller, Schneider, Degué, Legras and Daum also produced electroliers with a central light bowl on its own or surrounded by three or more shades in opaque, mottled glass in blues, purples, browns and beiges.

There were, of course, individual glassworkers who worked in styles different from Marinot's. Aristide Colotte used blocks of raw glass to carve a sculpture using prolonged hydrofluoric acid baths, direct wheel- and tool-carving and polishing, making his finished, polished designs stand out against the surrounding rough finish. While he frequently used large blocks, going up to a 500 lb block for a *Sorrowing*

Above
ARISTIDE COLOTTE: Deeply etched vase with geometric pattern, the inner section sand-blasted and stained. Unique. (Collection Robert Zehil, Beverly Hills)
Opposite, above
SCHNEIDER: Three Charder Le Verre Français overlaid glass vases, acid-etched in stylised geometric patterns, c 1925. (Private Collection, Münster)
Opposite, below
SCHNEIDER: Le Verre Français overlaid glass vase acid-etched in geometric patterns, c. 1925. (Editions Graphiques Gallery, London)

Christ, he also used smaller blocks for both sculpture and vases, which were treated in similar style, contrasting polished and rough sections. Jean Sala, born in Barcelona, came to Paris at the age of fifteen with his father, the glassworker Dominique Sala. Taught by his father, with whom he frequently collaborated, he devised a lightweight 'Malfin' glass, an incompletely refined impure glass, bubbled and textured. Sala trapped this normally porous product, plain or tinted, between two layers of transparent glass, fashioning it into simple shapes with serpentine or other shaped glass applications at the furnace. He also devised a range of blown and decorated glass fish. Wilhelm von Eiff, son of a craftsman at the German W.M.F. glassworks at Göppingen, trained as a glass and metal engraver before travelling to Paris, where he worked for René Lalique in his jewellery studio, then for Charles Michel as a glass engraver. In 1921 he worked briefly for Stefan Rath's Bohemian glassworks before joining the staff at the Stuttgart Art School. For the next two decades he designed and executed glass vessels in generally symmetrical shapes carved in high relief with figurative scenes, as well as abstract and geometric patterns.

In Sweden the Orrefors glassworks produced a vast range of creative glass, including 'Graal' glass, developed from the cameo technique, in which a design was acid-etched into a glass vessel of one layer or cased in two or more layers, then heated at the furnace to soften the etched lines, after which the whole was encased in a transparent glass layer and polished. Starting in 1916 with designs derived from Gallé's floralism, Orrefors' chief designers, the painters Simon Gate and Edward Hald, soon developed a variety of personal patterns varying from stylised dancing figures to abstract ornamentation. A further development occurred in 1930, when a new technique called 'Ariel' was launched in which patterns were sandblasted over the inner layer of the vessel, after which an outer layer was blown, enclosing the sandblasted air-channels which thus formed patterned air bubbles.

Gate and Hald also designed a wide variety of crystal vessels of rounded and panelled shapes, wheel-engraved with a variety of figural and abstract shapes, including classical and biblical subjects and a large number of nude figures. Orrefors, Gate and Hald were each awarded a Grand Prix at the 1925 Paris Exhibition, where five of their workers also received Gold Medals. 'Ça, c'est du verre. C'est bon,' was René Lalique's comment, while Marinot's verdict was: 'Il n'y a que ça.' Gate and Hald were equally struck with Marinot's glass, and they designed a number of vessels inspired by it.

In Italy Guido Balsamo-Stella designed a number of vases and plates in simple shapes, wheel-engraved with often humorous subjects inspired by Venetian life, mythological scenes, animals, nudes and decorative motifs in a simplified and stylised Cubist-inspired idiom. Often working in collaboration with his Swedish wife Anna, he was greatly influenced by the work of Gate and Hald.

Venetian glass had become largely derivative and tourist orientated when Paolo Venini and Giacomo Cappellini joined in 1921 to begin the production of simple glass which sought its inspiration in Venetian glass at the height of its creativity, the

Above
JOHN MONCRIEFF: 'Monart' vase in cased coral red glass, internally gold bubbled, c. 1930. The label indicates size VII, shape BA, colour code 299. (Private Collection, London)
Opposite
RENE LALIQUE: *Grenouilles et Nénuphars.* Frosted glass vase moulded in intaglio with black-patinated lily pads, green glass frogs set into wells on the surface of the lily pads. This model was exhibited at the 7th salon of the Société des Artistes Décorateurs in Paris, 1912. Only one or two exhibition models of this design were executed. (Christies, New York)

sixteenth century, as seen in the paintings of the period. They exhibited some of their designs at the 1925 Paris Exhibition with comparatively little impact. Shortly after the Exhibition Venini broke with his partner and set up on his own in Murano. Calling in a number of outside designers, including sculptors, to design for him, he quickly enlarged the range of glass with new colours and textures as well as the use of older techniques, but all in the plain, slick shapes that were becoming characteristic of modern Italian designs. In Paris the D.I.M. firm of Joubert et Petit became Venini's agent, and had a wide selection of his glass, including lamps, on permanent exhibition. Other Venetian glassmakers, such as Ercole Barovier, and the Salviati and Ferro-Toso glassworks, produced interesting glass in the Art Deco movement inspired by the 1925 Exhibition.

English glass was almost wholly traditional, though some interesting shapes were designed by James Hogan, Barnaby Powell and William J. Wilson at the James Powell & Sons (Whitefriars) glassworks. The furniture maker Gordon Russell designed some glass for Whitefriars and for the Brierly Hill, Stourbridge, firm of Stevens & Williams. Some interesting designs for Stevens & Williams were made by the New Zealand architect Keith Murray, who worked for the firm for three months a year from 1932 onwards for several years. The painters Paul Nash, Graham Sutherland, Dame Laura Knight and Eric Ravilious designed some glass for the Stourbridge firm of Stuart & Sons, but they had no real understanding of the medium. Most firms continued to produce fine quality crystal cut in traditional patterns, though Clyne Farquharson designed some interesting new patterns for John Walsh and Stevens & Williams. In Scotland the Perth North British Glassworks, founded by John Moncrieff, imported the Catalan glassworker Salvador Ysart in 1922, and he launched a range of internally decorated coloured glassware under the name 'Monart'.

Keith Murray was not the only architect to design glass; Tommaso Buzzi designed some for Venini in 1933, while K.P.C. de Basel, H.P. Berlage and Frank Lloyd Wright designed for the Royal Dutch Glassworks at Leerdam. Alvar Aalto designed rhythmically curved vases for Karhule-littale in Finland. Leerdam was in the forefront of modern glass design in Europe, employing Cornelis de Lorm, Chris Lanooy, Chris Lebeau and Andries Dirk Copier to design tableware and art glass, the latter produced as both unique, individual pieces and multiples. In the United States the Steuben Division of the Corning Glassworks, which had produced so many varieties of coloured ware under the direction of Frederick Carder, was reorganised in 1933 as a new company under the presidency of Arthur Amory Houghton Jr, great grandson of the founder of the parent company. His director of designs was a childhood friend, the architect John Monteith Gates, and Sidney Waugh, a sculptor, became principal designer. Using a newly developed formula for a particularly pure and brilliant crystal, Steuben began the production of an increasingly wide range of etched and engraved vessels as well as shaped and faceted ones. In 1937 Steuben began the practise of commissioning designs from internationally renowned artists, a practise they renewed several times in the post-World War II years.

In preparation for the 1925 Exhibition the Val Saint-Lambert works in Belgium launched a new line under the label 'Arts Décoratifs de Paris' (ADP) using crystal vases covered with transparent coloured glass intaglio-cut with repeating geometric patterns or alternating polished and mat panels or acid-etched, sometimes with multiple applied glass cabochons. Most of these were designed by Léon Ledru or Joseph Simon, while Philippe Wolfers designed a set of crystal tableware which was exhibited in the Belgian pavilion. The most striking Art Deco designs were, however, produced by Charles Graffart, a superlative glass artist.

Most firms producing glass turned out some glass for lighting or lighting fixtures, frequently in collaboration with such metalworkers as Edgar Brandt, Delion, Schwarz-Hautmont, Raymond Subes, etc. The Venetian glass firms specialised in elaborate glass chandeliers with intricately curled and modelled sections which gently diffused light. One French firm, Veronese, produced Venetian-style lighting fixtures, some of them designed by the painter Jean-Gabriel Domergue. Bagues, another French firm, produced elaborate lighting fixtures in the shape of sailing ships or artichokes, made of spun and blown glass, often with glass beads strung together. Süe et Mare produced a range of table and wall light fittings moulded in the shape of bowls of fruit and flowers. Jean Perzel devised luminous panels as well as attached and free-standing fittings consisting of mat glass panels set into lead, copper or brass fittings in geometric shapes. The glass was often acid-finished or sandblasted, sometimes with contrasting opal or enamelled sections. Desny used slabs of chunky glass cut to form futuristic shapes in conjunction with metal.

Glass was used architecturally in a number of different ways. Traditional stained glass panels were renewed with original designs by Jacques Gruber and Louis Barillet in France, Puhl & Wagner in Germany and Jaap Gidding and Theo van Doesburg in Holland. Non-leaded panels were created by Jacques Gruber, Francis Gruber, Valentine Prax and Touchagues; these were thick glass panels painted with designs in oils, varnished then acid-etched and sometimes painted with transparent coloured varnishes, forming a translucent whole. Mirrored glass panels were also painted and engraved by Paula and Max Ingrand, J.J.K. Roy, Labouret, René Buthaud, Etienne Cournault and Raoul Dufy; the mirror silvering being applied with both silver and gold leaf, the patterns painted or etched or sandblasted, glowing through the mirrored surface. Specially toughened mirrored glass panels were occasionally used as wall cladding or as a floor surface, as in the interiors for Suzanne Talbot designed by Eileen Gray.

The revival of the pâte-de-verre technique was initiated by Henri Cros in 1884. Unlike glass, which is shaped and coloured in its hot and molten state, pâte-de-verre is modelled in its cool state. Smashed, then finely crushed glass is mixed with a binding agent and water to make a malleable paste, and metallic oxides are added to give colour. This is modelled like clay, then wrapped in an investment, or else packed in a shaped refractory mould, and placed in the furnace. This is kept at a temperature sufficient to vitrify the paste without letting its different constituents mix together and fuse. When metallic oxides are mixed with the paste, the piece is

Above
GABRIEL ARGY-ROUSSEAU: Pâte-de-cristal winged nymph, modelled by Marcel Bouraine, 1927. (Sotheby's, London)
Opposite, above
ALMERIC WALTER: Pâte-de-verre plaque depicting Isadora Duncan dancing, modelled by Jean Descomps, c. 1920. (Private Collection, London)
Opposite, below
ALMERIC WALTER: Pâte-de-verre nude modelled by P. Duberry, c. 1925, 18 cms. (Editions Graphiques Gallery, London)

Left
GABRIEL ARGY-ROUSSEAU: Pâte-de-cristal bowl modelled with three butterflies, 8 cms. (Author's Collection)

Below, left
GABRIEL ARGY-ROUSSEAU: Pâte-de-verre vase modelled with a woman's head in different attitudes, 19 cms. (Author's Collection)

Below, right
GABRIEL ARGY-ROUSSEAU: Pâte-de-cristal vase modelled with stylised waves and a frieze of angelfish, 15 cms. (Author's Collection)

Opposite
GABRIEL ARGY-ROUSSEAU: Pâte-de-cristal nymph, modelled by Marcel Bouraine, 1927, 31 cms. (Author's Collection)

coloured through. Placing the metallic oxides in the bottom of the mould to which the paste is added, colours the surface. Thus polychrome pieces are possible.

Parallel with Cros's work, experiments with pâte-de-verre were carried out by Georges Despret in his glassworks, by Albert Dammouse the ceramist, and at the Daum works at Nancy, where Almeric Walter ran a pâte-de-verre atelier in which he could call on the design services of such artists as Henri Bergé, Victor Prouvé and Jean Descomps. When war broke out in 1914 Daum closed down its production of artistic glass. In 1919 Walter set up independently for the production of a wide range of pâte-de-verre using models by a large number of artists, including the models he had executed at Daum. His inspiration remained largely Art Nouveau or naturalistic, and several of the sculptures he made in pâte-de-verre were also made in ceramic (usually by Mougin Frères) or cast in bronze.

Pâte-de-verre is capable of being produced in a wide variety of finishes. Walter's was a heavy, opaque polychrome substance. The interwar years saw the rise of two great pâte-de-verre artists, Gabriel Argy-Rousseau and François Décorchemont. Each of them experimented with different finishes.

Décorchemont had been producing stoneware vases when he came across Dammouse's pâte-de-verre. Thin-walled, with open cloisonné sections filled in with translucent paste, Dammouse's pâte-de-verre looked like ceramic set with translucent plique-à-jour enamels. Indeed, he called it pâte-d'émail, or enamel paste, and it was believed by some critics to be soft porcelain. Décorchemont's first vessels were of a similar friable, thin-walled substance. He made his own raw glass which he crushed, using quince pips as a binding agent, then inserted this paste into moulds where it was allowed to dry. When dry, it was still malleable enough to be retouched before firing at low temperature for a long time. It was then taken out of the furnace, painted with coloured metallic oxides, given a last firing at high temperature for up to twenty-four hours, followed by the cooling or annealing process which took several days. All his early vessels were modelled with floral or Symbolist subjects in an Art Nouveau style.

Gradually both subjects and techniques changed. He began to use a lost-wax casting technique, and ordered his raw glass from the Saint-Denis glassworks, then later from Daum, and the thin-walled pâte-d'émail soon became a crystalline substance known as pâte-de-cristal. Naturalistic insects, nudes and flowers were simplified, in the 20s, to thick-walled vessels, with minor repeating patterns occasionally contrasted with figuration in the shape of nub handles modelled as nymphs, chameleons, or snakes. The richness of the colours was frequently alternated with colourless patches, swirls, veining, streaking and bubbling. He exhibited at Geo. Rouard's shop, selling at quite high prices.

Unlike Décorchemont, whose family had been artists for generations, Gabriel Rousseau was born into a family of poor farm workers, but his own ability and cleverness won him scholarships which enabled him to complete secondary studies and enter the National High School for Ceramics at Sèvres, where Henri Cros had his workshop. Cros's son Jean was a fellow student of Rousseau's. After graduating in 1906 Rousseau took over the management of a small ceramics laboratory,

Above
FRANCOIS DECORCHEMONT: Pâte-de-cristal vase moulded in relief with entwined snakes, 1924. (Sotheby's, Monaco)

268

experimenting with pâte-de-verre in his spare time. After his marriage in 1913 to the sister of a former classmate, he added the first part of her surname to his, and was henceforth known as Argy-Rousseau.

Argy-Rousseau's pâte-de-verre was an opaque, richly coloured, but surprisingly lightweight substance, moulded with classical theatrical masks, butterflies, fruit and flowers. He spent the war as a national defence engineer, and took out several scientific patents. After the war he produced a range of enamelled scent bottles which he sold to several expensive shops, principally that of Marcel Franck, and he exhibited his pâte-de-verre in several galleries, as well as at the Salon des Artistes Français. In 1921 Gustave-Gaston Moser-Millot, who owned a decorative arts gallery in the boulevard des Italiens, financed Argy-Rousseau. A limited company was formed with Moser-Millot as chairman and principal shareholder, and Argy-Rousseau as managing director. A comfortable workshop was opened, and all the new designs went on exclusive sale to Moser-Millot. The arrangement suited Argy-Rousseau, who could then concentrate wholly on the design and execution of his wares. He produced vases, bowls, lamps, night lights, panels in pâte-de-verre, and in the crystalline pâte-de-cristal his colours were even richer. He designed models with lions, wolves, deer, angel-fish, birds, classical mythological subjects and female nudes, as well as stylised, abstract and geometric patterns. In 1928 he executed a number of pâte-de-cristal sculptures from models designed by Marcel Bouraine, and signed by both of them.

The 1925 Paris Exhibition was a triumph for both men. Décorchemont's wares were on display in Ruhlmann's 'Hôtel d'un Collectionneur' and at Rouard's stand. Argy-Rousseau exhibited Hors Concours, and was a member of the jury. Both artists produced models which were executed in several examples, but by the very nature of the substance used these were multiple originals, since each item had to be individually coloured and finished, even though the same mould was used.

The financial Depression in the 30s was hard on both men. In December 1931 Moser-Millot wound up the Société de Pâte-de-Verre d'Argy-Rousseau, and Argy-Rousseau, never a businessman, was unable to launch a new firm and turned to small production in his own home. He executed a few commissions, including one for small religious plaques and images, made a few enamelled vases and mounted some of his earlier productions in gold, silver or platinum mounts. He also produced a range of chunky, geometric vases and bowls in translucent colours—rich greens, blues, pinks or ambers with internal swirls and streaks.

Décorchemont, whose parallel designs were also chunky and geometric and, indeed, sometimes identical with Argy-Rousseau's, also found it very difficult to make a living from the production of art glass. He concentrated increasingly on the production of large panels for decorative windows on commission, spending the years 1933 to 1938 almost exclusively on these for the Sainte-Odile Church in Paris. Daum had produced some enormous pâte-de-verre panels in the years before 1914, and Décorchemont carried on the tradition, executing some to various commissioned designs. Translucent and bright, they were a highly original alternative to leaded glass.

Above
FRANCOIS DECORCHEMONT: Pâte-de-cristal vase internally streaked and marbled, modelled with two circular handles, 1925. (Collection Musée des Arts Décoratifs, Paris)

CERAMICS

The renaissance of interest and research in ceramics in the latter part of the nineteenth century was largely due to the influence of Théodore Deck. Passionate in his search for new effects, he succeeded in combining decorative designs and patterns from various countries and eras with the results of his latest technical experiments, reinterpreting Persian pottery, Hispano-Mauresque faience and Italian majolica. He developed new coloured grounds and made two of them very much his own: gold, and a deep, rich turquoise blue that came to be known as 'Deck Blue'. His decorated plates are among the most beautiful produced, and he employed a number of artists to decorate them with portraits of women, plants and birds in shimmering colours, achieved with transparent vitrified enamels. Paul César Helleu, who was to become one of the great masters of the drypoint, was one of his decorators. Deck made no secret of his discoveries and in 1887 published a small handbook. Appointed director of the state-owned Manufacture de Porcelaine at Sèvres in 1887, he generously shared his knowledge until his death in 1891.

Parallel with Deck's later years, Ernest Chaplet was experimenting in the direction of decoration through firing. Born at Sévres in 1835, Chaplet learned the art of porcelain decoration at the age of fifteen, and spent over twenty years working for the firm of Laurin at Bourg-la-Reine, decorating tableware and other standard wares. Towards the end of his stay there, he was beginning to redevelop the technique of the 'barbotine', a soft paste of clay mixed with water and coloured with metallic oxides which was applied to the surface of the vessel after a first firing. Transparent and delicate, this paste would be used for painting the decoration as though the vessel were a canvas, and would survive firing without affecting the brush strokes, yet with a brilliant finish. In 1872 Charles Haviland, whose family had set up a china business in New York in 1921 and later built up a highly successful manufacture at Limoges, most of it geared to the American market, founded an experimental studio at Auteuil, run by Félix Bracquemond. Both Bracquemond and Haviland were admirers and collectors of the arts of the Far East: Charles Haviland, who was to form one of the greatest European collections of Japanese artifacts, paintings and books, even married the daughter of Philippe Burty, a noted art critic who was also a leading specialist on Japanese works of art. Bracquemond hired Chaplet, who quickly perfected the barbotine technique, which was used by a variety of artists with varying success, though strongly influenced by the Impressionists.

The high cost of production of the barbotine-decorated works of the Atelier Paris-Auteuil, as compared with cheap and often nasty reproductions, made it uneconomic to continue running this experiment. Bracquemond left in 1881 and the

Above
GEORGES BASTARD: Tennis player and golfer, polychrome ceramic decanters, the heads being the stoppers. (Private Collection, London)
Opposite
CARDINAL: Porcelain plate decorated with a design by Georges Lepape, c. 1927, 32 cms. diameter. (Private Collection, London)

271

Atelier ceased its production within a year. Chaplet, exhausted and discouraged by the departure of his friend Bracquemond, took a leave of absence during which he visited the traditional stoneware makers in Normandy. On his return he showed some of these wares to Charles Haviland, who set up in a small workshop at 153 rue Blomet at Vaugirard. Chaplet was soon experimenting with coloured glazes, though it was not until he worked with a research chemist that he succeeded in achieving copper-red flambés. He produced a variety of stoneware vases with mat glazes and deeply cut lines or cloisonné patterns, often designed by Frédéric Hexamer and the brothers Edouard and Albert Dammouse. As a result of competition from German stoneware factories and high tariff barriers in the United States, the rue Blomet atelier was no more successful financially than the Paris-Auteuil one had been. In 1886 Chaplet purchased the atelier from Haviland. Bracquemond introduced Paul Gauguin to him and the artist decorated vases for Chaplet before designing a number of sculptural vessels to be executed in stoneware. In 1887 Chaplet sold his works (but not his formulae) to Auguste Delaherche, a former student of Lechevallier-Chevignard at the School of Decorative Arts and former designer at the Christofle silver-plating works. Delaherche had become increasingly fascinated by ceramics and came to study briefly with Chaplet before purchasing the works, where he made high-fired stoneware vases, bowls and plates, both decorated and plain, sometimes in naturalistic fruit or flower shapes. He was to receive a Gold Medal at the 1889 Paris International Exhibition, and was also made a Knight of the Légion d'Honneur. After various moves and experiments Delaherche ceased to work with aides and, from 1904 until shortly before his death in 1940, turned, fired and decorated his stoneware vases and bowls entirely on his own, simplifying his shapes and concentrating on increasingly complex slips in a wide range of colours. He also produced a number of porcelain vessels in pierced and engraved patterns.

After selling his rue Blomet works to Delaherche, Chaplet settled at Choisy-le-Roi, where he continued to produce stoneware, including such large items as complete bathrooms and chimneys, but spent most of his time and energy working with porcelain, achieving flambé effects and a variety of rich colours on extremely simple shapes. In 1909, after losing his sight, Chaplet burned all his formulae and experimental notes and shot himself, though he languished in the hospital for several weeks before dying. He left all his collection to the Musée des Arts Décoratifs in Paris. His atelier was taken over by Emile Lenoble, who had married Chaplet's granddaughter.

Lenoble had already worked for seven years in a commercial ceramics factory before joining Chaplet. After taking over the Choisy-le-Roi works he soon began his own experiments, frequently painting designs on the finished vessels when he was not incising abstract designs. The 1914-18 War interrupted his work. He joined the army and was taken prisoner but after the war promptly returned to his work, the years between 1918 and 1930 proving very fertile for him. His first post-war vases and bowls were all decorated with incised friezes—geometric, abstract and of a stylised floralism—but he increasingly concentrated on developing a wider palette

Above
EMILE LENOBLE: Two stoneware vases, c. 1925, the one on the left 33 cms, the one on the right 23 cms. (Collection Robert Zehil, Beverly Hills)
Opposite, above, left
EMILE LENOBLE: Stoneware vase, c. 1925, 34.5 cms. (Collection Robert Zehil, Beverly Hills)
Opposite, above, right
EMILE LENOBLE: White stoneware vase with incised floral decoration, c. 1913, 35 cms., and brown and black stoneware vase with incised decoration, c. 1925-30, 36 cms. (Collection M. and H.-J. Heuser)
Opposite, below, left
HENRI SIMMEN: White flower-form stoneware bowl, c. 1925-30, 11 cms., red stoneware inkwell, c. 1925, 7 cms., and celadon stoneware vase with carved ivory stopper by Mme O'Kin Simmen, c. 1925-30, 20 cms. (Collection M. and H.-J. Heuser)
Opposite, below, right
ANDRE METHEY: Stoneware charger with polychrome glazes, c. 1910-20, 52 cms., and stoneware vase with polychrome glazes, c. 1910-20, 33.5 cms. (Collection M. and H.-J. Heuser)

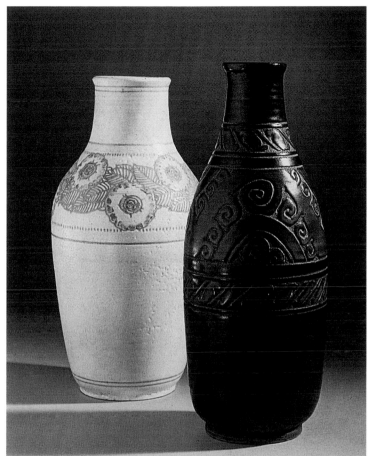

of colours, with particular emphasis on a range of blues and a predilection for celadon.

Henri Rivière, an artist whose total involvement with the arts of the Far East led him, at the turn of the century, to produce European subjects in traditional Japanese woodblock style, manner and technique, introduced his friend Lenoble to Korean and Chinese pottery. Lenoble succeeded in mixing his clay with kaolin to create a very light stoneware. Utterly different from Chaplet's pots, these were to become a standard feature of much Art Deco interior decoration. Lenoble was a friend of such interior decorators as Ruhlmann and Montagnac, and in the room settings these decorators designed for their showrooms and the annual Salons, pots by Lenoble were almost invariably displayed.

Art Deco furniture and room settings were ideally designed to display and set off complementary objets d'art, particularly ceramics and glass. The design studios of the great shops commissioned a variety of both, while specialist shops proliferated. Probably the most adventurous of these was Geo. Rouard's gallery, which comissioned, executed and displayed ceramics and glass by many of the leading artists and craftsmen. Lenoble was one of Rouard's artists. Another was Emile Decoeur.

Born in 1876, as was Lenoble, Decoeur, who had been orphaned when very young, entered Edmond Lachenal's studio as an apprentice at the age of fourteen. He was to spend ten years there, eventually working very closely with Lachenal and adding his own monogram to his master's signature on those ceramics which they had worked on together. On leaving Lachenal, Decoeur worked briefly with Fernand Rumèbe before setting up on his own. He had by now decided to abandon earthenware in favour of stoneware, to which he had been led by his admiration for Carriès, and his surface designs were largely based on Art Nouveau floralism. At the 1900 Paris International Exhibition he was awarded a Bronze Medal. He was soon exhibiting at the Salons of the Société des Artistes Français, where he was awarded an Honourable Mention in 1901, a 3rd Class Medal in 1902, a 2nd Class Medal in 1905 and a Travelling Scholarship in 1907. On his return he moved to Fontenay-aux-Roses, and there began to experiment with porcelain.

Decoeur essayed a wide variety of techniques, including high-fired stoneware and porcelain and surface decoration varying from incised or painted designs to dripped glaze. He soon developed in the direction of austerity of ambition, rejecting decoration in favour of increasingly simplified shapes with increasingly subtle glazes—he dismissed his early works as youthful errors. Honours continued to come his way: in 1910 he was awarded a 1st Class Medal, was awarded the French Legion of Honour in 1920, and was made an officer of that order in 1926. By 1927 he was working with a finer stoneware, achieved with a mixture of clay and kaolin, and was treating stoneware and porcelain in identical ways, so that it is often extremely difficult to tell them apart. The late 20s and 30s saw his most beautiful works, almost totally undecorated pots of pure, symmetrical shapes, each covered in a sumptuous single colour glaze—rich yellow, green, white, pink, blue or celadon.

Another of Lachenal's students was Henri Simmen. He had studied architecture and was planning to become an interior designer when he became fascinated by

French peasant pottery. After studying with Lachenal he set up his own studio and began working with salt-glazed pottery, as well as experimenting with flambés. At the end of the Great War he left for the Far East, travelling through China, Korea and Japan to study their ceramic arts and techniques. On his return he dedicated himself entirely to the craft. Rejecting extraneous aids, he modelled his ceramics entirely by hand, without the use of a mechanical potter's wheel. He used only natural products: 'rocks, minerals, lavas, basalts, oak, cornelian and bamboo ash, with no borrowings from modern chemistry,' he wrote. All minerals used in preparing glazes were crushed from their constituent materials, unrefined, and any remaining impurities were allowed to play their part in achieving the final results. His vessels were created by direct action of the fire, unprotected by an investment when placed in the kiln. He thus achieved a wide range of rich colours; he especially liked crackled glazes and created very personal shapes and colours, often inspired by nature. 'Any shape which presents itself to the potter's mind only presents itself in the usual shape of his thoughts,' he wrote. 'A flowing and graceful profile will not appear in a rustic's thoughts, a tortuous shape in a simple man's mind. Shapes which seem to emerge from a potter's fingers actually emerge from his soul and can only be triggered by an inner signal.' His Japanese wife, Mme O'Kin Simmen, frequently provided his creations with lids, finials or stands carved from ivory or precious woods.

Another centre of 'pure' pottery was to develop in Saint-Amand-en-Puisaye, in the Nièvre department, where a number of potters carried on the traditional business of utilitarian stoneware, generally in rustic shapes. Jean Carriès, a sculptor, first discovered Japanese pottery at the 1878 Paris Exhibition, then in the collection of his friend Paul Jeanneney. Ten years later, having made the decision to essay the technique himself, he moved to Saint-Amand-en-Puisaye, where he bought the Chateau of Montriveau, and took lessons from a local potter, Amand Lion. Combining local rustic elements with his own artistic fever, Carriès created new mat glazes, strange ornamentations, grotesque animals, figures and masks, as well as a number of vases, bottles and bowls in dull grey, blue or waxy colours with dripped glazes. Though he was to die before reaching his fortieth birthday, his influence was enormous and his castle became the centre of a movement which continued his style. Among the many potters who were to work there were his friend Georges Hoentschel, who was to buy the castle after the death of Carriès, Emile Grittel, Paul Jeanneney, William Lee, Henri de Vallombreuse, Count Nils de Bark and several local potters who changed to art pottery through the influence of Carriès, including Amand Lion, his son Eugène, Théo Perrot, the Abbé Pacton and Jean Pointu.

In total contrast to the work of the high-fired enthusiasts were the products of those to whom surface decoration was of prime importance. The critic Etienne Avenard, writing an article on André Méthey in *Art et Décoration* in 1912, described his aims thus: 'Colour, therefore, above all else. And, since one must choose, fine decoration rather than fine materials, the glorification of the artist rather than that of the fire, a thousand times and a thousand times again, art rather than craft.' Méthey was a professional carver in love with pottery, earning his living for years by carving the decorations on musical instruments while building kilns and experimenting. The years of failures and continual experimentation came to an end in about 1901, when he moved to Asnières. There, for the next six years, he produced a wide variety of vases and plates in rich colours, all with figurative designs by artists who were introduced to him by his friends Ambroise Vollard, the art dealer, and Théodore Duret, the critic and art historian. Among these artists were Georges Rouault, Edouard Vuillard, Odilon Redon, Maurice Vlaminck, Kees Van Dongen, Maurice Denis, Henri Matisse, Pierre Bonnard and André Derain. The discovery of Persian and Islamic pottery led Méthey to abandon faience, with its limited range of colours, for glazed clay pottery. Over the years he developed glowing, vibrant colours, achieving red shortly before his death in 1920. The last fifteen years of his life were highly productive, his first, purely geometric designs eventually giving way to stylised flowers and plants and, finally, human forms, often inspired by Hellenic decoration. His designs were usually friezes or sets of medallions containing related, but different figures or geometric designs, frequently connected by secondary motifs, the whole forming a dynamic composition in which design and colour combined to achieve the effect.

The works of Jean Mayodon were frequently similar in inspiration. Himself a painter, and the son of a painter, Mayodon first became interested in pottery in 1912, and he and his father built a kiln in which he produced his first essays. After the First World War he exhibited some of his vases at the Galliéra Museum and was sufficiently encouraged by public response to devote the rest of his life to ceramics. All his researches were directed towards obtaining richer colours, with frequent and lavish use of gold, and he perfected techniques in which successive firings, each at a lower temperature than the last, were used for each colour. Greek mythology provided him with his favourite subjects for decoration, though he also used other sources of inspiration. Vases, bowls and plates emerged from his kilns, but he also specialised in large-scale ceramic works, including large panels, fountains, monumental sculpture and swimming pools. Some of his panels were used in bathrooms, and others were commissioned for several French liners. Born in Sèvres, he became artistic director of the Manufacture de Sèvres in 1941.

Raoul Lachenal took over his father's studio shortly after the turn of the century when Edmond Lachenal decided to abandon ceramics for the stage. Raoul, fully trained by his father, experimented with high-fired stoneware before he decided he preferred high-fired porcelain. He first exhibited at the 1904 Salon. In 1911 he set up his own studio at Boulogne, and there produced a range of inventive and beautifully decorated vases, bowls and plates of uncomplicated, symmetrical shapes decorated with stylised floral or geometric patterns. He liked pure, strong colours, and used white, deep black, green, red, orange and gold to powerful effect. Several of his vessels were decorated in a cloisonné style, each colour section of the design being carefully outlined in a glaze of a different colour.

One of the most interesting artists to use ceramics rather than canvas or paper was René Buthaud. Trained as a silver chaser while studying at the Ecole des Beaux-

Above
RENE BUTHAUD: Green glazed mask, c. 1928.
(Private Collection, London)

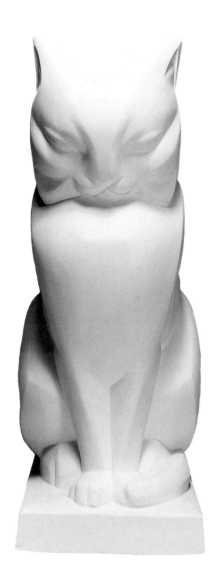

Arts in Bordeaux, he was awarded a scholarship in 1909 which enabled him to go to the Paris Beaux-Arts, where he studied painting and etching. He won a variety of prizes for both disciplines, culminating in a second Rome Grand Prix for etching in 1914. The war interrupted his studies and it was not until his demobilisation in 1918 that he began to experiment with ceramics. This was back in Bordeaux, where he rejoined two old friends, the painters Roger Bissière and Jean Dupas, who encouraged him in his new interests. A year later he married, and henceforth devoted himself to ceramics. In 1920 he exhibited at the Salon of the Société des Artistes Décorateurs at the Salon d'Automne, and Maurice Denis, Jean Dunand and Maurice Vlaminck soon bought some of his vases. Mrs. Florence Blumenthal, a wealthy American lady who had settled in Paris, set up a foundation which awarded prizes to young French war veteran artists. At Jean Dunand's suggestion, Buthaud was awarded one of the first of these prizes, 25,000 francs, which gave him financial freedom to spend some time at Golfe-Juan on the French Riviera, studying the techniques used in a major ceramics factory.

In 1923 René Guilleré, co-founder in 1901 of the Société des Artistes Décorateurs, and founder and director of the Primavera Studio set up in the Printemps department store in Paris in 1913, offered Buthaud the job of technical and artistic director of a new ceramics factory that Primavera had opened near Tours. He retained the position until 1926, when his wife's illness forced him to move. After her death he settled in Bordeaux, eventually marrying one of his late wife's sisters. His new kiln enabled him to fire ceramics at a higher temperature than previously, but still to work with a type of glazed faience. He produced vases and bowls of simple shapes which he then decorated in a linear, neo-classical style, reminiscent on occasions of the style of Dupas and the flowing line of Van Dongen. His subjects were most frequently culled from Greek mythology, with many others inspired by beautiful women: a simple profile or a full face, nude or dressed, dancing, seated, or holding a basket of flowers. As a member of the Ceramics Section jury at the 1925 Paris Exhibition he exhibited Hors Concours. In 1928 Lenoble introduced him to Geo. Rouard and he was to exhibit regularly in Rouard's gallery until 1961.

In 1931 Buthaud became Professor of Decorative Painting and Decorative Arts at the Bordeaux Ecole des Beaux-Arts. He also produced a small group of vases decorated with a 'snakeskin' glaze for an American dealer. Since he was still under contract to Rouard, he signed these with a pseudonym, 'J. Doris'. He also produced a small number of vases decorated with geometric abstract designs, but this was not of his own choosing. He was happier with a group of vases decorated with African subjects, both human and animal, inspired by the 1931 Colonial Exhibition. While he essayed the occasional stoneware vase or mask in the 1930s, the post-World War II years were devoted largely to ceramic statues loosely inspired by Staffordshire pottery.

The Sèvres Manufactory, which had had such conspicuous success at the 1900 Exhibition, proved equally adventurous twenty-five years later at the Exhibition of Decorative and Industrial Arts. Georges Lechevallier-Chevignard, who had taken over as director in 1920, set up a new faience department under the direction of

Maurice Gensoli shortly before the opening of the Exhibition. Open to a variety of artists in other fields, the new range consisted of both vases and tableware, with decorations designed by artists as varied as Robert Bonfils, Jean Dupas, Henri Rapin, Suzanne Lalique (daughter of the jewellery and glass manufacturer), Jean Dufy (Raoul's brother), the sculptor brothers Joël and Jan Martel, Eric Bagge, Jacques-Emile Ruhlmann and Louis Jaulmes. Suzanne Lalique and Jean Dufy also designed extensively for Théodore Haviland at Limoges. The twin Sèvres pavilions at the Exhibition displayed an incredibly wide range of ceramics, vases of all shapes and sizes for indoor and outdoor use, lamps, wall lights, fittings, tableware, ornaments of all shapes and sizes, statuettes and sculpture, wall and floor cladding and tiles. The sculpture included a number of designs by François Pompon, as well as a range of small sculptures in white bisque porcelain. Simon Lissim, the stage designer and book illustrator, decorated some porcelain vases and plates for Sèvres with both abstract, geometric patterns and figurative designs inspired by such Russian legends as that of the Firebird, in glowing colours and gold. He also designed and decorated such oddities as pipes and cigarette holders with matching tobacco jars, cuff-links, buttons and clocks. At the 1937 Paris International Exhibition, where he was awarded two Grand Diplômes d'Honneur, he exhibited a large aquarium of decorated porcelain panels with a glass front and, a year later, began designing very similar decorations for porcelain executed by the American firm of Lenox, Inc. of Trenton, New Jersey. Porcelains and other ceramics decorated in similar patterns, often with gold, were also executed at the various Limoges factories.

The design studios of the Paris department stores were not slow to produce decorative ceramics for the 1925 Exhibition. Primavera had the widest range, employing a variety of decorators, including Madeleine Sougez, Marcel Renard, Claude Lévy, Mme Chauchet-Guilleré and Colette Gueden, as well as commissioning both plain and highly decorated pieces from the Longwy ceramics factory. La Maitrise produced a wide range, much of it designed and decorated by its director, Maurice Dufrêne, though its team of designers included Reschofsky, Peltier and Mlle Maisonée. Süe et Mare's Compagnie des Arts Français sold a wide range of ceramics, both tableware and decorative and useful objects, frequently treated architecturally, and almost invariably made of white majolica. Francis Jourdain designed tableware for sale in his shop. Geo. Rouard, of course, maintained the widest range of tableware, with designs by Marcel Goupy, Hermann-Paul, Drésa, Bonvallet, and many others. Jean Luce designed coordinated tableware and glassware, using the same decorative motif to unite both, though frequently ringing the changes by subtly altering the angle by which the motif was viewed on individual items of the set.

The French section of the Goldscheider complex edited several artists who worked in a variety of sculptural media. Edouard Cazaux, who exhibited at the annual Salons of the Société Nationale des Beaux-Arts and the Salon d'Automne, designed and decorated a wide variety of vessels as well as some very striking and colourful ceramic statuettes. He also frequently decorated ceramic statuettes de-

Overleaf, left
LIMOGES: Gilt and polychrome glazed porcelain vase, c. 1925. (Editions Graphiques Gallery, London)
Overleaf, right, above
JEAN LUCE: Red and black glazed box and cover, c. 1927, and vase with repeating design of a dove in silver resist, c. 1925. (Editions Graphiques Gallery, London)
Overleaf, right, below
JEAN LUCE: Teapot and sucrier, c. 1925-30. (Private Collection, London)

signed by fellow members of the La Stèle and L'Evolution groups, particularly those by his close friend Sibylle May. Both used a Cubist-inspired angularity allied with a simplification of features.

André Fau and Guillard executed ceramic statuettes by Léon Leyritz and Do Canto, while E.M. Sandoz designed an extraordinary variety of tea sets, decanters and boxes in the shape of various birds, animals and human figures which were executed by Théodore Haviland and Achille Bloch. The Adnet brothers designed a series of pigeons, executed in white glazed pottery by the Faiencerie de Montereau, while the Robj and Aladin firms produced a wide range of somewhat humorous decanters, night lights, and plain statuettes based on grotesque characters and pretty women.

While most countries pursued traditional local pottery, a number of individual firms produced work within the Art Deco movement. In the Netherlands Theodore Colenbrander adapted the highly decorative techniques, launched in the wake of the Art Nouveau movement there, to abstract and geometric patterns. Georges de Feure also experimented in that direction, executing a few highly decorative ceramics, while Chris Lanooy turned to the more rigorous stoneware of Oriental inspiration. In Belgium Charles Catteau designed a wide range of vases, plates and bowls in decorated stoneware as well as glazed faience with cloisonné patterns, all executed at the Keramis works of Boch Frères. In Sweden Wilhelm Käge designed a wide range of faience tableware in open modern shapes, as well as a range of green glazed pottery vases, bowls, plates and boxes decorated with nudes, mermaids and abstract motifs in inset silver, all executed at the Gustavsberg works.

In Italy, the firm of Richard Ginori produced quirky, original decorative designs by the architect Gio Ponti and the sculptor Saponaro, while the Cantagalli firm reproduced Renaissance designs on modern faience, bringing them as much into the Art Deco image as the French ceramists had brought in the Hellenic.

The Soviet Union produced some curious decorative patterns in the Leningrad State Factory, as well as at those at Novgorod, Dimitrov and Doulevo, where such artists as Sergei Tchekhonin, Nattalia Danko and Alexandra Shchkotikhina-Pototskaia designed a number of revolutionary commemorative plates in which a variety of motifs were interspersed with the hammer and sickle, and typographical motifs and abstract patterns were used. Other products included vases, chess sets and figures.

Denmark's several factories produced a wide variety of art pottery. The Royal Copenhagen factory turned out the most exquisite delicate glazes on decorated ceramics, as well as high-fired stoneware vases and sculptures in a somewhat primitive style by Jais Nielsen, and a range of animals by Knud Kyhn. Bing and Gröndahl produced an even wider range, with a group of artists each having his or her own speciality, from sculptured porcelain to under- and over-glaze decoration, and the use of a mat glaze on small objects and figurines of great elegance. Jean Gauguin, son of the French painter, was one of the leading artists here, sculpting in glazed faience as well as a substance he devised himself, which he called 'roche céramique', easy to model, resistant to distortion by fire and extremely hard after firing, therefore highly suitable for architectural as well as outdoor use.

Above
EDOUARD CAZAUX: Gilt and polychrome faience vase decorated with the story of Adam and Eve, c. 1930-35, 28 cms., gilt and polychrome faience vase, c. 1930-35, 28 cms., and gilt and polychrome faience bowl decorated with Bacchanalian nudes, c. 1930, 6 cms. diameter. (Collection M. and H.-J. Heuser)
Opposite
EDOUARD CAZAUX: *Josephine Baker.* Gilt and polychrome faience figure, c. 1928, 36 cms. (Editions Graphiques Gallery, London)
Overleaf, left
SYBILLE MAY: Decorated faience figure, c. 1925, 20.5 cms. Edouard Cazaux frequently decorated her ceramic sculptures. (Editions Graphiques Gallery, London)
Overleaf, right
BOYER: Decorated porcelain kneeling nude figure, made at Limoges, c. 1927, 30 cms. (Private Collection, London)

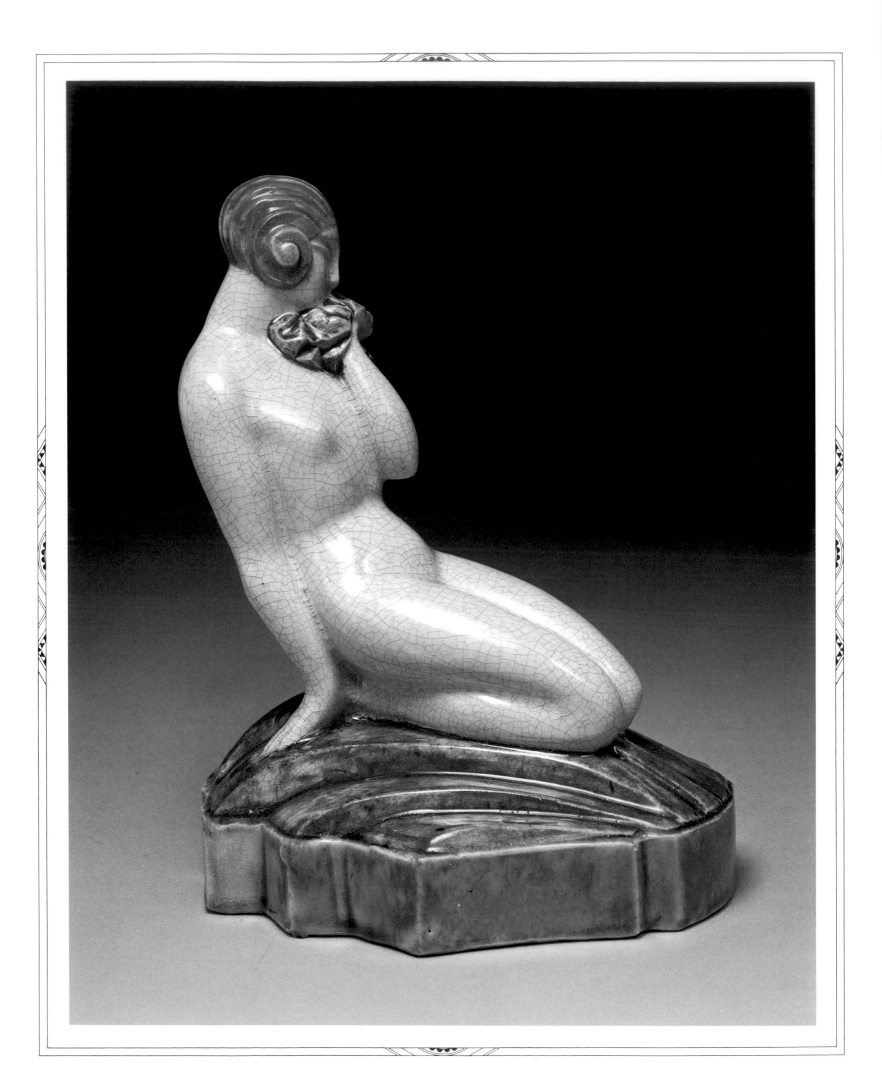

Ceramic figurines in delicate pastel colours, with striking use of rich contrasting colours, were produced in Germany in several ceramic works, particularly Philipp Rosenthal at Selb, the Fraureuth works at Sachsen, and the Gebruder Heubach works at Lichte. Large figurines in strong, glazed colours, inspired by the Ballets Russes and Hollywood, were produced at the Royal Dux works in Bohemia, which had been part of Czechoslovakia since the end of the First World War. Smaller, delicately coloured figurines of bathers and other pretty girls were produced by the Royal Doulton works in England.

Royal Doulton also produced several different ranges of ceramics in the Art Deco mood. These included salt-glaze stoneware decorated with coloured slips by Margaret E. Thompson, Harry Simeon, William Rowe, Vera Huggins, J. H. Mott and Elise Simmance; ceramic sculpture by Richard Garbe, Gilbert Bayes, James Woodford and others; 'Sung' ware, a transmutation glaze developed by Charles J. Noke, in which a flambé glaze was coated with various metallic oxides to achieve veined, mottled effects in a wide range of colours; and, most beautiful of all, 'Chang' ware, introduced in 1925 by Noke, his son Cecil and Harry Nixon, in which a heavy body was coated with several layers of different coloured transmutation glazes, the top one crackled and allowed to run thickly at different levels down the sides of the vessel. Outside artists occasionally contributed to Royal Doulton: Reco Capey, professor of design at the Royal College of Art, designed a small number of Cubist-inspired ceramics. The firm also produced a small range of tableware decorated with Cubist and abstract patterns.

Other English firms developed highly coloured decorated pottery. Clarice Cliff, who had joined the firm of A.J. Wilkinson Ltd. in Stoke on Trent at the age of sixteen as a transfer-print pattern decorator, soon created a range of table and other wares decorated with abstract geometric, stylised floral, landscape and figure designs in bold, raw, often crude colours which became enormously popular. She eventually became artistic director of both Wilkinson and its sister Newport Pottery Co., extending her range from the brightly coloured 'Bizarre' wares which made her reputation, to sophisticated Art Deco designs in green or black and silver, and even produced a small group of ceramics decorated by a number of well-known British artists, including Vanessa Bell, Duncan Grant, Barbara Hepworth, John Armstrong, Laura Knight, Graham Sutherland, Dod Procter, Ernest Procter, Ben Nicholson, Paul Nash, Albert Rutherston and Frank Brangwyn. Susie Cooper designed for the firm of A.G. Grey from 1925 to 1932, painting strong Cubist and abstract patterns in bold colours. She later formed her own company and eventually became a leading designer for Wedgwood.

Wedgwood itself produced a few Art Deco designs in the mid 20s, including designs by Marcel Goupy. In the 1930s Keith Murray designed vases, bowls, boxes, mugs and coffee sets, usually elegant, engine-turned shapes decorated with parallel lathe-cut grooves, with a mat finish in green, grey, cream, celadon or black, though some of the coffee sets were silver. They also produced a range of stylised animal sculpture by John Skeaping. In Poole, Dorset, a subsidiary of the ceramics firm of Carter & Co. Ltd., called Carter, Stabler & Adams, was set up in 1921.

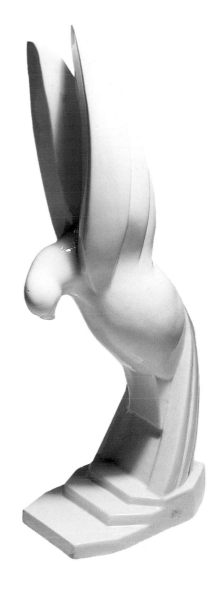

Above
J. & J. ADNET: White glazed faience dove, c. 1930. (Gallery 1925, London)
Opposite, above, left
EDOUARD MARCEL SANDOZ: Coffee pot, milk jug and sucrier in glazed and decorated porcelain, executed by Théodore Haviland at Limoges, c. 1927. (Editions Graphiques Gallery, London)
Opposite, above, right
CHARLES CATTEAU: Glazed stoneware vase decorated with polar bears, executed at the Faiencerie de Keramis of Boch Frères, 1925, 24 cms. (Editions Graphiques Gallery, London)
Opposite, below, left
ROBJ: *Napoléon*. Glazed decanter, c. 1927. (Private Collection, London)
Opposite, below, right
GEORGES DE FEURE: Group of experimental decorated and glazed plates. (Collection Laurence and Barlach Heuer, Paris. Photo: Sully Jaulmes)

Above
ROYAL DUX (CZECHOSLOVAKIA): Glazed and
unglazed porcelain figure, c. 1926, length 44
cms. (Private Collection, London)
Below
CLARICE CLIFF: Milk jug with geometrical design,
c. 1929. (Private Collection, London)

Above
CLARICE CLIFF: *Biarritz*. Decorated plate, c.
1930, 21 cms. (Private Collection, London)
Opposite
CARLTON WARE: Glazed vase with gilt and
polychrome decoration, c. 1928, 34 cms.
(Editions Graphiques Gallery, London)

With models from Harold and Phoebe Stabler, John Adams, Truda Carter and others, this firm produced a range of ceramics decorated with stylised geometric, floral and bird patterns in neat, quiet colour combinations with a satin finish, as well as items decorated solely in unusually coloured glazes.

At the Ruskin Pottery in Smethwick, W. Howson Taylor produced a variety of wares, of which the finest were the high-fired vases and bowls. Frequently mottled, with splashes of colour, speckling or spotting, each individual pot emerged from the fire in rich red and purple glazes, with strong greens and rough oatmeals and occasional black spots. Taylor went on producing these until just before his death in 1935, when he closed down the works and destroyed all his formulae and materials. Charles Vyse and his wife Nell set up their studio in Chelsea in 1919, and there produced a number of ceramic sculptures, generally modelled by Charles and coloured and glazed by his wife. In the late 20s they also began to produce stoneware inspired by the Chinese, though some of their shapes were purely European and of this decade. William Staite Murray produced decorated stoneware with coloured glazes as well as undecorated, sculptured pieces, while Bernard Leach, who had studied in Japan, set up a pottery at St. Ives in Cornwall with Shoji Hamada. Leach made stoneware fired at high temperatures, as well as low temperature faience. Several of his students and apprentices became well-known potters in their own right, including his son David Leach, Michael Cardew, Katherine Pleydell-Bouverie and Norah Braden.

The Viennese firm of Goldscheider produced a wide range of decorative ceramics, including a number of decorative wall-masks in rich, contrasting colours. Several artists of the Vienna Secession designed and decorated ceramics, mostly executed in the Wiener Keramik works, and while most showed the design preoccupations of the Secession, some can properly be considered within the Art Deco context.

Opposite, above
VALLY WIESELTHIER: Glazed pottery candle-holder with figures of Diana and her hounds, executed at the Wiener Werkstätte, c. 1924, 36 cms. Exhibited at the 1925 Paris Exhibition. (Editions Graphiques Gallery, London)
Opposite, below
CARTER, STABLER & ADAMS: Ceramic decorated vase designed by Truda Carter, c. 1927, 14 cms. (Private Collection, London)
Below, left
KEITH MURRAY: Ceramic vase with engine-turned incisions, made by Wedgwood & Co., c. 1935. (Editions Graphiques Gallery, London)
Below, right
JOHN SKEAPING: Deer, ceramic sculpture made by Wedgwood & Co., c. 1930. (Private Collection, London)
Overleaf
GOLDSCHEIDER, VIENNA: *Tragedy.* Glazed pottery mask, c. 1922. (Editions Graphiques Gallery, London)

BIOGRAPHIES OF THE ARTISTS

ADLER, Rose. Paris (1890–1959) Paris
Bookbinder and designer. She studied bookbinding at the Ecole d'Art Décoratif of the Villa Malesherbes then in the rue Beethoven under Andrée Langrand, taking private lessons in gilding from Noulhac (1866–1931). In 1923 Jacques Doucet purchased three bindings she had exhibited at a student show in the Pavillon de Marsan, and employed her regularly until his death. She met and fell under the spell of Pierre Legrain at Doucet's and followed his principles of spare, uncluttered design and the use of abstract patterns to give free rein to the imagination as well as the use of unusual materials. She, however, modified his geometricism to a freer, less constricted line using a wide though subtle range of colours hitherto unusual in bookbinding. After Doucet's death in 1929 she continued to work for his literary foundation and other patrons and she increasingly approached figuration using crocodile, lizard and snakeskin, ivory and precious stones. She exhibited at the SAD (1925–1929) and was a founder member of the UAM. She exhibited at the Exposition Internationale du Livre (1931), with the Chareau-Cournault-

Garnier group (1934), and the International Exhibitions in Paris (1937), San Francisco (1939) and New York (1949), and was a founder member of the Société de la Reliure Originale (1947). She designed and occasionally executed furniture for Doucet and others, frequently covering the wood with tinted shagreen, reptile skin or leather. LH (1951).

ADNET, Jacques (1900-1984) & Jean. Chantillon-Coligny
Architects and interior designers. Jacques trained with Henri Rapin then went to work for Maurice Dufrêne in 1920. In 1922 the Galeries Lafayette department store set up a design studio called La Maîtrise. Maurice Dufrêne was put in charge, and Jacques joined the studio, specialising in the design of plain, simplified, functional furniture, using fine and rare woods and fine fabrics. His twin brother Jean also joined the firm, and both brothers frequently designed and exhibited together. At the 1925 Paris International Exhibition of Decorative and Industrial Arts they exhibited in the French Embassy pavilion. They also designed a wide range of highly stylised and simplified birds in white glazed ceramic. In 1928 Jean was put in charge of the window display department at the Galeries Lafayette, to which he devoted much of his life. That same year Jacques left La Maîtrise and took over the running of the Compagnie des Arts Français in succession to the founders, Süe and Mare. He soon changed the direction of the firm towards Modernism, the use of metal and glass, chromium plating and simplified geometric patterns. He carried out many important private and public commissions, and was awarded the Grand Prix for Architecture at the 1937 Paris Exhibition of Arts and Tech-

niques for his Saint-Gobain pavilion. He closed down the Compagnie des Arts Français in 1959 and was put in charge of the Ecole Nationale Supérieure d'Art Décoratif, where he remained until he retired in 1970.

ALASTAIR (Baron Hans Henning Voigt, known as).
Karlsruhe (1887-1968) Munich
Artist, dancer, composer, musician, poet and translator. A mysterious, romantic figure, he toured Europe in the years before the First World War, staying with and dancing for such people as Gabriele d'Annunzio, the Italian poet. Largely self-taught as an artist, he was launched by John Lane as the natural successor of Aubrey Beardsley, though his line was more exotic and his subjects even more decadent than Beardsley's. Highly literary in his inspiration, he illustrated a number of books for Lane in England and for Harry and Caresse Crosby's Black Sun Press in Paris and held exhibitions of his drawings and watercolours in New York, Paris and Brussels. He abandoned drawing during the harsh years from the late 30s to 1964, earning a precarious living by translating dozens of novels and other books. In the last five years of his life he finished about 150 drawings very similar in style to his early ones.

ARGY-ROUSSEAU, Gabriel. Meslay-le-Vidame, Eure-et-Loire (1885–1953) Paris
Glass artist. Born Joseph-Gabriel Rousseau, he entered the National High School for Ceramics at Sèvres in 1902, and was a fellow pupil of Jean Cros, son of the Henri Cros who had rediscovered the technique of pâte-de-verre. In 1913, after his marriage, he adopted part of his wife's surname to become Argy-Rousseau. He first exhibited his

pâte-de-verre in 1914 and, in 1921, went into partnership with G. G. Moser-Millot, who owned a retail shop in the boulevard des Italiens and financed a proper workshop. He produced a superb body of designs in opaque pâte-de-verre and the more translucent pâte-de-cristal, using animal and human as well as abstract decorative motifs. From 1909 onwards he also produced a range of enamelled scent bottles. In 1928 he executed a group of pâte-de-cristal sculptures designed by Marcel Bouraine. He exhibited at the SAF, where he was awarded an Honourable Mention (1920), a Bronze Medal (1923), a Silver Medal (1926), and a Gold Medal (1927), as well as at the SA and the SAD. At the 1925 Exhibition his pâte-de-verre was on display in the Glass Section in the Grand Palais and in the French Embassy; he was a member of the Jury for Glass and exhibited Hors Concours.

BAGGE, Eric. Anthony, Seine (1890–1978)
Architect and interior decorator who also designed fabrics and wallpapers. He exhibited at the SAD from its foundation and at the SA from 1919. At the 1925 Exhibition he designed the Hall of Jewellery in the Grand Palais after winning a contest organised by Georges Fouquet, the boudoir and bathroom in the French Embassy, the tapestries room of the Manufactures Nationales de Tapisserie des Gobelins et de Beauvais and other installations and was the official 'Rapporteur' of the International Jury, himself exhibiting Hors Concours. He was a member of the Groupe des Architectes Modernes, a member of the French Exhibitions Committee of the Société d'Encouragement à l'Art et l'Industrie and director of the Practical School for Drawing organised by the Jewellery Guild. LH.

BAKST, Léon. St. Petersburg (1866–1924) Paris
Painter and stage designer. He was a founder of the Mir Iskoustva (World of Art) group and magazine in Russia before accompanying Diaghilev's Ballets Russes to Paris in 1909. He designed costumes and settings for several ballets for Diaghilev, Ida Rubinstein and others in an exciting Eastern burst of colour and contrasts which helped transform French and other Western concepts of acceptability in interior design.

BARBIER, George. Nantes (1882–1932)
Primarily a book illustrator, he also designed fabrics, wallpapers and posters and commercial wrappings, boxes and postcards. He designed costumes and settings for several theatrical productions and for Rudolph Valentino's movie Monsieur Beaucaire. A regular contributor to La Gazette du Bon Ton, the Journal des Dames et des Modes, Fémina, Vogue, Comoedia Illustré and other journals, his illustrations were frequently reproduced in the pochoir process. His finest book illustrations were those interpreted in woodcuts by F. L. Schmied.

BASTARD, Georges. Andeville (1881–1939)
A master tabletier. He studied at the Paris Ecole des Arts Décoratifs in addition to the training he received at home from his family steeped in the crafts for several generations. He exhibited at the SAF, SA (1910–1912), and the ST

(1933 and 1934). He was awarded an Honourable Mention (1902), Medal 3rd Class (1908), 2nd Class (1909), 1st Class (1912), Travel Scholarship (1910) and LH (1925). At the 1925 Exhibition he exhibited in the tabletterie section in addition to collaborating with a number of furniture designers, including Ruhlmann and Montagnac. He was director of the Ecole des Arts Décoratifs of Limoges until 1938, when he was appointed director of the Manufacture Nationale de Porcelaine at Sèvres.

BENEDICTUS, Edouard. Paris (1878–1930)
Painter and designer. He executed bookbindings, designed various fabrics and published an album of abstract Art Deco motifs useful in decoration. He regularly designed furnishing fabrics for the firms of Tassinari et Châtel and Brunet, Meunié et Cie., and designed various ranges of carpets and carpeting. He exhibited at the SAF and was awarded a Honourable Mention (1899), Medal 3rd Class (1902), 2nd Class (1907), 1st Class (1909), LH (1921) and LHO (1926).

BENITO, Edouard Garcia. Valladolid, Spain (b. 1892)
Painter and graphic artist. He illustrated a number of books and published stylised fashion illustrations in various magazines. He also designed for advertising. He exhibited at the SNBA until 1934 and at the ST in 1923. His portraits of Paul Poiret and his wife were included in the Poiret auction sale in November 1925.

BERNARD, Joseph. Vienne, Isère (1866–1931) Paris
Sculptor. Son of a stonemason, Bernard studied briefly at the Beaux-Arts schools of Lyon and Paris and then developed on his own, eschewing modelling in favour of direct carving of marble and dry plaster, the latter then being cast in bronze. He exhibited at the SAF from 1893, the SA from 1910 to 1927 and the ST from 1923 to 1927. His awards include a Medal 3rd Class (1893), 2nd Class (1898), Honourable Mention (1900 Universal Exhibition), LH (1910) and LHO (1926). His frieze on 'The Dance' in the Ruhlmann pavilion at the 1925 Exhibition was one of several statues by him purchased by the French state. Even his smaller statues have a monumental quality about them; they are sculpted in a modified classical style stripped of excess ornamentation or detail.

BONET, Paul. Paris (b. 1889)
Bookbinder. Born of Belgian parents, he was in turn an electrician, an errand boy for his mother's millinery shop and dress designer. Wanting to have some bindings executed for his books, he found no one able to satisfy his requirements and began to design his own. He had no technical ability, so commissioned workers to execute his designs, which he exhibited at the SAD in 1925 and 1926 without great success. One collector, however, admired his designs at the 1926 SA and commissioned him to design a large number of bindings for him. Bonet soon employed the services of several superb technicians and the sale of his first patron's collection in 1930 brought him great fame and increasing orders. He was acclaimed in the 1930s and the post-war years as one of France's

greatest designers of bookbindings.

BONFILS, Robert. Paris (1886–1971)
Graphic artist painter and designer. After studying at both the Ecole des Arts Décoratifs and the Ecole des Beaux-Arts in Paris he exhibited paintings of nudes, landscapes, still lifes, flower studies and portraits at the same time as becoming a considerable graphic artist mastering all the techniques. He illustrated a vast number of books, albums and periodicals, designed some exceptionally fine bookbindings, designed porcelain for Sèvres, designed fabrics and wallpapers and executed several schemes of interior designs. He exhibited at the SA from 1909, the ST from its foundation, both until 1938, and the SAD from 1910. He was a member of the Committee of the SA and a member of the Society of Original Wood Engravers. At the 1925 Exhibition, of which he was one of the organisers, he exhibited in nine different categories in addition to designing one of the posters and the cover of the catalogue. LH.

BOUTET DE MONVEL, Bernard. Paris (1884–1949)
Drowned off the Azores
Painter and graphic artist. He was a pupil of Luc-Olivier Merson and Jean Dampt and frequently exhibited his paintings in settings by Süe et Mare, including the 1925 Exhibition in their pavilion. He exhibited at the SNBA, the SA, the ST (being a member of its committee from 1923 to 1928), the Salon des Humoristes and the 1926 retrospective of the Indépendants. LH.

BRANDT, Edgar-William. Paris (1880–1960) Paris
Smith. The son of an engineer, he followed a technical education at the Vierzon professional school, later designing and making jewellery and wrought-iron work, often in collaboration with other designers. He set up his own workshop in 1919 and always installed the newest equipment. He worked with several architects and designers, particularly Louis Favier, who designed his showroom in 1921. He exhibited at the SAF, the SAD and the SA and nearly all the International Exhibitions throughout his life. His awards include a Medal 3rd Class (1905), 2nd Class (1907), 1st Class (1908), Médaille d'Honneur (1923), many international Grand Prix, LH (1920) and LHO (1926). At the 1925 Paris Exhibition he executed the Porte d'Honneur with Favier and Ventre, a vast quantity of metalwork both inside and outside several pavilions, the French Embassy and also had his own display stand, which encouraged him to expand his showrooms to encompass a full range of decorative works and also open a New York branch.

BRANDT, Paul-Emile. La Chaux-de-Fonds, Switzerland
Jeweller. Swiss, he moved to Paris to study under Chaplain and Allard. He became a naturalised Frenchman and set up in the rue des Saints-Pères, designing and executing a range of jewellery and watches in an elegant floral Art Nouveau style which later changed to rigorously geometric patterns. He worked in gold, platinum and silver, often with lacquer, and executed a quantity of silverware and boxes. He exhibited at SA, the SAF and the 1925 Paris Exhibi-

tion. His awards include an Honourable Mention (1906), Medal 3rd Class (1911) and Gold Medal (1923) after which he exhibited Hors Concours.

BUTHAUD, René. Saintes (1886-1986)

Painter, ceramist and graphic artist. After studying at the Ecole des Beaux-Arts in Bordeaux, then in Paris, he was awarded the first Second Prix de Rome for engraving. In about 1919, encouraged by his friends Jean Dupas and Roger Bissière, he made his first essays in ceramics. He worked primarily with stoneware, though he also worked with faience and porcelain, and developed a crackled glaze. He devised broad, simple shapes giving him fine surfaces as a variety of canvas. Between 1923 and 1926 he ran the Primavera ceramics factory at Ste. Radegonde, only to return to Bordeaux to continue his own work. He exhibited portraits and landscapes at the SAF from 1911 and ceramics at the SA also from 1920. He also exhibited regularly at the Rouard Gallery in Paris from 1928 to 1961. He continued to draw and painted several pictures on mirror-glass.

BUZON, Camille-Frédéric de. Bordeaux (1885-1964)

Painter. A student of Paul Quinsac at the Ecole des Beaux-Arts in Bordeaux, he was awarded a travelling scholarship in 1906 which enabled him to travel to Spain, after which he studied under Gabriel Ferrier at the Ecole des Beaux-Arts in Paris, receiving another travelling scholarship in 1909 for his history painting. He exhibited at the Paris Salon from 1911 onwards, and was elected a member of the Société des Artistes Français. He taught painting and drawing at the Ecole des Beaux-Arts in Bordeaux from 1929 to 1955. He was greatly influenced by his brother Marius and like him was involved in the neo-classical movement centred in Bordeaux. He painted a vast fresco on the subject of the port of Bordeaux for its Labour Exchange between 1936 and 1937.

BUZON, Marius de. Bayon (1879-1958) Algiers

Painter. Like his brother Camille-Frédéric, a student of Paul Quinsac at the Ecole des Beaux-Arts in Bordeaux and Gabriel Ferrier at the Ecole des Beaux-Arts in Paris. He exhibited regularly at the SA and the ST in Paris and at the Société des Amis des Arts in Bordeaux from 1905. A frequent traveller to North Africa, he was awarded a scholarship in 1913 which enabled him to settle in Algeria. Much of his time was spent as an orientalist painter, depicting the luminous landscapes of North Africa, but he was greatly influenced by the neo-classical movement, and executed many vast decorative paintings, including one of the four huge frescoes for the Wine Pavilion at the 1925 Paris International Exhibition of Decorative and Industrial Arts, and one for the Salon des Ambassadeurs at the Palais Bourbon in Paris, and several in Bordeaux and in Algeria. He was awarded a Gold Medal at the SAF in 1922.

CARLU, Jean. Bonnières-sur-Seine (1900-1983)

Poster artist and painter. After studying to become an architect, Carlu, whose right arm had been amputated when he was barely eighteen years old, became one of the leading poster artists in the years following the First

World War. Using Cubist conventions, he devised a variety of memorable designs which varied from painted to photomontage as well as neon signs which he also pioneered. He spent the latter years of the 30s and the Second World War years designing posters in the United States, resuming his career in France in the post-war years. He also illustrated several books.

CASSANDRE (Adolphe Mouron, known as). Kharkov, Russia (1901–1968) Paris

Poster artist and typographer. Born in Russia of French parents, he arrived in Paris in 1915 and later studied at the Académie Julian. His first poster was for Boucheron in 1924 and this was rapidly followed by a group of highly inventive posters which won him the Grand Prix for posters at the 1925 Paris Exhibition. In 1927 he went into partnership with Maurice Moyrand to form a new advertising agency, the Alliance Graphique, which was later to be joined by Loupot. Using a variety of typographic, photographic and other effects, he succeeded in largely transforming the style of poster design. After Moyrand's death in 1934 Cassandre gradually abandoned poster design in favour of designing new typefaces and typographical work.

CAZAUX, Edouard. Canneilec (1889–1974) La Varenne

Ceramist and sculptor. Born into a family of potters, he was too poor to pursue his studies, so was apprenticed first to his family's works at La Negresse then at Tarbes. In 1906 he went to work in a ceramics factory in Paris while waiting to be called up for his military service. He was billeted at Mont-de-Marsan, where he took lessons in drawing in his spare time and was discovered by the sculptor Charles Despiau. On his return to Paris in 1912 he was at last able to discover the beauties of Chinese and Korean pottery while simultaneously studying sculpture with Despiau. The First World War, which he spent as a stretcher-bearer, interrupted his work, and it was not until 1919 that he was able to resume his career. Aged thirty, he married and settled at La Varenne. He executed several monuments to the War dead, and was introduced to the ST in 1922 and the SA and the SAD in 1923 by Despiau. He was appointed a Member of the Jury at the 1925 International Paris Exhibition of Modern Decorative and Industrial Arts, at which he was awarded a Silver Medal by the Society for the Encouragement of Art and Industry. He also had two one-man shows in Paris that year. From 1928 he supplied Degué with designs for art glass, generally adaptations to pressed glass of his sculptural pots. He continued to produce both stoneware in monochrome enamels (though he succeeded in mixing flambe oxblood glazes with turquoise) and Art Deco pots with abstract patterns and painted designs of nudes, animals and plants, often with crackled gold backgrounds or polychrome patterns. In 1929 he was awarded Grand Prix at the International Exhibitions in Cairo and Barcelona, in 1931 a Gold Medal at the SA, in 1933 the French Légion d'Honneur, in 1937 a Gold Medal at the Paris International Exhibition. He was by then executing monumental sculptures, including fountains and church fittings in ceramic, in addition to his smaller scale sculpture. He ex-

ecuted several decorative items for the Normandie steamship, and continued to work in both sculpture and pottery to the end of his life.

CHANAUX, Adolphe. (1887–1965)

Designer. Specialising in designing fine furniture for several of the great interior design firms in Paris, including Groult, Printz, Jean Michel Franck and Ruhlmann. These were usually signed by Chanaux and the firms for which they were supplied except those for Groult, which were normally only signed by Chanaux since Groult hardly ever signed. Some of his designs used such unusual materials as tortoiseshell and shagreen, and Marie Laurencin decorated some of his designs for André Groult. He became a partner in the firm of Jean-Michel Franck.

CHAREAU, Pierre. Bordeaux (1883–1950) New York

Architect, interior decorator and furniture designer. Born into a family of shipbuilders, Chareau studied architecture and worked for a British firm of architects in Paris. While on leave from the army during the First World War he designed a study and bedroom for his friend Dr. Jean Dalsace, which were exhibited at the SA in 1919. He turned increasingly to designing furniture and lighting fixtures with occasional architectural commissions. In 1927 he designed a Golf Club House at Beauvallon, in 1929 the reception rooms of the Grand Hotel at Tours and from 1929 to 1931 he worked with the Dutch architect Bijvoët on his masterpiece, the Glass House for Dr. Dalsace. At the 1925 Exhibition he designed the study-library in the French Embassy. Though modernist in his outlook, this was tempered by his love of fine materials and rare woods. With the fall of France in the war he went to the United States, where he designed a Nissen-hut type of house made of army surplus sheet iron for Robert Motherwell and built himself a one-room open-plan house.

CHAUCHET-GUILLERE, Charlotte. Charlesville (1878–1964)

Painter and designer. She joined the Société des Artistes Décorateurs, which had been founded by René Guilleré in 1904. Two years later she married him. In 1913 Guilleré set up a design studio called Primavera for the Printemps department store, and she became its Manager. She designed vast numbers of sober, handsome, dark-coloured room settings and furniture, much of which was exhibited in the various Salons in Paris and elsewhere. She took complete control of Primavera on the death of her husband in 1931, taking on as her assistant Colette Gueden, who took over from her in 1939.

CHAUVIN, Louis. Rochefort-sur-Mer (1889-1976)

Sculptor. He arrived in Paris at the age of eighteen to study at the Ecole des Arts Décoratifs, later studying sculpture under Antonin Mercié at the Ecole des Beaux-Arts. He very soon abstracted his sculptures to smooth, elongated, machine-inspired forms, which he exhibited at the SA and the Salon des Indépendants without marked success or recognition—a situation which turned him into a bitter recluse though he continued to produce roughly one new sculpture per year, rarely shown or sold. He was given a retrospective show at the 1962 Venice Biennale and was expected to win the Grand Prix but gave an interview on the eve of its opening in which he announced that he was not interested and expected the result to be rigged. He did not win.

CHERMAYEFF, Serge. Russia (b. 1900)
Architect and furniture designer. He was educated in England and travelled extensively through Germany, Austria, France and Holland studying their avant garde art and design. He was made joint director with Paul Follot of Waring and Gillow's department of modern French furniture, set up in 1929. His own furniture designs consisted of simple shapes with jazzy decoration, frequently painted or silver-leafed and incised or with contrasting veneers In the 1930s he began to design Modernist furniture in addition to architecture. He moved to the United States in 1933, first practising as an architect and later becoming chairman of the department of Design and professor of Architecture at Brooklyn College, New York.

CHEURET, Albert. Born in Paris
Sculptor and designer. A pupil of Perrin and Lemaire, Cheuret exhibited regularly at the SAF to which he was elected a full member in 1907. He was awarded a Medal 3rd Class in 1908. He designed a large number of light fittings of bronze and alabaster in naturalistic (storks, other birds and animals) as well as abstract shapes. At the 1925 Exhibition he designed a complete shop in addition to displaying light fittings and small bronzes.

CHIPARUS, Demetre (Dimitri Chiparus, known as). Born in Rumania
Sculptor. A student of Antonin Mercié and Jean Boucher, he exhibited at the SAI from 1914 to 1928 and was awarded an Honourable Mention in 1914. Though his figures were often cast in bronze, he specialised in chryselephantine figures in cold painted or patinated bronze and carved and tinted ivory on elaborate polychrome stepped marble or onyx bases, which were made for the Etling firm of publishers and bronze founders. He also designed a number of figures which were executed in polychrome ceramics by Etling.

COARD, Marcel. Paris (1889–1975)
Furniture designer. Having begun architectural studies which were interrupted by the First World War, Coard set up as an interior designer in 1919. His shop in the boulevard Haussmann was run on strictly commercial lines and he supplied antique furniture, reproductions and classic interiors. His own creations were reserved for a few private patrons such as Jacques Doucet, for whom he designed and executed furniture in simplified geometric shapes in rare and unusual materials or cladding including shagreen, lacquer, tinted mirror-glass, mother-of-pearl, lapis-lazuli and other hardstones; he was one of the first designers to cover furniture in stretched parchment. He also designed a number of African-inspired pieces

COLIN, Paul. Nancy (1892-1985)
Painter, poster artist and decorator. In 1923 he was chosen by Rolf de Maré as stage designer and poster artist for the Théâtre des Champs-Elysées. Two years later he did the poster for the Revue Nègre, the start of a long association with Josephine Baker, whose favourite poster artist he became. He also painted a number of variations on her dancing and on black American Jazz musicians. He designed over 500 sharply delineated and stylised posters and designed a number of costumes and stage sets for the Paris Opéra, the Comédie Française and other theatres. He exhibited at the SA and at a number of International Exhibitions including Paris 1925 and the Colonial Exhibition, where he was awarded the Grand Prix for posters. He founded a free school in which he taught the guiding principles of modern poster design. LH.

CRETTE, Georges. Créteil (1893-1969)
Bookbinder. After studying at the Ecole Estienne he became Marius-Michel's pupil, taking over his mentor's studio after his death and signing his bindings until about 1930 'Georges Cretté Successeur de Marius-Michel'. He first exhibited a range of his designs at the 1925 Paris Exhibition and later developed a range of sober designs using the most beautiful leathers, perfectly executed, devising original gold tooled designs in an extension of classical workmanship. He was awarded the Grand Prix for Bookbinding at the 1937 Paris Exhibition.

CREUZEVAULT, Louis. (1879–1958)
Bookbinder. Creuzevault took over the Dodé studio in 1904 and continued to execute plain bindings until 1914. After the war he changed to art bindings, executing highly elaborate mosaics of polychrome leathers with equally elaborate gilding. His son Henri, born in Paris in 1905, joined him when very young, and the two together designed a series of original bindings which were exhibited at the SAD, the Galliéra Museum and various International Exhibitions. Henri designed on his own from 1937 and was a founder member of the Reliure Originale society. He began to publish and deal in pictures in his gallery and finally abandoned bookbinding in favour of art dealing in 1959.

CZAKY, Joseph. Szeged, Hungary (1888–1971) Paris
Sculptor. He arrived in Paris in 1908 after studying at the Budapest School of Decorative Arts and became a naturalised Frenchman in 1914. Greatly attracted by Cubism, he was one of the first to essay the style in sculpture while never abandoning figuration, and later moved towards a smooth stylisation of shape. He exhibited at the SA from 1911, the SNBA and the ST.

DECOEUR, Emile. Paris (1876–1953) Fontenay-aux-Roses
Ceramist. He was first apprenticed to Edmond Lachenal at the age of fourteen and spent some ten years there before being allowed to collaborate sufficiently closely with his mentor to add his signature to jointly made pots. After leaving Lachenal he was briefly associated with Fernand Rumèbe, but soon set up on his own, specialising in working with stoneware, though he later worked with porcelain. He soon abandoned his early Art Nouveau designs in favour of increasing simplification, his final works being absolutely simple, symmetrical shapes, undecorated except for ravishingly coloured glazes.

DECORCHEMONT, François-Emile. Conches, Eure (1880–1971)
Pâte-de-verre and leaded glass worker. The son of a sculptor, he and his father together built a kiln and experimented with a glass paste which, treated rather like ceramics, produced opaque, thin-walled vessels, generally referred to as pâte-d'émail (enamel paste). In about 1907 Décorchemont succeeded in creating true pâte-de-verre using powdered glass which he purchased from the Cristalleries de Saint-Denis. His early Art Nouveau-inspired designs gradually gave way in the 20s to stylised fruit, flowers, animals and reptiles in the style of the day, then moving to 'monumental', simplified geometric shapes from 1928. The years from 1933 to the outbreak of war were largely devoted to leaded glass windows for churches, the glass panels being, in fact, usually pâte-de-verre. He exhibited at the SAF, the SA, the SAD and several International Exhibitions. He was awarded a Honourable Mention (1903), a Medal 3rd Class (1905), 2nd Class (1906), 1st Class (1911), a travelling scholarship (1908), LH (1920) and LHO (1926).

DELAUNAY, Robert. Paris (1885–1941) Montpellier
Painter, graphic artist and stage designer. He began his career as a stage scenery painter at the age of seventeen. Three years later he abandoned this in favour of pure painting. First attracted by neo-Impressionism, he became fascinated with Cubism without losing his primary interest in depicting light and colour. Chevreul's theories of simultaneous contrasts led him to create a prismatically brilliant and colourful series of paintings which he called simultaneous paintings, but which Guillaume Apollinaire (who had recently written Le Bestiaire, ou le cortège d'Orphée) dubbed 'Orphism'. Though independent, he greatly influenced other artists of his generation. He exhibited at the Salon des Indépendants from 1904 as well as at the ST. His painting of a woman and the Eiffel Tower (one of his favourite themes) was exhibited in the Mallet-Stevens hall in the French Embassy at the 1925 Exhibition. He worked for Diaghilev's Ballets Russes, illustrated several books and executed a number of lithographs.

DELAUNAY-TERK, Sonia. Odessa (1885–1980) Paris
Painter and designer, wife of Robert Delaunay. Following the same evolution in her painting as her husband, she began experimenting with embroidery and fabric design, transferring her painted rhythmical patterns and, in the process, transforming them into the new medium of fabrics. Her first dresses date from about 1914, but in the post-war years she opened her own fashion workshop, and designed fabrics, shawls and clothes for women and men as well as furs for Jacques Heim. She also designed for Diaghilev's Ballets Russes, and illustrated several books. She had her own boutique devoted to her designs on the Alexandre III Bridge at the 1925 Paris Exhibition. After the 1920s she concentrated more on painting, though she continued to design fabrics.

DELORME, Raphaël. Caudéran (1885–1962) Paris
Painter. After studying at the Ecole des Beaux-Arts in
Bordeaux, he became a stage designer in Paris, specialising in effects of perspective. Mme Métalier, a wealthy
cousin, offered him the hospitality of her castle at Valesnes
in the Indre-et-Loire if he would abandon the stage for easel
painting. This he did, combining his love of perspective
with handsome, fleshy, somewhat indifferent female nudes.
He exhibited at the SA, the SNBA, the ST and in one-man
shows in Tours and Bordeaux, largely unsuccessfully, and
was only 'discovered' after his death.

DESPRES, Jean. Souvigny (b. 1889)
Jeweller and silversmith. He was apprenticed as a young
boy to a silver and goldsmith in the old Marais quarter of
Paris, and also took night-classes in drawing, later essaying
painting. After the Great War he set up his own workshop
and retail shop, making and selling silver, gold and pewter
objects (tableware, vases, boxes) and jewellery in an
almost modernistic, machine-inspired style. Some of his
jewellery was designed in conjunction with miniature
paintings on glass by Etienne Cournault. He exhibited a
dressing table set at the 1925 Paris Exhibition, and exhibited regularly at the Salon des Indépendants and at
various International Exhibitions.

DESPUJOLS, Jean. Salles, Gironde (1886–1965)
Shreveport, Louisiana
Painter. After studying at the Bordeaux Ecole des Beaux-
Arts, where he was awarded the City of Bordeaux Prize
in 1910, he studied at the Paris Ecole des Beaux-Arts,
where he won the First Grand Prix de Rome for painting
in 1914, though he was only able to take up study-
residence in Rome after the end of the war. In Rome he
became close to Jean Dupas and Robert Eugène
Poughéon, both of whom had also won Rome prizes, and
with them founded the French neo-classical style of the
interwar years. He taught painting at the Fontainebleau
American School of Art from 1924 to 1936, then travelled
extensively throughout the Far East before finally settling
in the United States, becoming an American citizen in
1945. He exhibited at the SAF, the Salon des
Indépendants and the ST. He was awarded an Honourable Mention (1931) and a Gold Medal (1935). He
later composed music, wrote poetry, essays on philosophy
and metaphysics, and published six illustrated autobio-
graphical volumes.

D. I. M. (Décoration Intérieure Moderne)
Interior designers. Founded after the First World War by
Joubert and Mouveau. Joubert was the moving force, with
several years of pre-war experience with the decorating
firm of Jansen. Mouveau, whose previous experience had
been entirely connected with stage design, left the firm in
1924 to return to the stage, and was replaced by Philippe
Petit, a former student at the Ecole Bernard Palissy. The
firm, now frequently referred to as Joubert et Petit, undertook a wide range of commissions, and went in for both
extremely costly and relatively cost-conscious schemes.
Joubert and Petit designed furniture both individually and
together, executed in the firm's works. Their costlier de-

signs involved the use of rare veneer, marquetry and
parquetry panels and ivory and mother-of-pearl inlays, and
their workmanship was of the finest quality. Petit, who was
a fine draughtsman, generally drew all their schemes on
paper in gouache and watercolour. D. I. M. had its own
boutique on the Alexandre III Bridge at the 1925 Exhibition, and designed the dining room in the French Embassy.

DJO-BOURGEOIS. Bezons, Seine-et-Oise (1898–1937)
Architect and interior designer. He was a student and
disciple of Robert Mallet-Stevens and worked for the
Studium-Louvre for several years. At the 1925 Exhibition
he designed the study in the Studium Louvre pavilion. He
really came into his own after 1926, designing built-in
furniture with frequent use of metal on rigorously plain and
uncluttered lines. He also designed several private homes
and apartment buildings.

DOMERGUE, Jean Gabriel. Bordeaux (1889–1962) Paris
Painter. Studied at the Ecole des Beaux-Arts under Tony
Robert-Fleury, Jules Lefebvre, Adler, Humbert and Flameng,
and won the Prix de Rome in 1913. His early landscapes
gave way to portraits of celebrities and beautiful women,
and he soon developed a characteristic style, elongating
his models, all of whom develop long, slender necks, long,
slender and shapely arms and legs, sensual lips and eyes
and adopt elegant clothes and posture. He exhibited at
the SAF from 1906, receiving an Honourable Mention
(1908), a 3rd Class Medal (1912) and a Gold Medal
(1920). He also exhibited at the Royal Academy in London
and the Carnegie Institute in Pittsburgh. He was elected
to the Académie des Beaux-Arts in 1950, and became
Curator of the Jacquemart-André Museum in Paris in 1956
   He illustrated several books with original etchings and
lithographs, frequently in colour. LH.

DOMINIQUE
Interior designers. Founded in 1922 by André Domin
(1883-1962) and Marcel Genevrière (1885-1967), who
designed fairly elegant Art Deco furniture, frequently in a
moderate price bracket. They designed and furnished Jean
Puiforcat's home as well as the Houbigant perfume factory
at Neuilly. They frequently used shagreen, parchment and
leathers to cover their furniture, which gradually moved
towards more simplified and more geometric lines. At the
1925 Exhibition they designed the salon in the French
Embassy (Private Section), in addition to their contribution
in the Musical Instruments, Arts of the Street and other
Sections. After 1926 they joined with Pierre Chareau,
Pierre Legrain, Jean Puiforcat and Raymond Templier to
exhibit at the Galerie Barbazanges as the Groupe des
Cinq (Group of Five). Domin also illustrated a number of
books and periodicals and designed some advertisements,
posters and brochures.

DRESA (André Saglio, known as). Versailles (1869–1929)
Painter and decorator. He designed several stage productions for the Paris Opera and other theatres, designed
fabrics and wallpapers for André Groult and others, and
wrote a number of books on the arts. He worked for a
number of years in the Beaux-Arts administration, or-

ganising exhibitions of French art in other countries. He
exhibited paintings, watercolours and costume designs at
the SAF, the ST, and the 1900 Paris Exhibition, when he
was awarded a Bronze Medal, and at the 1925 Paris
Exhibition.

DUBOST, Michel. Lyon (1879–1952) Grasse
Fabrics designer. A student at the Lyon Ecole des Beaux-
Arts, he specialised in textiles, eventually teaching there
and at the School of Weaving (Ecole de Tissage). From
1922 to 1933 he worked for François Ducharne, the
textile manufacturer, in Paris, designing patterns based on
nature until his meeting with Edouard Monod-Herzen
opened the doors of abstraction and geometrical design
to him. Ducharne later published an album of Dubost's
designs with a preface by Colette.

DUCHAMP-VILLON, Raymond. Damville, Eure (1876–
1918) Cannes
Sculptor. Brother of Raymond Duchamp and Jacques Villon,
he abandoned medicine for sculpture, exhibited at the
SNBA and the SA. Influenced by Cubism, he attempted
to apply its analytical methods to sculpture, and pursued
a few themes over and over again, particularly his ob-
sessive development of the depiction of his 'Grand Cheval'
(Great Horse). In 1912 he designed the façade of the
'Cubist House' which André Mare furnished at the SA. He
died in 1918 of wounds received in the latter stages of
the war.

DUFAU, Clémentine-Hélène. Quinsac, Gironde (b. 1879)
Painter. Arriving in Paris in 1889, she studied at the
Académie Julian and with Bougereau and Tony Robert-
Fleury, developing great sensuality in her treatment of
women and a talent for large, decorative compositions.
She exhibited at the SAF, was a founder member of the
SA, exhibited at the Galerie Manzi Joyant from 1900, the
ST from 1926, and was awarded an Honourable Mention
(1895), the Marie Bashkirtseff Prize (1895), a Medal 3rd
Class (1897), Travel Scholarship (1898), Silver Medal
(1900 Paris Universal Exhibition), Medal 2nd Class
(1902) and LH (1909). She also designed a number of
lithographed posters.

DUFET, Michel. Déville-lès-Rouen (1888-1985)
Interior designer and journalist. After studying painting and
architecture at the Ecole des Beaux-Arts, he founded the
M. A. M. (Mobilier Artistique Moderne) in 1913 to
manufacture modern furniture, which he exhibited at the
SAD and the SA from 1919. In 1924, after closing down
his firm, he founded the art periodical *Feuillets d'Art* and
became editor in chief of another magazine, *Décor
d'Aujourd'hui*. He also ran, simultaneously, the Red Star
firm of interior decorators in Rio de Janeiro and Le Sylve,
the newly set up design gallery of Le Bûcheron in Paris,
which exhibited and sold a wide range of furniture, carpets, objets d'art and pictures. Among his more important
commissions were those for the liners Foch, Ile-de-France
and Normandie, and the layout of the Antoine Bourdelle
Museum. He attempted to design for mass-production, but
with little interest from manufacturers and retailers, so the

bulk of his production was in the medium to expensive range.

DUFRENE, Maurice. Paris (1876–1955) Nogent-sur-Marne
Interior decorator. He began working for Julius Meier-Graefe's Maison Moderne in 1899 while still a student at the Ecole des Arts Décoratifs, and there learned the practical side of designing complete interiors. Though working for an Art Nouveau gallery, he tended to use Art Nouveau ornamentation sparingly, and by 1906 was designing furniture in fairly plain, solid shapes with a minimum of ornament. He was also designing stoneware and porcelain for Dalpayrat, as well as objects in wood, metal, glass and leather. He was a founder member of the SAD in 1902, regularly exhibiting there as well as at the SA, was awarded an Honourable Mention in 1900, and taught at the Ecole Boulle from 1912 to 1923. In 1921 he was put in charge of the newly created La Maîtrise design workshop at the Galeries Lafayette, and himself designed furniture, fabrics, carpets, wallpapers, silverware, glassware, ceramics and complete schemes. He designed the interior of the La Maîtrise pavilion at the 1925 Exhibition. LH (1920), LHO (1926).

DUFRESNE, Charles Georges. Millemont (1876–1938)
Painter and designer. Studied sculpture and painting at the Ecole des Beaux-Arts, then spent two years in Algiers on a scholarship. He was a founder member of the SI in 1923 and, a year later, designed some tapestries for Süe et Mare, who used them to upholster a suite of furniture exhibited at the 1925 Paris Exhibition. He was then commissioned by the Mobilier National to design a set of upholstery tapestries for a suite of furniture, and chose a sequence based on the story of Paul and Virginie, which was woven at the Beauvais manufactory. He also exhibited at the SNBA from 1910, the SA and at the Salon des Indépendants, designed sets and costumes for 'Antar' at the Odéon, painted strange Cubist-orientated jungle scenes, and executed a large number of etchings. He consistently refused all honours and awards except the Carnegie Prize, awarded in Pittsburgh.

DUFY, Raoul. Le Havre (1877–1953) Forcalquier
Painter, designer and graphic artist. He illustrated a number of books with woodcuts, etchings and lithographs. In 1911 Paul Poiret commissioned him to design fabrics, and set up a studio for him. A year later he moved to Bianchini-Férier, for whom he designed dress and upholstery fabrics until 1930, as well as printed panels. In 1925 he designed fourteen large hangings for Poiret's houseboats moored within the Exhibition area. From 1930 to 1933 he designed printed silks for Onondaga of New York. He also executed a series of lithographs as fashion designs using his fabrics for La Gazette du Bon Ton. He exhibited at the SAF from 1901, then at the SA, the Salon des Indépendants, and a vast number of group and one-man shows and exhibitions. At the 1937 Paris International Exhibition he painted what was then the world's largest picture, 60 metres x 10 metres, on the subject of electricity for the Pavilion of Light.

DUNAND, Jean. Lancy, Switzerland (1877–1942) Paris
Dinandier, lacquerer, painter and designer. After studies at the Geneva School of International Art and a period of apprenticeship with the sculptor Jean Dampt in Paris, he worked as a sculptor until 1902, and began to work as a coppersmith a year later. Using all the techniques open to him, he produced a range of hammered, encrusted, inlaid and etched vessels varying from Art Nouveau designs to increasingly geometric patterning. In 1912 he began to experiment with lacquerwork and, in 1919, set up a large workshop to deal with both lacquerwork and dinanderie. He introduced the use of eggshell into lacquer, which he also used to extend the possibilities of dinanderie, and designed and executed furniture, panels, screens and jewellery in addition to supplying lacquer panels for other furniture designers, such as Ruhlmann, Legrain and Printz, and commissioning designs from friends. At the 1925 Exhibition he designed the smoking room in the French Embassy, and supplied lacquer panels for many other displays. He supplied lacquer panels for several ocean liners.

DUPAS, Jean. Bordeaux (1882–1964) Paris
Painter. He studied at the Bordeaux Ecole des Beaux-Arts, then at the Paris one under Gabriel Ferrier. Awarded the First Grand Prix de Rome in 1910, he studied in Rome under Carolus Duran and Albert Besnard, and later made friends there with Robert Poughéon and Jean Despujols, leading them into the neo-classicism he was developing. He exhibited regularly at the SAF and was awarded an Honourable Mention (1909), Medal 3rd Class (1910) and Gold Medal (1922). At the 1925 Exhibition his large decorative panel Les Perruches was the focal point of the salon in Ruhlmann's pavilion, in which several more paintings of his were hung. His large painting on the subject of La Vigne et le Vin (Vine and Wine) was hung in the Bordeaux Wine Tower pavilion. He painted both easel paintings and murals, designed a number of posters and illustrated books, periodicals and brochures, and executed a number of paintings on glass panels for the liners Ile de France (1930), Normandie (1935) and Liberté (1949). He was elected to the French Institute in 1941, taught painting at the Ecole des Beaux-Arts from 1942 to 1954, and was curator of the Marmottan Museum in Paris. LH (1926).

ERTE (Romain de Tirtoff, known as). St. Petersburg (1892–1990) Paris
Graphic artist. Studied with Ilya Repine in St. Petersburg, architecture at Cronstadt, then painting at the Académie Julian in Paris, before going to work for Paul Poiret in 1913 as fashion designer, along with José de Zamora. He also provided a number of fashion illustrations for La Gazette du Bon Ton before moving to Monte Carlo in 1914, where he lived for eight years, supplying Harper's Bazaar with a vast number of covers, fashion illustrations and a regular illustrated column. He also designed costumes and sets for the Folies Bergère and other theatres, nightclubs and revues, including George White's Scandals and the Ziegfeld Follies, and designed collections of clothes for the New York fashion house of Henri Bendel and for B.

Altman & Co. In 1920 he designed the sets and costumes for the movie Restless Sex, starring Marion Davies and financed by William Randolph Hearst, while he spent most of 1925 in Hollywood under contract with M. G. M., designing both costumes and sets for a number of actresses and films. In 1929 and 1930 he designed a collection of fabrics and dress models for the Amalgamated Silk Corporation of New York. He remained busily designing for theatre, opera, music hall, film, advertising and magazine and book illustrations, cleverly retaining the majority of his original drawings until the major resurgence of his fame which started in the middle 1960s.

FEURE, Georges de (George Joseph van Sluijters, known as). Paris (1868–1943)
Painter and decorator. His early career as a great Symbolist painter, watercolourist and illustrator, poster artist, and designer of Art Nouveau furniture, fabrics, stained glass, wallpapers—much of it for S. Bing's L'Art Nouveau—as well as glass and ceramics was rounded off when he became professor of Decorative Arts at the Ecole Nationale des Beaux-Arts. As fashion turned away from Art Nouveau he left for England, spending several years there as a stage designer. He was back in France in the 20s, his major commission in 1924 being the design and furnishing of Madeleine Vionnet's fashion house in the avenue Montaigne, for which he designed carpets, stained glass panels, large decorative frescoes, moulded glass lights, mirrors, fabrics and all the furniture, with special display areas for furs and lingerie and eighteen changing cubicles, each with a different character. He continued to design furniture, frequently ornamented with stylised figuration, women's fashions, stage costumes, and essayed some ceramic designs combining traditional Dutch patterns with modern stylisation. At the 1925 Paris Exhibition he designed and decorated the Roubaix & Tourcoing pavilion, which displayed the clothing, curtains and upholstery fabrics from these areas.

FOLLOT, Paul. Paris (1877–1941) Sainte Maxime
Interior decorator. A student of Eugène Grasset, whom he was to succeed as professor of decorative arts at the rue Vavin school, he joined Meier-Graefe's Maison Moderne in 1901, there meeting Maurice Dufrêne. A firm believer in reinterpretation of traditional design in a contemporary idiom, he began by designing sensible furniture with Art Nouveau decoration, modified the decoration over the years to stylised floral, fruit and garland designs, then gradually moved towards lacquer, marquetry and ivory inlays. He always preferred to design complete room settings, the wood carvings in his furniture designs executed by his friend Laurent Malclès, while painted panels or pictures hung on the walls were normally by his wife, Hélène Follot. He exhibited at the SNBA, the SAF, the SAD and the SA, receiving an Honourable Mention in 1905. In 1923 he became director of Pomone, the design studio of Au Bon Marché department store, and continued to design everything from furniture to fabrics, wallpapers (his father had been a leading wallpaper manufacturer), carpets and ceramics. Several of his designs for tableware were executed in England by Wedgwood & Co. At the

1925 Exhibition he designed the interior of the Pomone pavilion, the antechamber at the French Embassy, and the Textiles Section in the Grand Palais with René Crevel. In 1929 he became co-director with Serge Chermayeff of the Modern French Furniture design section of Waring & Gillow, an English firm which had long been established in Paris. His designs became much simpler, using contrasts of finely figured woods, and gradually moved towards Modernist lines.

FOUJITA, Tsuguharu. Tokyo (1886–1968) Paris
Painter and graphic artist. Studied at the Tokyo Imperial School of Fine Arts, sold a picture for the emperor's collection and painted the portrait of the emperor of Korea in 1911 before travelling to London in 1912 and to Paris the following year. Painting, drawing and etching in a uniquely personal style, he depicted beautifully stylised nudes and cats as well as larger and complex compositions, and became totally involved in the social and intellectual life of Paris. He exhibited at the SA, the ST and private galleries, decorated the Japanese House at the Cité Universitaire and the Barroom at the Cercle Interallié, was elected to membership of the Tokyo Fine Arts Academy and, in 1919, president of the Association of Japanese Artists in Paris. At the 1925 Paris Exhibition he was a member of the Jury. He illustrated a number of books, two albums of etchings, a number of individual etchings and lithographs and a few lithograph posters. LH.

FRANCK, Jean Michel. Paris (1893–1941) New York
Designer. He first established himself by executing the furniture for the living room for the Vicomte de Noailles in 1927. Never exhibiting in the Salons or in galleries, he designed geometric furniture using rare and costly woods in conjunction with materials like shagreen, parchment, leather, bronze, copper, brass or mica. A characteristic invention was his use of straw marquetry, used on furniture, as well as cladding in a variety of patterns, such as sunburst or fan-shapes. Executed for a small number of wealthy patrons such as Guerlain, Elsa Schiaparelli or Nelson Rockefeller, they were never the subject of any publicity. In 1935, however, Franck opened a shop in the rue Saint-Honoré in Paris with his partner, Chanaux, who executed Franck's designs. He commissioned both furniture and decorative items from various Surrealist artists, including Alberto and Diego Giacometti, Christian Bérard and Salvador Dali. Franck left for the United States shortly before the outbreak of the Second World War.

GESMAR, Charles. (1900–1928)
Poster artist and stage designer. Attached himself as a star-struck youth to the actress Spinelli. Dismissed by her, he attempted to commit suicide, but was taken up by Mistinguett, to whom he devoted himself for the rest of his short life. He designed the most extravagant costumes for her, executed in the workshop set up in the Moulin Rouge by Miss and himself, and was her constant companion and chaperone. Miss, who always called him 'maman' (mother), referred to him as 'her whole family'. He also designed her posters, some stage sets, and several pro-gramme covers for the Casino de Paris and the Moulin Rouge.

GOULDEN, Jean. Charpentry, Meuse (1878–1947) Reims
Enameller. Born into a wealthy farming family, he studied medicine in Paris. While working in the Paris hospitals, he spent his spare time meeting a number of artists, and following his hobbies of painting and music. As a medical officer during the First World War, he was sent on the Macedonian Campaign. After the war he spent some months living in the Monastery on Mount Athos, where he discovered the beauty of Byzantine enamels and ikons. On his return to France he prevailed on Jean Dunand to teach him the techniques of enamelling, and specialised in champlevé enamelling. He became very friendly with Dunand, Jouve and Schmied, and frequently acted as their patron. In 1925 he married Schmied's daughter. The four artists exhibited together as a group at the Georges Petit Gallery. In 1927 he left Paris to settle in Reims, where he continued to execute enamelled boxes, lamps, clocks and other objects decorated in random geometric patterns.

GOUPY, Marcel. Paris (b. 1886)
Designer. After studying architecture, sculpture and interior decoration at the Ecole des Arts Décoratifs in Paris, he essayed painting and worked as a silversmith and jew-eller until 1909, when he met Georges Rouard, who had recently opened the Maison Geo. Rouard in the avenue de l'Opéra. He joined Rouard as artistic director, a post he retained until 1954, designed a large variety of utilitarian and decorative glass, much of it enamelled, some both inside and out, as well as often matched porcelain or other ceramics, most of it made by Théodore Haviland at Limoges. He also designed silver. He exhibited his designs at the 1923 Exhibition of Contemporary Decorative Arts, and at the 1925 Paris Exhibition he displayed a wide range of his works in various pavilions as well as in the Rouard boutique, and was vice-president of the Glass Jury.

GRAY, Eileen. Enniscorthy, Eire (1879–1976) Paris
Designer and architect. After studying the rudiments of lacquering in London, she studied the intricacies of the art in Paris under a noted Japanese lacquerer, Sougawara. She designed some exceptionally fine lacquer furniture for a few discerning patrons, notably Jacques Doucet and Suzanne Talbot, some of which she exhibited at the SAD and the SA. In 1922 she opened her gallery under the name of Galerie Jean Désert, in which she exhibited her lacquered furniture, screens, small objects and rugs which she designed from about 1910. These were executed in her studio under the direction of Evelyn Wyld, who left in 1927 to set up a partnership with an American painter and furniture designer called Eyre de Lanux. Eileen Gray began to design tubular steel furniture in about 1925, though her increasing geometrisation of design and use of abstract patterns were obvious in the room setting she designed for the 1923 SAD which brought her work to the attention of J. J. P. Oud, a leading De Stijl architect, and led to a special number of the Dutch magazine Wendingen being devoted to her work in June 1924. She became increasingly interested in architecture, closed down her gallery in 1930 and thereafter concentrated on architecture with Jean Badovici, the editor of Architecture Vivante, an avant garde publication, until his death, then on her own. She continued to design very advanced furniture capable of mass-production, but this did not go into actual production until she was in her nineties.

GROMAIRE, Marcel. Noyelles-sur-Sambre, Nord (1892–1971) Paris
Painter and graphic artist. Close to the followers of Matisse and impressed by Cubism, he was largely self-taught and devised his own pictorial language, remaining firmly apart from all dogmatic movements. He remained staunchly figurative, with a touch of Cubism and Expressionism, and executed an exceptional body of etchings including some to illustrate books. He depicted scenes of the First World War, scenes of peasant life, industrial scenes, landscapes and some powerful nudes.

GROULT, André. (1881–1967)
Interior decorator. A sensitive decorator who sought to harmonise colour, pattern and design of each room setting not only with every aspect within it, but also with the room's function (i.e., a man's room should be seen to be 'masculine', a woman's to be 'feminine', a dining room should invite one to gourmandise, etc.). He first exhibited at the 1910 SA and SAD, and commissioned a cross-section of painters and designers to produce a range of new and colourful fabric designs. He was married to Paul Poiret's sister Nicole, who set up her own fashion house which she decorated and supplied with original fabric designs. Related to Marie Laurencin, he incorporated her paintings in many of his design schemes, and himself designed painted frames which frequently incorporated strips of tinted mirror-glass for her pictures. At the 1925 Exhibition he designed the lady's bedroom in the French Embassy, and parts of the Fontaine and Christofle/Baccarat pavilions, and participated in the design of the Musical Instrument and Art of the Garden Sections in the Grand Palais.

GRUBER, Jacques. Sundhausen, Alsace (1870–1936) Paris
Stained glass artist. Gruber was one of the most distinguished Art Nouveau artists. A pupil of Gustave Moreau at the Paris Ecole des Beaux-Arts on a Nancy scholarship, he worked for the glassmaking firm of Daum Frères from 1894 to 1897, designing some exceptionally complex figurative vases, taught Decorative Art at the Nancy Ecole des Beaux-Arts, designed furniture for Majorelle, ceramics for Mougin Frères and bookbindings for René Wiener, painted, and was one of the founders of the School of Nancy. Among his pupils were Paul Colin (the poster designer), and the brothers Jean Lurçat (painter and designer of tapestries) and André Lurçat (architect). In 1900 he set up his own workshop to design and manufacture furniture, acid-etched cameo glass panels which he incorporated in his furniture, and stained glass. He closed down at the outbreak of war in 1914, reopening in Paris

to concentrate solely on religious and secular stained glass, no longer in his pre-war Art Nouveau style but in a fully stylised geometricism which, however, never abandoned figuration. His son Jean-Jacques Gruber joined him and took over his studio after his death. He exhibited at the SAD from 1908, the SAF, the SA and the Galliéra Museum and was awarded an Honourable Mention (1911), a Bronze Medal (1920), a Silver Medal (1921), a Gold Medal (1923) and LH (1924). At the 1925 Exhibition stained glass panels designed by him were to be found on a number of pavilions and were also on display in the Stained Glass Section.

GUILLEMARD, Marcel. Paris (1886–1932)
Designer. Employed as a furniture designer at the Krieger firm, he and his fellow designer Louis Sognot were hired by René Guilleré for his newly founded Primavera Design Studio. Guillemard was to become head of its Design and Decoration division from 1918 to 1929. His designs evolved from historicism to contemporary classicism through Cubist shapes, ending in a mildly modernist use of metal in conjunction with wood.

GUILLERE, René. (1878–1931)
Decorator. Worked for several years for the Société des Sculpteurs-Modeleurs, rising to become their lawyer and counsel. In 1901 he founded the Société des Artistes Décorateurs, becoming its president in 1911. He persuaded, with some difficulty, the Board of Directors of the Printemps department store to set up a design studio to encourage modern design and decoration. He set this up in 1913, and remained in overall charge for the rest of his life, appointing his wife, Charlotte Chauchet-Guilleré as manager, and hiring excellent designers as well as working with fine individual artists.

HEILIGENSTEIN, Auguste. Saint-Denis (1891–1976) Montreuil
Glass and ceramics designer. Apprenticed in the Legras glassworks at the age of eleven, he studied various aspects of design and decoration there, at Prestat and at the Baccarat works, working as a commercial artist after 1910. During the war he was awarded the military LH in 1917. In 1919 he joined the firm of Geo. Rouard, where he executed enamelled glass to Goupy's designs, all signed by Goupy. In 1923 he left Rouard, married the ceramist Odette Chatrousse and pursued a twin career in enamelled glass and ceramics, exhibiting at Rouard's gallery until 1926 when he switched to Edgar Brandt's gallery. He executed glass with enamelled decoration by Bakst for Mrs. Florence Blumenthal, designed a range of glass for Pantin (1931–1935) and exhibited at the SAF, where he was awarded an Honourable Mention (1923), a Gold Medal (1924) and a Medal of Honour (1947). LHO (1960).

HENRY, Hélène. Champagney (1891–1965)
Textile designer. Self-taught painter and amateur musician, she set up a workshop in Paris in 1918 equipped with hand looms to produce modern fabrics to her own design, alternating abstract printed patterns with textured ones. She supplied upholstery fabrics to several friends who were furniture designers, including Emile-Jacques Ruhlmann, Pierre Chareau, Maurice Dufrêne, Francis Jourdain and Robert Mallet-Stevens, and her fabrics appeared in several pavilions at the 1925 Exhibition. She was a founder member of the UAM in 1930, and later received a number of state commissions for national monuments.

HERBST, René. Paris (1891-1982)
Architect and interior designer. After working in architectural practices in London and Frankfurt, he settled in Paris to become a leader of those who believed in functionalism and rejected unnecessary ornamentation. He exhibited in all the International Exhibitions, and was a member of the Jury at the 1925 Paris Exhibition, where he also designed a number of shopfronts and interiors. He was the leader of the group which walked out of the SAD to found the UAM in 1930.

IRIBE, Paul. Angoulême (1883–1935) Menton
Painter and designer. He began his career by supplying cartoons and illustrations to a variety of publications, including L'Assiette au Beurre and, in 1908, founded his own Le Témoin (The Witness), to which André Lhote, Raoul Dufy, Sem and Jean Cocteau contributed. He illustrated an album of fashion plates for Paul Poiret, which was sent to all the 'great ladies of Europe', then set up a decorating studio in which he designed furniture, fabrics, wallpaper and objets d'art, his great patron being Jacques Doucet, who commissioned him to entirely design and furnish his new apartment at 46 avenue du Bois. Iribe employed Pierre Legrain as his assistant. In 1914 Iribe left for the United States, and there worked as a theatrical designer, as well as working in Hollywood for Cecil B. De Mille and other producers. On his return to France he illustrated a number of books and periodicals, including a trilogy for Nicolas wines, designed costume jewellery for his very close friend Chanel, and in 1935 founded another chauvinist magazine, Le Mot.

JALLOT, Léon. Nantes (1874-1967)
Furniture designer. After some years as manager of the furniture workshops at Bing's L'Art Nouveau, he set up on his own in 1903, designing and manufacturing not only furniture, but fabrics, carpets, tapestries and screens, and drew the plans for his own house and for that of André Derain. His son Maurice Jallot, who had studied at the Ecole Boulle, joined him in 1921, and the two jointly designed a wide variety of furniture, etc. The actual furniture shapes are of the simplest, providing large flat surfaces which were either lacquered, painted or covered in shagreen or leather, sometimes with a simple geometric design. At the 1925 Exhibition he supplied furniture for the Grand Salon designed by Henri Rapin and Pierre Selmersheim and decorated the man's bedroom with Georges Chevalier, both in the French Embassy. In the late 20s the Jallots made increasing use of synthetic materials and metal in their designs.

JANNIOT, Alfred. Paris (1889–1965)
Sculptor. Awarded a First Grand Prix de Rome for Sculpture, he met Jean Dupas at the Villa Medicis there, becoming a firm friend. Encouraged by Dupas, he settled in Bordeaux, where he was befriended by a group of artists which included René Buthaud and Raphael Delorme. He adapted their neo-classical style to sculpture, becoming Bordeaux's unofficial 'official' sculptor. At the 1925 Paris International Exhibition of Decorative and Industrial Arts he exhibited a massive group, supplied two bas reliefs for the Nice Monument to the war dead in 1928, and an extensive one for the Colonial Palace built for the 1931 Colonial Exhibition in Paris. He executed a number of commissions in Bordeaux, including a bas-relief for the Employment Exchange in 1936. An over-life-size statue of an athlete, commissioned for the Bordeaux municipal stadium was, however, never placed there.

JAULMES, Gustave-Louis. Lausanne (1873–1959) Paris
Painter and designer. He studied architecture before specialising in decorative painting which he exhibited at the SNBA from 1906, the SA from 1908, and the Salon des Artistes Indépendants from 1909. In 1910 he began exhibiting furniture, in 1915 he began to design tapestries: one of his tapestries, executed at the Gobelin works, was a gift of the French government in 1919 to the City of Philadelphia, Pa. In 1918 he, André Mare and Louis Süe were jointly commissioned to decorate the avenue des Champs-Elysées and build a cenotaph for the victory celebrations. When Süe and Mare founded the Compagnie des Arts Français, Jaulmes joined as a leading designer of tapestries and upholstery fabrics, generally executed by his wife, as well as furniture and murals. At the 1925 Exhibition Jaulmes decorated the Salle des Fêtes in the Grand Palais (with Süe as architect), the Salon d'Honneur in the Sèvres pavilion, exhibited furniture and paintings in the Süe et Mare pavilion, and paintings in the Ruhlmann pavilion and the Grand Salon in the French Embassy. He painted the curtain for the Lyon Municipal Theatre and painted murals for the Rodin Museum and the Musée des Arts Décoratifs in Paris.

JENSEN, Georg. Raavad, Denmark (1866–1935) Copenhagen
Silversmith, jeweller, potter and sculptor. After studying under Mogens Ballin and at the Copenhagen Academy from 1887 to 1892, he practised as a potter and sculptor before becoming a silversmith. His company soon expanded considerably, with retail outlets in several cities. He exhibited forty-nine silver items in the 1913 SA and was awarded a First Prize at the San Francisco World's Fair in 1915. Though he only briefly worked with gold, his silver and jewellery designs established him as one of the leading creative designers in his field.

JOURDAIN, Francis. Paris (1876-1958)
Painter, graphic artist and designer. The son of Frantz Jourdain, he was largely self-taught, though he briefly studied with Eugène Carrière and Albert Besnard. He exhibited luminous paintings, many of mysterious floral gardens, and mastered the complex techniques of etching in colour, exhibiting at the SNBA and the SA, and was awarded a Grand Prix at the 1911 International Exhibi-

tion in Turin. In 1912 he opened his Ateliers Modernes (Modern Workshops) to design and build plain simple furniture adapted to the shrinking modern environment and usually adaptable to mass-production. By the end of the war this had expanded to a fully operational factory with a separate showroom and retail shop. He designed furniture, fabrics, wallpapers and ceramics, and tackled everything from apartments to offices, factories, aeroplanes or railway carriages. At the 1925 Exhibition he designed the smoking room and gymnasium in the French Embassy, as well as a smoking carriage commissioned by the Paris-Orléans railway company for the Exhibition. He was a founder member of the UAM, which was largely based on principles he had advocated for years.

JOURDAIN, Frantz. Antwerp (1847–1935)
Architect, writer and critic. Firmly committed to all forms of art, he was a champion of the avant garde and campaigned for a long time to found the SA, of which he was the first president, dedicated to being a showcase for all that was new or had been hitherto neglected. As an architect, he designed the striking Samaritaine department store in its original form, though his son was involved in its later transformation into an Art Deco idiom. LHO.

JOUVE, Paul. Marlotte, Seine-et-Marne (1880–1973)
Painter, illustrator, ceramist and sculptor. Totally fascinated by animals, particularly the great cats, then the elephants, then birds of prey, he devoted his life to depicting them. He exhibited a painting of Ethiopian lions at the SNBA at the age of fifteen, and was barely eighteen when he designed the great ceramic frieze of animals for the Binet gate at the 1900 Paris Universal Exhibition. He studied the beasts at the Paris, Antwerp and Hamburg zoos, then travelled to Algeria on a scholarship, spending three years there. He illustrated Kipling's *Jungle Book*, his many drawings being cut on wood by F. L. Schmied. This book, which needed several years of gestation, was only published in 1918, by which time he was on his way to Cambodia to research elephants for his illustrations of Pierre Loti's *Un Pèlerin d'Angkor* (A Pilgrim from Angkor). He illustrated a number of books, painted and etched a variety of beasts, and designed panels for Jean Dunand. He exhibited at the Georges Petit Gallery with Dunand, Goulden and Schmied.

KIS, Paul.
Smith. Born in Belafalva in Rumania, he travelled throughout Europe before settling in Paris, where he soon established himself as a leading designer in wrought metal. Early exuberant designs gave way to geometric patterns derived from Cubism, and he exhibited his wares at the SAD from 1922 onwards. Established in the rue Léon-Delhomme (15e) in Paris, where he maintained workshops and a display gallery, he set up a personal commercial stand on the Alexandre III bridge at the 1925 International Exhibition of Modern Decorative and Industrial Arts. He executed a number of commissions for various firms, including that of Paul Poiret, and created a sensation at the 1926 SAD by displaying a complete room setting in which all the furniture, lighting and accessories were made of

matching wrought iron. He executed a number of wrought-iron light fittings in conjunction with glass executed by Sabino, Lalique and other firms. His public commissions included some monumental gates for the King of Thailand's Palace in Bangkok.

LAHALLE, Pierre. (1877–1956)
Furniture designer and interior decorator. He began designing furniture in about 1902 in association with Maurice Lucet, and they were later joined by Alfred Levard, a graduate of the Ecole des Arts Décoratifs. While their earlier designs were strongly influenced by Art Nouveau, they soon moved towards Art Deco, shapes based on eighteenth-century designs, simplified and stylised, using fine figured woods with inlays of ivory and mother-of-pearl, and made use of dramatic colour contrasts in lacquer, polychrome painting and gilding. The three worked together and separately, frequently exhibiting at the SA and the SAD. Lahalle and Levard designed furniture for the Studium-Louvre, often in collaboration with André Fréchet; Levard occasionally designed for Primavera.

LALIQUE, René. Ay, Marne (1860–1945) Paris
Jeweller, sculptor, painter, glass designer. At the turn of the century he was recognised as the leading Art Nouveau jeweller, and as a distinguished sculptor in bronze, ivory and silver. He began to experiment with glass, designed a moulded glass panelled door for his house, and designed a series of scent bottles as well as sculptures which were executed in glass. He used two methods, cire perdue (lost wax) casts and moulded glass, and held his first all-glass exhibition in 1912. The outbreak of war interrupted his activity, and he was never to produce precious jewellery again. His small glassworks at Combs-la-Ville was insufficient to start a new career (at the age of fifty-eight) so he purchased a new one at Wingen-sur-Moder, close to the German border. He there perfected semi-industrial techniques, both blowing into moulds and using a stamping press, each item then being finished by hand by engraving, polishing, etc. He produced an extremely wide range of objects in glass, using clear, coloured, opalescent and stained glass, and was greatly imitated. At the 1925 Exhibition he had his own pavilion, designed and furnished the dining room in the Sèvres pavilion, and was present wherever glass was used, in the cascades of the Porte d'Honneur, those of the perfumery section, the pebbles in the Primavera dome, and many other places. Though production was interrupted during the German occupation, he saw the reopening of his factory shortly before his death, and this was run by his son Marc, and now by his granddaughter, Marie-Claude.

LALIQUE, Suzanne. Paris (b. 1899)
Painter and decorator. René Lalique's daughter, she was largely self-taught, though she studied briefly with Eugène Morand. She first exhibited at the SA at the age of sixteen, later exhibiting at the ST, the SNBA, the SAD and the Bernheim Jeune gallery in 1930, when her exhibition catalogue had prefaces by three noted writers, Jean Giraudoux, Paul Morand and Edouard Bourdet. In ad-

dition to her paintings (which included a portrait of her father) she designed porcelain for the Sèvres Manufactory and for Limoges, fabrics and wallpapers for various interior designers, and painted a screen for Jacques Doucet.

LALLEMENT, Robert. Pau (1902–1954) Davos
Ceramist and designer. Brought up in Dijon by his grandmother and an aunt as his mother had died when he was eight months old, he studied at the Ecole des Beaux-Arts there, where the head, Ovide Yencesse, a fine medallist, sculptor and painter, detected his talent for ceramics. He was joined in Paris by his father, Théodore Lallement, who had lived and worked in Russia until forced to flee from there by the Revolution. Robert worked for Lachenal in 1921 and 1922 in order to perfect his technique, after which his father bought him a small ceramics works at 5 Passage d'Orléans (13e), where he worked with him until his death. Robert devised techniques which enabled him to sell his wares fairly inexpensively, specialising in the production of ivory glazed pots of cubic, cylindrical, global and flat shapes using square, round, spherical and rectangular sections, decorated with Cubist patterns or designs based on sports, battles, sins and virtues, popular songs, kings, signs of the zodiac, the seasons, composers, animals, castles, architecture, ballooning, fruit, popular cries, old crafts, boats, and Swedish subjects, all taken from his own drawings. He also designed a series of abstract pots in high-fired iridescent black glaze, and sometimes used gold and platinum in his design. The patterns were always fired at low temperatures. He executed a number of ceramic sculptures designed by the Martel brothers, Hubert Yencesse, son of his former teacher, and his wife. He later moved to larger premises on the Quai d'Auteuil, where he displayed furniture by his friends Charlotte Perriand, Djo-Bourgeois, Pierre Barbe and René Herbst, as well as some he designed himself, using metal and glass as well as wood. He was a founder member of the UAM, although he had previously exhibited at the Salons of the SAD from 1926. He received many private commissions, but gave up all original work in 1933 to work for his father-in-law's building company. He joined the Navy when war broke out, then joined the Free French Forces in the Far East after he was demobilised, finally returning to France in 1947. He died of a heart attack after a ski race at the age of 52.

LAMBERT-RUCKI, Jean. Cracow (1888–1967)
Sculptor and painter. After studying at the Cracow School of Fine Arts under Mehoffer, he moved to Paris, where he exhibited at the SA, the Salon des Indépendants from 1920, the Salon des Artistes Modernes, the ST from 1933, with the Section d'Or group from 1922 to 1924, and at Léonce Rosenberg's gallery in 1924. He carved a number of Cubist-influenced works in wood which he frequently lacquered, covered in gold and silver leaf, or set with glass or mirror mosaics. He worked frequently with Jean Dunand, whom he supplied with designs for lacquer panels, and executed a number of mosaics and sculptures for churches.

LAMOURDEDIEU, Raoul. Fouquerolles (1877–1953) Paris
Sculptor. Exhibited at the SA and the SNBA, and became

professor at the Ecole des Beaux-Arts in Paris. He executed a number of small bronzes as well as bronze and silver medals. He was a member of the La Stèle and L'Evolution groups, and exhibited with them in the Goldscheider pavilion at the 1925 Exhibition. LH.

LAURENCIN, Marie. Paris (1883–1956) Paris
Painter and graphic artist. Introduced to the Bateau-Lavoir by Georges Braque, she was introduced to Cubism and Fauvism, but retained a very personal pastel palette, delicate treatment, and evanescent subjects. Her favourite themes revolved around girls, flowers, amazons, horses, dogs, cats and does with the occasional monkey. She supplied André Mare's Cubist House at the 1912 SA with paintings, exhibited frequently at Léonce Rosenberg's gallery, illustrated a number of books, etched and lithographed extensively, designed the costumes and sets for Francis Poulenc's ballet 'Les Biches' in 1924 for Diaghilev's Ballets Russes in a very modish and fashionable style and designed sets and costumes for several plays. She regularly contributed paintings to room settings by André Groult, including the lady's bedroom in the French Embassy at the 1925 Exhibition.

LE BOURGEOIS, Eve-Marie. Paris (b. 1904)
Sculptor. Daughter of Gaston Le Bourgeois, she was thoroughly trained by him, and became an exceptionally fine sculptor in ivory. She exhibited at the SA, the SAD and the 1925 Paris Exhibition.

LE BOURGEOIS, Gaston-Etienne. Vire, Calvados (1880–1954) Paris
Sculptor. Primarily an animalier sculptor, he specialised in wood carving, and produced a number of stylised and naturalistic figures of small animals. He also carved a number of wood panels in low relief for use in decorative schemes and in furniture designed by several of the leading Art Deco designers. He also designed some decorative door furniture for the Maison Fontaine. He was the director of the sculpture workshop of the Union Centrale des Arts Décoratifs, and exhibited at the SNBA, where he was awarded a travelling scholarship in 1911, at the SA, the SAD, the 1925 Paris Exhibition, and was given a one-man show at the Pavillon de Marsan in 1922.

LE CHEVALLIER, Jacques. Paris (b. 1896)
Designer. A graduate of the Ecole des Arts Décoratifs, he went into partnership with Louis Barillet, the two setting up a stained glass workshop which lasted for a quarter of a century. He designed and executed secular and religious stained glass panels, designed a number of tapestries, painted, executed a number of wood engravings, illustrated several books and designed a number of very personal lamps, all powerfully machine-inspired using metal, exposed rivets and hinged or counterweighted sections, many executed with Raymond Koechlin. He was a founder member of the UAM. In 1945 he set up his own stained glass workshop.

LE FAGUAYS, Pierre. Nantes (b. 1892)
Sculptor. A student of Vibert, he exhibited at the SAF from 1922, receiving Honourable Mentions in 1926 and 1927. He carved ivory, wood and stone, and executed a number of stylised bronzes. He was a member of the La Stèle and L'Evolution groups and exhibited with them in the Goldscheider pavilion at the 1925 Exhibition.

LEGRAIN, Pierre. Levallois-Perret (1889–1929) Paris
Designer. As a student at the Ecole des Arts Appliqués Germain Pilon, he had met Robert Delaunay and Robert Bonfils. In 1908 he went to work for Paul Iribe, assisting him in his furniture designs as well as submitting illustrations to the publications Iribe edited. Legrain met Jacques Doucet when Iribe decorated Doucet's apartment in the avenue du Bois. In 1914 he joined the army, but was invalided out in 1916. He eked out a precarious living illustrating various magazines, then approached Doucet for a job. In 1917 Doucet commissioned him to design 'unusual' bookbindings for him. Legrain, who knew nothing about bookbinding, soon renewed the craft, bringing in such unusual materials as shagreen, wood and mother-of-pearl, as well as using geometric and calligraphic designs. He used a number of professional binders to execute his designs, but more particularly René Kieffer, with whom he worked exclusively from 1919 when he left Doucet, until 1922 when he was financed by Briant & Robert to set up his own workshop in their establishment. In 1926 he set up entirely on his own with fine craftsmen to execute his designs. Parallel with binding, he designed a wide range of leather items and furniture, the latter using rare and unusual woods or treated as books, covered in leather, shagreen or parchment. Doucet commissioned him to decorate his Neuilly studio in about 1925. Much of his furniture was inspired by African art, but he was eclectic in his choice of influences, so also designed highly sophisticated and smooth furniture. He designed a piano for Pleyel whose glass case showed the mechanism. His bindings were one of the sensations of the 1925 Paris Exhibition.

LELEU, Jules. Boulogne-sur-Mer (1883–1961) Paris
Sculptor and designer. A pupil of Théophile Deman, he exhibited sculpture at the SAF from 1905. After the war he set up as an interior decorator with his own furniture workshop, exhibiting at the SAD from 1922, then at the SA and the ST. At the 1925 Exhibition he supplied the chairs for the Grand Salon designed by Rapin and Selmersheim and the music room designed by Sézille, both in the French Embassy, and exhibited a complete suite of living room furniture in his stand on the Esplanade des Invalides. He received a number of official commissions to decorate and supply furniture for several liners and French Embassies.

LEMPICKA, Tamara de. Warsaw (? 1902–1980)
Painter. Arriving in Paris after reputedly studying at the St. Petersburg Academy, she studied with Maurice Denis and André Lhote, the latter influencing her greatly. Her connections with society brought her many portrait commissions, and her first solo exhibition in Milan was followed by one in Paris at the Colette Weill gallery in 1930. She exhibited at the ST, the SA, the Salon des Indépendants and the Salon de l'Escalier. She was awarded the Prix d'Honneur at the 1927 Bordeaux International Exhibition, and a Bronze Medal at the 1929 Posen International Exhibition. In the late 1930s, she and her family moved to the United States, where she continued to paint despite a hectic social life. She executed about one hundred paintings of exceptional charm, often heavily charged with sensuality, which are models of the Art Deco style. In the 1940s she briefly painted in the pictorial style of the day before turning to abstraction. She also executed some etchings.

LENOBLE, Emile. Choisi-le-Roi (1876–1940) Morget
Ceramist. He spent seven years working with commercial faience before joining Chaplet in Choisi-le-Roi to work with stoneware. In about 1910 he began using painted designs on his stoneware in addition to mastering the art of engraving and incising the surface. Inspired by Far Eastern pottery, he devised a thinner and lighter clay, and spent a lifetime developing new shades in his glazes. Many interior decorators of the Art Deco period, like Montagnac and Ruhlmann, used his pots in their decorative schemes.

LEPAPE, Georges. Paris (1887–1971)
Painter, illustrator and designer. He illustrated an album of fashion designs for Paul Iribe in 1911, following the success of the previous album illustrated by Iribe, and was one of the principal illustrators of La Gazette du Bon Ton, supplying Poiret not only with occasional original models, but also with some fabrics designs. He illustrated books, including the complete works of Alfred de Musset, executed a vast number of covers and fashion illustrations for Vogue and other publications, executed colourful posters, advertising brochures, and designed sets and costumes for plays, music hall and movies.

LHOTE, André. Bordeaux (1885–1962)
Painter. Studied decorative sculpture at the Bordeaux Ecole des Beaux-Arts, then practised as a wood carver before approaching painting, to which he was to devote the rest of his life. Greatly influenced by Cézanne and by Cubism, he yet remained a figurative artist. He exhibited at the SA, the Salon des Indépendants, commercial galleries and several International Exhibitions. He founded his own art school in 1918, and trained, taught or influenced a vast number of artists, reaching many more through his numerous books and frequent lecture tours. He was also an exceptional draughtsman and fine graphic artist.

LINOSSIER, Claudius. Lyon (1893–1955) Paris
Dinandier, sculptor, medallist and silversmith. Apprenticed to a silversmith at the age of thirteen, later moving to Paris where he worked as a silver and goldsmith before joining Jean Dunand for three months to learn dinanderie. After the war he settled in Lyon, where he practised as a dinandier, specialising in geometric and abstract decoration. He exhibited at the SAF, the SA, the SAD and at the 1925 Exhibition, where he had his metalware on view at the French Embassy, the dinanderie section and other pavilions. He was awarded a travelling scholarship (1924) and the LH (1932).

LOUPOT, Charles. Nice (1892–1971)
Poster artist and illustrator. After studying at the Ecole des Beaux-Arts in Lyon with Bonnardel, he moved to Switzerland, where he executed a number of posters. In 1923 he moved to Paris, briefly illustrated for *La Gazette du Bon Ton*, then executed two posters for the Voisin car, one in his spacious illustrator's style, the other in a stylised, almost schematised, style which he was to pursue. He joined Cassandre and Moyrand in their Alliance Graphique and exhibited his posters with Cassandre at the Salle Pleyel. He illustrated and designed covers for a number of publications, including *Art et Industrie* and *Fémina*. He resumed his career as a leading poster artist after the Second World War.

LUCE, Jean. Paris (1895–1964)
Ceramics and glass designer. After working for his father's firm he set up his own firm in 1923, though he was only to take over its direction in 1931. Using simple, well-proportioned shapes allied with geometric motifs for ceramics and thick-walled, often mirrored glass with surface decoration either acid-etched or sand-blasted, contrasting polished and rough areas, he designed a wide variety of tableware and decorative pieces. He designed the tableware and glassware for the liner Normandie, and these designs were later used by the Campagnie Générale Transatlantique for all their ships. He exhibited at the Galliéra Museum in 1911, the SA, the SAD and was a member of the Jury at both the 1925 and 1937 Paris Exhibitions, where he also displayed his designs. He taught at the Applied Arts School, and was a technical advisor at the Manufacture de Sèvres.

MALLET-STEVENS, Robert. Paris (1886–1945)
Architect and designer. Greatly influenced by Josef Hoffmann, he was the first architect in France to seek to adapt the new concepts of simplification and functionalism to the rich tastes of his country, and designed houses whose imbricated cubes formed intricate planar contrasts in complete opposition to the matchbox shapes predicated by the strict functionalists. His most complete complex is at Auteuil in the rue Mallet-Stevens, a short street in which he designed all the houses, including one for himself and another for the Martel brothers, with whom he worked very closely. This street still exists, though all the houses have since been modified to some extent. He designed several shopfronts, using unusual materials such as polished brass with thick rivets and protruding display windows. He first exhibited his furniture designs at the 1913 SA, and frequently used tubular steel, lacquered or painted in bright colours. In 1924 he designed some interiors for Marcel L'Herbier's film *L'Inhumaine*. At the 1925 Exhibition he designed the Tourism pavilion, the Habitation Moderne garden, which he planted with concrete Cubist trees by the Martel brothers, and the hall of the French Embassy, where he placed paintings by Robert Delaunay and Fernand Léger. A founder member of the UAM, he became its first president.

MARINOT, Maurice. Troyes (1882–1960)
Glass-maker and painter. After exhibiting his paintings with the Fauves group, he discovered glass at the Viard works at Bar-sur-Seine, and soon threw himself into the exploration of this fascinating medium. He began by designing decoration which was applied in enamel by an artisan, learned to apply the enamel himself, then learned to make the glass on his own, developing thick-walled, internally decorated pieces which he first incised deeply with repeated prolonged acid baths, later working his pots exclusively at the furnace. When the Viard works closed down he returned to painting. Much of his glass production was destroyed by the Allied bombardment during the Second World War.

MARTEL, Jan and Joël. Nantes (1896–1966) Paris
Sculptors. Twin brothers, they always worked together. Influenced by Cubism, they experimented with a variety of materials, executing sculpture in glass, cement, sheet-steel, reconstituted stone, mirror-glass, ceramics, reinforced lacquer and synthetic materials. They executed small sculptures as well as vast monuments, and frequently worked with Mallet-Stevens, who designed a house for them. At the 1925 Exhibition they executed low relief carvings for the Concorde Gate and the plinth of its figurehead statue, and for Mallet-Stevens' Tourism pavilion, executed the interior decoration for the bathroom exhibited at the Sèvres pavilion, and the concrete Cubist trees for the Mallet-Stevens garden. Founder members of the UAM, both died in 1966, one of illness, the other in an accident.

MARTIN, Charles. Montpellier (1848–1934)
Illustrator, graphic artist and designer. He studied at the Montpellier Ecole des Beaux-Arts, the Académie Julian and the Paris Ecole des Beaux-Arts under Cormon. He was a prolific illustrator, working for *La Gazette du Bon Ton*, *Le Journal des Dames et des Modes*, *Feuillets d'Art*, *Fémina*, *Le Sourire*, *Le Rire*, *Vogue*, *Harper's Bazaar* and *Vanity Fair*, and illustrated a large number of books. He exhibited at the SA and the Salon des Humoristes, and designed sets and costumes for a number of plays, revues and ballets. He also designed furniture, fashions and wallpapers for several decorators, including André Groult, for whom he executed painted panels and screens. He was an exceptional draughtsman, and executed a number of erotic drawings and watercolours.

MARTINE
Interior design studio established by Paul Poiret in 1911, largely to market the designs and talents of the young pupils of his Ecole Martine, though it later employed the design talents of a number of artists, including some girls from the school. They specialised in naive and colourful fabrics, wallpapers and murals, cube-shaped furniture in brightly painted wood or highly figured veneers, and a vast number of colourful limp bolsters with long tassels. Martine decorated Poiret's three houseboats at the 1925 Exhibition.

MARTY, André Edouard. Paris (1882–1974)
Painter, illustrator, etcher and enameller. He studied philosophy before entering the Ecole des Beaux-Arts in Paris where he studied under Cormon. Like a number of his fellow students, he began to illustrate for *La Gazette du Bon Ton*, then *Fémina*, *Comoedia Illustré* and *Vogue*. He illustrated a large number of books, many with original etchings, designed a number of sets for the Théâtre des Arts, and exhibited regularly at the SAD and the SA, and was a member of the Jury at the 1925 Exhibition. He was one of the regular designers for the Compagnie des Arts Français, both under Süe et Mare and later, and had some of his designs for fabrics and screens exhibited in both the Süe et Mare and the Fontaine pavilions at the 1925 Paris Exhibition. He worked closely with Camille Fauré at Limoges, designing fine geometric polychrome decorations executed in enamels on copper, vases, bowls and small jewellery. Marty designed for Fauré's workshops until well into the 1960s.

MAYODON, Jean. Sèvres (1893–1967)
Ceramist. After training as a painter he began experimenting with pottery in 1912, exhibiting his first production at the Galliéra Museum in 1919. His polychrome ceramics were immediately admired, and he exhibited thereafter at the SA and the SAD, with a permanent display of his wares at the Geo. Rouard gallery. He executed important commissions for the France and Normandie steamships, as well as many fountains, screens, bathroom and patio settings and other large compositions, in addition to vases, bowls and other smaller items. Often inspired by Persian and Far Eastern ceramics, he loved gold backdrops and decoration, using archaic and Hellenic images of athletes, archers, nudes and leaping and running animals. He was artistic director of the Sèvres Manufactory from 1941–1942.

MERE, Clément. Bayonne (b. 1870)
Painter, tabletier and designer and maker of furniture. Studied painting under Gérôme, then joined Julius Meier-Graefe's Maison Moderne in about 1900. He met Franz Waldraff there, and the two designed and executed incised, painted and gilt ivory panels, turned wood and ivory boxes, and supplied a number of dress designers with fabrics, carved and incised buttons, and other small items. Together and after their separation, Mere on his own designed and executed highly individual items of furniture, with carved woods covered in incised, stained and polished leather, inlaid with carved or stained ivory, wood marquetry, enamelled metal, lacquered sections, marbling, shagreen and other materials. He exhibited at the SA, the SAD and the SNBA.

MERGIER, Paul Louis. Orthez, Basses Pyrénées (b. 1891)
Painter, enameller and decorator. While following a career as an aeronautical engineer, he researched the various techniques of enamelling from 1920 onwards. He designed a number of new methods and applications, using pastes rather than powders, and executed a number of enamel plaques, including some very large panels. He painted still lifes, portraits and landscapes using oil paints mixed with rubber which he made himself, though he also worked in pastel, gouache, and watercolour. He executed a quantity of dinanderie decorated with figurative scenes, designed furniture, much of it clad in various leathers and

inlaid with mother-of-pearl, ivory and other precious materials, and wrote a book discussing the relationship between the fine arts and sciences and another on enamelling technique. He exhibited at the SA, the SAF, the SAD, the ST, the Salon des Indépendants, the 1937 Paris International Exhibition and the 1939 New York World's Fair.

METTHEY, André. Laignes (1871–1920) Asnières
Ceramist. After a period spent as a painter, sculptor and interior designer, he settled in Asnières in 1901 and set up as a ceramist. For several years he designed traditional pots which he asked his artist friends to decorate for him. These friends included Maurice Denis, Pierre Bonnard, Odilon Redon, Ker-Xavier Roussel, Kees Van Dongen, Maurice Vlaminck and Edouard Vuillard. In about 1905 he began to experiment with glazed earthenware pots, which he decorated himself with geometric patterns. He later became more adventurous, and extended his range of decoration to highly stylised plants, animals and figures, firing his pots three or more times and achieving a wide range of rich colours, including a crackled gold. A major exhibition of his ceramics was held at the Galliéra Museum in 1909, after which he fell ill with tuberculosis and was unable to work for some two years. A flood destroyed his studio, but he was able to resume work in 1911. The following few years were very successful for him, and his fame, reputation and popularity remained high until the outbreak of war in 1914, when he closed down his workshop. After the war his failing health prevented him from resuming his career.

MIKLOS, Gustave. Budapest (1888–1967) Oyonnax
Sculptor, painter and designer. Studied at the School of Decorative Arts in Budapest and various academies in Paris. He volunteered for service in the French Foreign Legion in 1914. During the Greek campaign he was fascinated by Hellenic and Byzantine art. On his return to France he met Jacques Doucet, and designed carpets, silverware and enamels for him. In about 1923 he began to sculpt, and executed a number of sculptures for Doucet, mostly of Cubist inspiration. He became friendly with F. L. Schmied, and both designed for him and carved some of Schmied's own designs. He also supplied Dunand with some designs, himself designed some furniture and supplied painted panels for furniture by others. He left Paris with his wife in 1940 to settle in the provinces and spent the rest of his life teaching. He exhibited at the SA and the SAD as well as Léonce Rosenberg's gallery L'Effort Moderne in 1922 and La Renaissance in 1928. He later joined and exhibited with the UAM.

MONTAGNAC, Pierre-Paul. Saint-Denis (1883–1962)
Painter and designer. He studied at the free academies, under Eugène Carrière and at the Grande Chaumière, then divided his time equally between painting and the applied arts. He exhibited his paintings only at the SA, where he was awarded a travelling scholarship in 1920, and became its president in 1947. He designed a large number of tapestries for the Gobelins Manufactory, and furniture for a number of firms, exhibited at the SAD, the

Salon des Architectes Modernes, of which he became a member of the Jury, and International Exhibitions in Barcelona and Leipzig. He was also president of the SAD for many years. At the 1925 Exhibition he designed a Reception Room displayed in the Esplanade des Invalides and supplied some furniture for the Grand Salon designed by Rapin and Selmersheim for the French Embassy. LH and LHO (1938).

NAVARRE, Henri. Paris (1885–1970)
Sculptor, architect, silversmith and glass-maker. Born into a family of architects, he studied with them, studied wood carving at the Bernard Palissy School of Applied Arts, went through a complete apprenticeship as goldsmith and silversmith, studied at the Ecole des Beaux-Arts, then took a course in stained glass and mosaics at the Conservatoire des Arts et Métiers. He executed a number of monumental sculptures and decorative carvings on buildings, and executed the sculpture frieze on the Monumental Gate at the Paris 1925 Exhibition. Greatly influenced by the work of Marinot, he began to work with glass in about 1924, making thick-walled, simply shaped vessels with internal decoration, as well as a number of masks and other sculptures, including a large glass figure of Christ and a gilded reredos for the chapel in the liner Ile-de-France in 1927. He designed the Grille of Honour for the Colonial Museum in 1931. He exhibited at the SNBA, the SA and the SAD, and was elected president of the Jury for sculpture at the SA. He also exhibited in Brussels, Cairo, Stockholm, Copenhagen, Oslo, Athens, and in New York in 1928 and 1930. LH.

NICS Frères.
Smiths. Born in Hungary, Michel and Jules Nics moved to France and set up a factory and showroom at 98 Avenue Félix Faure in Paris. They began to exhibit at the salons of the SAF in 1914, manufacturing a wide range of wrought-iron stair rails, radiator covers, grilles for gates as well as lamps and accessories. The firm was run by Jules Nics on his own after 1935.

PERZEL, Jean. Bruck, Germany (b. 1892)
Designer of light fittings and systems. As a very young man he studied and practised as a stained glass artist. After touring Europe, he arrived in Paris at the age of eighteen, then went on to Algeria. He returned to Paris in 1919, and went to work for Jacques Gruber in his new Paris workshop. In 1923 he left to set up on his own, specialising in designing light schemes. His fittings combined metal supports and reflectors with clear, opaque and tinted glass, frequently given a rough edge. He exhibited at the SA, the SAD, and the SNBA as well as in various International Exhibitions, and received a number of awards. His firm still exists.

PICABIA, Francis. Paris (1879–1953) Paris
Painter and graphic artist. After studying at the Ecole des Arts Décoratifs in Paris, he painted in the style of the Impressionists and etched a number of views of Paris and landscapes. He interested himself in the Fauves and the Cubists, met Marcel Duchamp in New York in 1915, and

was one of the founders of the Dada movement. A writer, publisher, painter and publicist of his ideas, he painted a number of haunting images in which an apparently straightforward figurative design is split, decorated or overlaid with disturbing effectiveness.

POMPON, François. Saulieu (1855–1933) Paris
Sculptor. The son of a cabinet-maker, he learned carving from his father, then practised as a marble cutter at a Dijon stonemason's before studying architecture, etching and sculpture at the Dijon Ecole des Beaux-Arts, after which he moved to Paris. There he worked as a stone carver of caryatids and other decorations for house fronts while following the evening classes of Aimé Millet and Caillé at the Ecole des Arts Décoratifs, and sculpting small figures inspired by characters of fiction. The sculptor Antonin Mercié hired him as a practitioner to work on his large compositions. From Mercié he moved to Falguière, Saint-Marceaux, then on to Rodin in 1891, remaining as his chief assistant for fifteen years. Encouraged by Rodin he sculpted in his spare time, executing some portraits but many animals, developing his own smooth, stylised manner, capturing the essence of the creatures he depicted. He exhibited at the SAF from 1881 to 1922, and was awarded an Honourable Mention (1886), a Medal 3rd Class (1888), an Honourable Mention at the 1889 International Exhibition and a Bronze Medal at the 1900 Universal Exhibition. Fame, however, only began to touch him when at the age of sixty-seven he moved to the SA in 1922 where he exhibited his massive white Polar Bear, which was again displayed at the 1925 Exhibition in Ruhlmann's pavilion. The last ten years of his life were very prolific; he executed a number of commissions in addition to his chosen work, and left some 300 sculptures to the state, which set up a museum in his name in the Paris Zoo, later transferring it to the Dijon Museum. LH (1925), LHO.

POPINEAU, François Emile. Saint-Armand-Montrand (b. 1887)
Sculptor. He executed several Monuments to the Dead of the First World War and some garden and park statuary, as well as a number of stylised female nudes in bronze and in wood. He exhibited at the SNBA, the SA, the ST and the Salon des Indépendants.

POUGHEON, Robert Eugène. Paris (1886–1955) Paris
Painter. A student of Jean Paul Laurens and Lameire, he began exhibiting at the SAF in 1911, and was awarded the Théodore Ralli Prize (1911), an Honourable Mention (1913) and a Grand Prix de Rome (1914). He joined the Académie de France in Rome after the war to study under Albert Besnard, and there became very close to two other Rome prizewinners, Jean Dupas and Jean Despujols, the three developing a glacial neo-classical stylisation which each, however, interpreted with different symbols. Back in Paris he was awarded a Silver Medal (1927) and a Gold Medal (1929). In 1935 he became a professor at the Ecole des Beaux-Arts, became Inspector of the Beaux-Arts, then member of the Institute Français in 1942. He later became curator of the Jacquemart-André Museum.

PRINTZ, Eugène. Paris (1889–1948) Paris

Furniture designer and manufacturer. Trained in his father's furniture factory, he designed both simple, functional furniture and highly complex items, using exotic wood veneers and unusual solutions to the placing and movement of doors and drawers. After working with his father for several years he set up on his own at 12 rue Saint-Bernard, where he showed paintings and tapestries in addition to his furniture. He exhibited at the 1925 Paris International Exhibition of Modern Decorative and Industrial Arts as well as the SAD and the 1931 and 1937 International Exhibitions. His furniture, signed and numbered, was produced in limited quantities of each design, and frequently incorporated lacquer panels and wrought silver or bronze sections by Jean Dunand, enamels by Jean Serrière, as well as complex gilt or patinated metal legs or substructures in addition to the more usual handles. He executed a vast number of private and public commissions in France, Great Britain, Belgium, the United States and Mexico, and opened his own gallery at 81 rue de Miromesnil. He designed expensive furniture, though shortly before his death he turned out some designs for mass production which, however, were never carried out.

PUIFORCAT, Jean E. Paris (1897–1945) Paris

Silversmith and sculptor. His early schooling was interrupted by the outbreak of war, and he joined up at the age of seventeen, returning decorated with the Croix de Guerre. After the war he entered his father's workshops to study the art and craft of the silversmith, simultaneously studying sculpture with Louis Lejeune. He began designing and exhibiting his silverware in 1921, rejecting traditional decoration in favour of simplified, often geometrical forms based on mathematical equations, allying the smooth, highly polished silver surfaces with lapis-lazuli, ivory, jade, rock crystal and other semi-precious materials. He exhibited at the SA from 1921—becoming a member of both Admissions and Awards Juries and Reporter on Metal— at the SAD, the Galeries Barbazanges (1926–1928), the Galerie Renaissance (1929) and at Grenoble, Milan, Madrid, New York, San Francisco, Buenos Aires and Tokyo. At the 1925 Exhibition he was a member of both Admissions and Awards Juries, Reporter on the Metals Class, and exhibited in the Ruhlmann pavilion, the French Embassy dining room designed by Henri Rapin, the Metals Class in the Grand Palais and in the pavilion designed by Henri Pacon and shared between the magazine *Art et Décoration* and the Artisans Français Contemporains, one wing taken by Geo. Rouard to show his stable of ceramists and glass designers, the other wing taken by Puiforcat. In 1929 he unveiled his monumental statue of a football player at the Colombes Olympic Stadium. He was a founder member of the UAM.

RAPIN, Henri. Paris (1873-1939)

Painter, illustrator and decorator. After studying with Gerome and J. Blanc, he began to exhibit at the SAF from 1900, and was awarded a Medal 3rd Class (1904), and a Medal 2nd Class (1910) in the Applied Arts for the generally simple furniture he designed. In response to the challenge from the Munich designers exhibiting at the SA in 1910, he began to design furniture that was more stylised and executed in rich materials, often using carved wood panels by Le Bourgeois and Hairon. At the 1925 Exhibition, he designed the display of the art school established by the Ladies Committee of the Union Centrale des Arts Décoratifs, whose artistic director he was; designed the Grand Salon in the French Embassy with Pierre Selmersheim; and designed its dining room, which housed a huge carved panel by Max Blondat, executed shortly before his death, a stained glass panel by Jacques Gruber, carved panels by Charles Hairon and Eve Le Bourgeois, wrought iron by Subes and silver by Puiforcat. LH (1920), LHO (1926).

RATEAU, Armand-Albert. Paris (1882–1938)

Designer. Studied drawing and wood carving at the Ecole Boulle in Paris, then worked as a freelance designer for a number of interior decorators before becoming manager of the decorating workshops of the Maison Alavoine in 1905, remaining there until 1914 when he joined the army. After the war he set up on his own, and executed a number of important commissions, particularly for Jeanne Lanvin, a leading dressmaker, for whom he designed and furnished her home and her fashion house, as well as running the department of interior design she had set up; and for George and Florence Blumenthal's numerous homes. Hardly ever exhibiting his designs, he was kept busy by his wealthy private clients, his preferred materials being solid oak and bronze, the latter executed with the sculptor Paul Plumet. He frequently used motifs of stylised flowers and birds in patinated bronze, with occasional use of lacquer.

ROGANEAU, François-Maurice. Bordeaux (1883–1974) Nice

Painter. After studying at the Ecole des Beaux-Arts in Bordeaux as well as the one in Paris, he was awarded a First Grand Prix de Rome in 1906. On his return to Bordeaux, he rejoined the Ecole des Beaux-Arts as a teacher, and succeeded Paul Quinsac as its head in 1929. A close friend of the city's then mayor, Adrien Marquet, he was commissioned to execute a vast number of large paintings for public buildings, both secular and sacred. He also received several commissions from other countries, particularly Colombia and Argentina. A highly skilled academic artist, several of his large frescoes showed the influence of neo-classicism in his decorative formal groupings. He executed one of the four large frescoes for the Wine Pavilion at the 1925 Paris Exhibition of Decorative and Industrial Arts, and another for the 1934 Paris Exhibition.

ROUSSEAU, Clément. Saint-Maurice-la-Fougereuse (1872-1950) Nevilly-sur-Seine

Sculptor and designer. A student of Léon Morice, he established himself at Neuilly where he executed some highly personal furniture for a few wealthy clients. His designs are among the most interesting produced in the Art Deco style, but are extremely rare. He used marquetry, inlays of various unusual woods, shagreen and various leathers as well as ivory and mother-of-pearl inlays. He exhibited at the SAF from 1921, his furniture gaining him an Honourable Mention (1923) and a Bronze Medal (1926). He was also awarded an Honourable Mention (1930) for his sculpture.

ROUX-SPITZ, Michel. Lyon (1888–1957)

Architect and interior designer. After studying with Tony Garnier, he was commissioned by Charles Plumet to design two room settings for the 1925 Paris Exhibition of Modern Decorative and Industrial Arts. He specialised thereafter in designing furniture and room settings based on the character, personality and psychology of those for whom they were destined, using luxurious materials and fine workmanship. He exhibited regularly at the SAD, incorporating within his room settings silver by Jean Puiforcat, metalwork by Raymond Subes, Perzel lights and the works of other leading designers. At the 1929 Salon he exhibited a complete dining room commissioned by the Société des Glaces de Boussois. He executed both public and private commissions.

RUHLMANN, Emile-Jacques. Paris (1879–1933) Paris

Designer. The son of a well-to-do builder, he soon learned the essentials of cabinet-making, and began exhibiting at the SA from 1913, later exhibiting in a number of European cities. After the First World War he took over the direction of his father's firm and greatly expanded it with workshops specialising in furniture-making and other aspects of interior design, and associated his name with well-executed furniture in a modified and often stylised traditional form, using rare veneers and discreet inlays of ivory. At the 1925 Paris Exhibition he presented his own pavilion, displaying in it the combined talents of a large number of artists who regularly worked for him, and participated in the French Embassy while his building firm worked on a number of other pavilions and shops. In his later years he began to use metal fairly extensively, designed modular furniture, and began to design simple, somewhat Modernist furniture. His nephew, the architect Alfred Porteneuve, who had earlier worked with Süe et Mare, joined him and, after his death, repeated a number of his earlier designs. LH.

SANDOZ, Edouard-Marcel. Basel (1881–1971)

Sculptor. Studied at the Ecole des Beaux-Arts in Paris with Mercié and Injalbert. He specialised in animalier sculpture, and executed a wide range of animals in bronze, treated in a somewhat impressionist way to capture the fleeting movements of the animals, though he also produced a few highly stylised, smooth, hieratic bronzes like his *Condor*. He also designed a series of decanters, bottles, boxes and tea and coffee sets in humorous shapes (birds, animals, babes in swaddling clothes, etc.) executed in polychrome porcelain by Haviland at Limoges. He exhibited at the SNBA as well as in Brussels and Barcelona. LH.

SANDOZ, Gérard-Roger. Paris (b. 1902).

Jeweller and painter. In about 1920 he began to design mechanistically-inspired jewellery executed in his father's firm of jewellers, continuing to do so for about ten years.

He also designed some posters and contributed some designs for his uncle Paul Follot. In 1932 he made a film with Michel Bernheim, *Panurge*, in which he starred along with Paul Poiret and Danielle Darrieux, made a filmed documentary in 1939, and wrote for radio and television, as well as writing the script and designing the sets for another film in 1954. From 1930 onwards, however, he devoted himself largely to abstract painting. He exhibited at the SA and the SAD, and was one of the founder members of the UAM.

SCHMIED, *François Louis*. Geneva (1873–1941) Tahanaout, Morocco

Painter, engraver, printer and publisher. A pupil of B. Menn, B. Bodmer and Alfred Martin at the Geneva School of Industrial Arts, he followed his friend Jean Dunand to Paris where he set up as a wood engraver, exhibiting at the SNBA from 1904 and publishing his first illustrated book in 1911. Paul Jouve was so impressed that he commissioned him to carve on wood his illustrations for *The Jungle Book*, a task which took several years, the book only being published after the war. Schmied was severely wounded during the war, losing an eye, but he returned to work and soon established himself as a leading illustrator, engraver and printer, publishing his own books and often designing the most sumptuous bindings. He travelled frequently with Jean Dunand and his son Bernard Dunand, designed lacquer panels for them, and himself painted and executed a number of large enamel plaques, some of which were used to decorate the liner Normandie. He exhibited his graphics, paintings and books at the SAD, the Salon des Peintres Orientalistes and at the Galerie Georges Petit. At the 1925 Paris Exhibition he exhibited as editor. LH.

SUBES, *Raymond*. (1893–1970)

Smith. Student at the Ecole Boulle and the Ecole des Arts Décoratifs, then worked for three years for Emile Robert, who was then one of the leading wrought-iron designers. He succeeded Robert as artistic director of the Borderel et Robert works in 1919. He rapidly established himself as a leading designer and executant, using a variety of metals, and worked closely with a number of architects, as he had a direct and creative ability to use metal in virtue of its architectural function without monotony. He executed a lacquered metal bookcase with Ruhlmann for the latter's pavilion at the 1925 Exhibition, to which he contributed a large number of screens, consoles and grilles in various sections. In the 1930s he executed furniture for Porteneuve, Ruhlmann's nephew, using chromium-plated tubular metal.

SUE ET MARE

Founded as the Compagnie des Arts Francais in 1919 by Louis Süe (1875–1968), an architect and painter, and André Mare (1887–1932), a painter. Both had designed furniture from 1910 onwards, and Mare had designed fabrics and decorated parchment bookbindings. With their own group of designer/friends they established themselves as interior designers, prepared to tackle every aspect of interiors, their style in furniture being heavily indebted to the Louis-Philippe style, allied with a massive theatricality

and a love of gilding, with white ceramics and glass beads used in lighting and objets d'art. They published an album illustrating some of their designs in 1921 called *Architecture*. In the 1925 Paris Exhibition they designed and decorated twin pavilions, one for themselves called the Musée des Arts Contemporains, the other for the Maison Fontaine, which took them over in 1928, Süe resuming his architectural and design practise, Mare returning to painting.

SYLVE, LE

Design studio of the Bûcheron department store. Though Le Bûcheron had commissioned some Art Nouveau furniture at the turn of the century, it did not really get involved with Art Deco until shortly before the 1925 Exhibition, when its director, M. Boutillier, commissioned a modern interior for its shop in the Exhibition. An order to design and furnish the 2nd Class dining room on the liner Ile-de-France encouraged Boutillier to set up a new design studio under the direction of Michel Dufet and Léandre Vaillat, with furniture designed by Guerin, Sénéchal and Dufet, sculpture by Bourdelle, Chana Orloff, Pierre Traverse, Drivier, Guenot, Yvonne Serruys and Albert Marque, glass by Jean Sala and Cuppellin, ceramics by Serré and Goupy, silver by Jensen, dinanderie by Dunand and paintings by Utrillo, Vlaminck, Van Dongen, Marquet, Goerg and others. Separated from the main shop, it had its own entrance on the rue de Rivoli with a gate carved by Binquet using the motif devised by Cassandre in his very first poster.

SZABO, *Adalbert G*. Born in Hungary.

Smith. Established himself as a leading metalworker in the years before the First World War, executing a number of wrought-iron light fittings, lamps, screens and other smaller items. He exhibited at the SA and the SAF, and was awarded an Honourable Mention (1907), Medal 3rd Class (1908), 2nd Class (1911) and 1st Class (1912). LH (1932).

TEMPLIER, *Raymond*. Paris (1891–1968) Paris

Jeweller. Born into a family of jewellers, he studied at the Ecole des Beaux-Arts from 1909 to 1912, then joined his father. He designed a number of geometrically-shaped pieces, preferring platinum and diamonds, enamel and lacquer. He exhibited at the SA, becoming its vice-president, the SAD, the SNBA, the 1925 and 1937 Paris Exhibitions, and was a founder member of the UAM.

TRAVERSE, *Pierre*. Saint-André-de-Cubzac (b. 1892)

Sculptor. A student of Injalbert, he executed both large and monumental sculptures and stylised smaller figures. He exhibited at the SAF, where he was awarded a Silver Medal (1921), a travelling scholarship (1923), a Gold Medal (1926) and a Medal of Honour (1942). He also exhibited at the SA and the SAD. He was a member of the La Stèle and L'Evolution groups, and exhibited with them in the Goldscheider pavilion at the 1925 Paris Exhibition. He was awarded a Diploma of Honour at the 1937 Paris International Exhibition. He also exhibited in London, New York, Detroit, etc. LH (1938).

VERTES, *Marcel*. Budapest (1895–1962)

Painter, graphic artist and illustrator. A student of K. Ferenczy in Budapest, he moved to Vienna where he quickly established a fine reputation as a poster artist, then on to Paris in 1925, when he was commissioned by Maurice Exteens, Gustave Pellet's son-in-law and successor, to illustrate two albums of lithographs, one in black called *Maisons*, the other in colour called *Dancings*, the latter somehow reminiscent of Toulouse-Lautrec's album *Elles*, published by Pellet. Vertès had a difficult time establishing himself in France, though his mordant wit, sharp observation and choice of subject, the twilit world of brothels, nightclubs, swingers and discreetly unfaithful couples did not make things easier for him. He moved to the United States in the late 1930s, greatly sweetening his choice of subjects and their treatment, portraying circuses, romantic lovers and horseback rides. He painted a number of murals for stores, restaurants and private houses, including one for Gypsy Rose Lee. He exhibited at the SA, the Salon de l'Araignée and a large number of galleries.

VINCENT, *Rene (René Maël, known as)*. Bordeaux (1879–1936) Paris

Poster artist, illustrator and designer. After studying architecture at the Paris Ecole des Beaux-Arts he turned illustrator, working for *La Vie Parisienne* and *L'Illustration*, and published his first illustrated book in 1905. Though his earlier work was inspired by Art Nouveau, he soon moved to an angular representation that became typical of the Art Deco style, and from about 1920 he concentrated on designing posters, signed 'René Vincent', 'Rageot' or 'Dufour'. He designed a number of vases, table services, clocks and other items, some of which were executed in ceramic by Jean Besnard at Ivry. In 1924 he opened a workshop at Sèvres which he called Vinsard.

WLERICK, *Robert*. Mont-de-Marsan (1882–1944) Paris

Sculptor. As a student at the Ecole des Beaux-Arts in Toulouse, he was awarded a Rome Grand Prix for Sculpture in 1924. Two years later he moved to Paris, where he attended some courses at the Ecole des Beaux-Arts and spent time with his old friend, the sculptor Charles Despiau. He exhibited at the SNBA from 1907 onwards. During the First World War he and Jean Dupas worked for the facial plastic surgery unit run by Professor Moure in Bordeaux. In 1923 he joined with the sculptors Henri Bourdelle, Charles Despiau and Aristide Maillol to found the annual ST, where he was to exhibit henceforth. He taught drawing at the Ecole Germain Pilon in Paris before moving to the Ecole des Arts Appliqués à l'Industrie (School of Arts Applied to Industry) until 1943. He succeeded Antoine Bourdelle as professor at the Académie de la Grande Chaumière after the latter's death. He was commissioned to execute a large number of monumental sculptures, particularly for the 1937 Paris International Exhibition, but he also executed a number of smaller works, particularly portrait heads and busts and full-length nudes. A major retrospective of his work was held in 1982 at the Despiau-Wlerick Museum at Mont-de-Marsan.

BIBLIOGRAPHY

BOOKS

Adler, Rose. *Reliures,* Paris 1931.

Affiche Illustré, L'. Paris n.d. (c. 1944).

Albis, Jean d'. *Histoire de la fabrique Haviland de 1842 à 1925,* Limoges 1969.

Alexandre, Arsène. *L'Art décoratif de Léon Bakst,* Paris 1913.

Allemagne, Henry René d'. *Le Fer forgé à l'Exposition des Arts Décoratifs et Industriels Modernes,* Paris 1926.

Allen, Paul. *Beresford Egan,* London 1966.

Annuaire des Arts Décoratifs et Industriels Modernes, Paris 1924.

Architecte, L', Paris 1925.

Arwas, Victor. *Art Deco Sculpture,* London & New York 1975.

———. *Glass: Art Nouveau to Art Deco,* London & New York 1977.

———. *Alastair, Illustrator of Decadence,* London 1979.

Badovici, Jean. *Intérieurs Süe et Mare,* Paris 1924.

———. *Maisons individuelles,* Paris 1925.

Baker, Josephine, and Bouillon, Jo. *Josephine,* London 1978.

Balagny, Hugues. *Avant-propos sur la prochaine exposition internationale d'art appliqué. Avons-nous un style nouveau?,* Paris 1913.

Barbe-Despond, Arlette. *L'Union des Artistes Modernes,* Paris 1986.

Barillet, Louis. *Le Verre,* Paris n.d. (c. 1928).

Barrelet, James. *La Verrerie en France de l'époque Gallo-Romaine à nos jours,* Paris 1953.

Baschet, Jacques. *Sculpteurs de ce temps,* Paris 1946.

Basler, Adolphe. *La Sculpture moderne en France,* Paris 1928.

Battersby, Martin. *The Decorative Twenties,* London 1969.

———. *The Decorative Thirties,* London 1971.

Bayard, Emile. *Le Style moderne,* Paris 1919.

———. *L'Art appliqué français d'aujourd'hui,* Paris n.d. (1926).

Bayer, Patricia. *Art Deco Interiors,* Paris 1990.

Bayer, Patricia and Waller, Mark. *The Art of René Lalique,* London 1988.

Bénédictus, Edouard. *Variations,* Paris n.d.

Bénézit, E. *Dictionnaire critique et documentaire des peintres, sculpteurs, dessinateurs et graveurs,* Paris 1948.

Benoist, Luc. *Les Tissus, la tapisserie, les tapis,* Paris 1926.

Besnard, Charles-Henri. *L'Art décoratif moderne et les industries d'art contemporaines,* Paris 1925.

Blum, Stella. *Designs by Erté—Fashion Drawings and Illustrations from Harper's Bazaar,* New York 1976.

Bodelsen, Merete. *Gauguin Ceramics in Danish Collections,* Copenhagen 1960.

Bossaglia, Rossana. *Il Deco italiano,* Milan 1975.

Bouilhet, Tony. *L'Orfèvrerie française au XXe siècle,* Paris 1941.

Brielle, Roger (Introduction). *François Pompon,* Paris n.d.

Bröhan, Karl H. *Kunsthandwerk I. Jugendstil, Werkbund—Art Deco,* Berlin 1976.

Brunhammer, Yvonne. *The Nineteen-Twenties Style,* London 1959.

———. *Le Style 1925,* Paris n.d. (c. 1975).

———. *1925,* Paris 1976.

———. *Les Styles des Années 30 à 50,* Paris 1987.

Bujon, Guy and Dutko, Jean-Jacques. *E. Printz,* Paris 1986.

Cabanne, Pierre. *L'Epopée du Cubisme,* Paris 1965.

Camard, Florence. *Ruhlmann,* Paris 1983.

———. *Michel Dufet,* Paris 1988.

Cassandre, A. M. *Publicité,* Paris n.d. (c. 1929).

Casson, Stanley. *Some Modern Sculptors,* London 1928.

———. *XXth Century Sculptors,* London 1930.

Cendrars, Blaise (Introduction). *Le Spectacle est dans la rue,* Paris 1935.

Chanaux, Adolphe. *Jean-Michel Frank,* Paris 1980.

Chapsal, F. *Rapport à monsieur le Ministre du Commerce, de l'Industrie, des Postes et des Télégraphes sur le projet d'Exposition Internationale des Arts Décoratifs Modernes à Paris,* Paris 1916.

Chareau, Pierre. *Mobilier,* Paris n.d.

Chaumeil, Louis. *Van Dongen,* Geneva 1967.

Chavance, René. *Une Ambassade française,* Paris 1925.

———. *L'Art français depuis vingt ans: la céramique et la verrerie,* Paris 1928.

Claris, Edmond. *L'Exposition Internationale des Arts Décoratifs et Industriels Modernes,* Paris 1925.

Clouzot, Henri. *La Ferronnerie moderne,* Paris 1925 et seq.

———. *La Ferronnerie moderne à L'Exposition des Arts Décoratifs,* Paris 1925.

———. *Style moderne dans la décoration intérieure,* Paris 1926.

Cohen, Arthur A. *Sonia Delaunay,* New York 1975.

Cohen, Arthur A. (ed.). *The New Art of Colour: The Writings of Robert and Sonia Delaunay,* New York 1978.

Colvile, Georgiana M. M. *Vers un langage des arts autour des années vingt,* Paris 1977.

Contreau, Pierre. *Le Grand Négoce, organe du commerce de luxe français,* Paris 1926.

Courrières, Ed. des. *Van Dongen,* Paris 1925.

Crespelle, Jean-Paul. *La Folle Epoque,* Paris 1968.

Damase, Jacques. *Sonia Delaunay, rythmes et couleurs,* Paris 1971.

Damase, Jacques (ed.). *Sonia Delaunay 1925,* Paris n.d.

Dayot, Armand. *Animaux décoratifs,* Paris n.d. (c. 1930).

———. *Animaux stylisés, plumes,* Paris n.d. (c. 1930).

———. *Animaux stylisés, poils,* Paris n.d. (c. 1930).

Delaunay, Sonia. *Tapis et tissus,* Paris n.d. (c. 1930).

Delevoy, Robert. *Fernand Léger,* Geneva 1962.

Delhaye, Jean. *Art Deco Posters and Graphics,* London 1977.

Dervaux, Adolphe. *L'Architecture étrangère à l'Exposition Internationale des Arts Décoratifs,* Paris 1925.

———. *Les Pavillons étrangers à l'Exposition Internationale des Arts Décoratifs,* Paris 1926.

Descargues, Pierre. *Fernand Léger,* Paris 1955.

Deshairs, Léon. *Une Ambassade française,* Paris 1925.

———. *Exposition des Arts Décoratifs, Paris 1925, Intérieurs en couleurs,* Paris n.d.

———. *L'Hôtel du Collectionneur,* Paris 1926.

———. *Modern French Decorative Art,* London 1926–1930.

Deshairs, Léon (ed.). *L'Art Décoratif français 1918–1925,* Paris 1925.

Devauchelle, Roger. *La Reliure en France des origines à nos jours,* Paris 1961.

Deville, Etienne. *La Reliure française,* Paris & Brussels 1931

Devinoy, Pierre, and Janneau, Guillaume. *Le Meuble léger en France,* Paris 1952

Devinoy, Pierre, and Jarry, Madeleine. *Le Siège en France du moyen âge à nos jours,* Paris 1948.

De Vos, Jacques. *Jean Lambert-Rucki,* Paris 1988.

Diehl, Gaston. *Les Fauves,* Paris 1943.

———. *Van Dongen,* Milan n.d.

Djo-Bourgeois, *Répertoire du goût moderne,* Paris 1928.

Dowling, Henry G. *A Survey of British Decorative Art,* London 1935.

D'Uckerman, P. *L'Art dans la vie moderne,* Paris 1937.

Dufrêne, Maurice. *Intérieurs français au Salon des Artistes Décorateurs en 1926,* Paris 1926.

———. *Ensembles mobiliers à l'Exposition Internationale de 1925,* Paris 1928.

Duncan, Alastair. *Art Deco Furniture,* New York 1984.

Duthuit, Georges. *Les Fauves,* Geneva 1949.

Edouard, Joseph. *Dictionnaire biographique des artistes contemporains,* Paris 1930–1937.

Elsen, Albert E. *Modern European Sculpture, 1918–1945,* New York 1979.

Erté. *Erté Fashions,* London 1972.

———. *Things I Remember,* London 1975.

Exposition Internationale des Arts Décoratifs et Industriels Modernes, Circulaire, Projets, Paris 1924.

Exposition Internationale des Arts Décoratifs et Industriels Modernes, Projet, Paris 1922.

Exposition Internationale des Arts Décoratifs et Industriels Modernes, Projet de règlement, Classification générale, Paris 1922.

Fanelli, Giovanni and Rosalia. *Il Tessuto moderno,* Florence 1976.

Fare, Michel. *La Céramique contemporaine*, Paris 1953 .

Fierens, Paul. *Van Dongen*, Paris 1927.

Follot, Paul. *Intérieurs français au Salon des Artistes Décorateurs de 1927*, Paris 1927.

Fontaine, Georges. *La Céramique française*, Paris 1946.

Fouquet, Georges, et al. *La Bijouterie, la joaillerie, la bijouterie de fantaisie au XXe siècle*, Paris 1934.

Fouquet, Jean. *Bijoux et orfèvrerie*, Paris n.d.

——. *Objets usuels*, Paris n.d.

Frantz Kery, Patricia. *Art Deco Graphics*, London 1986.

Fréchet, André. *Intérieurs modernes, mobilier et décoration*, Paris 1923.

Gaffe, René. *Connaissance de Paul Bonet*, Brussels 1933.

Geffroy, Gustave. *René Lalique*, Paris 1922.

George, Waldemar. *Intérieurs et ameublements modernes*, Paris 1927.

Giacomotti, Jeanne. *La Céramique*, Paris 1933–1935.

Gregorietti, Guido. *Il Gioielli nei secoli*, Milan 1969.

Gruber, Jacques. *Les Vitraux*, Paris 1925.

Haggar, Reginald G. *Recent Ceramic Sculpture in Great Britain*, London 1946.

Hald, Arthur, and Wettergren, Erik. *Simon Gate—Edward Hald*, Stockholm 1948.

Hammacher, A. M. *L'Evolution de la sculpture moderne*, Paris 1971.

Hautecoeur, Louis. *Sculpture décorative*, Paris 1937.

Henriot, Gabriel. *La Ferronnerie moderne*, Paris 1923.

——. *Ferronnerie du jour*, Paris 1929.

Herbst, René. *Les Devantures, vitrines, installations de magasins*, Paris 1925.

——. *Jean Puiforcat, orfèvre, sculpteur*, Paris 1951.

——. *Un Inventeur, l'architecte Pierre Chareau*, Paris 1954.

——. *25 années d'U.A.M.*, Paris 1956.

Hesse, Raymond. *Le Livre d'art du XIXe à nos jours*, Paris 1927.

Hillier, Bevis. *Art Deco*, London 1968.

——. *Posters*, London 1969.

Hughes, Graham. *Modern Jewellery*, London 1963.

——. *Modern Silver throughout the World, 1880–1969*, London 1967.

Huisman, Georges. *Eloge de Marcel Vertès*, Paris 1951.

Hutchison, Harold F. *The Poster, An Illustrated History from 1860*, London 1968.

Jamot, Paul. *A. Perret et l'architecture de Béton Armé*, Paris 1927.

Janneau, Guillaume. *Emile Decoeur, céramiste*, Paris 1923.

——. *Le Fer, ouvrages de ferronnerie et de serrurerie dûs à des artisans contemporains*, Paris 1924.

——. *L'Art décoratif moderne, formes nouvelles et programmes nouveaux*, Paris 1925.

——. *Le Fer à l'Exposition Internationale des Arts Décoratifs*, Paris 1925.

——. *Le Verre et l'art de Marinot*, Paris 1925.

——. *Le Luminaire et les moyens d'éclairages nouveaux*, Paris 1926.

——. *L'Art Cubiste, théories et réalisations*, Paris 1929.

——. *Modern Glass*, London 1931.

Janneau, Guillaume, and Benoist, Luc. *L'Exposition Internationale des Arts Décoratifs et Industriels Modernes*, Paris 1925.

Joel, David. *The Adventure of British Furniture 1851–1951*, London 1953.

Johnson, Stewart. *Eileen Gray: Designer 1879–1976*, London 1979.

Jourdain, Frantz, and Rey, Robert. *Le Salon d'Automne*, Paris 1928.

Kahle, Katharine Morrison (McClinton). *Modern French Decoration*, New York 1930.

Karshan, Donald. *Archipenko, The Sculpture and Graphic Art*, Tübingen 1974.

Kjellberg, Pierre. *Art Deco*, Paris 1986.

Klein, Dan. *All Colour Book of Art Deco*, London 1974.

Kramer, Hilton, et al. *The Sculpture of Gaston Lachaise*, New York 1967

Kyriazi, Jean Mélus. *Van Dongen et le Fauvisme*, Lausanne & Paris 1971.

——. *Van Dongen après le Fauvisme*, Lausanne 1976.

Lajoix, A. *La Céramique en France 1925-1947*, Paris 1983.

Lalique, Marc and Marie-Claude. *Lalique par Lalique*, Lausanne 1977.

Lalique, Marie-Claude. *Lalique*, Geneva 1988.

Laprade, Albert. *L'Exposition de Paris*, Paris 1937.

Laude, Jean. *La Peinture française 1905–1914 et l'art Nègre*, Paris 1968.

Lechevallier-Chevignard, Georges. *Les Oeuvres de la Manufacture Nationale de Sèvres, 1738–1932*, Paris n.d.

——. *Verriers et céramistes*, Paris 1932.

Legrain, Jean-Antoine; Blaizot, Georges; and Bonfils, Robert. *Pierre Legrain, relieur*, Paris 1965.

Legrain, Pierre (ed.). *Objets d'art*, Paris n.d.

Lesieutre, Alain. *The Spirit and Splendour of Art Deco*, New York & London 1974.

Leymarie, Jean. *Le Fauvisme*, Geneva 1959.

Iorac-Gerbaud, Andrée. *L'Art du laque*, Paris 1974.

Maenz, Paul. *Art Deco 1920–1940*, Cologne 1974.

Magne, Henri Marcel. *L'Architecture, L'Art français depuis vingt ans*, Paris 1922.

——. *Les Enseignements de l'Exposition Internationale des Arts Décoratifs et Industriels Modernes*, Paris 1926.

——. *Décor du tissu*, Paris 1933

Mallet-Stevens, Robert. *Grandes Constructions*, Paris n.d.

Mannoni, Edith, and Bizot, Chantal. *Mobilier 1900–1925*, Paris n.d.

Marcilhac, Félix. *Jean Dunand His Life and Works*, London 1991.

——. *René Lalique Maître-Verrier*, Paris 1989.

Martel, Jan and Joël. *Sculptures*, Paris n.d.

Martinie, A. H. *La Sculpture. L'Art français depuis vingt ans*, Paris 1928.

——. *La Ferronnerie*, Paris 1929.

Maryon, Herbert. *Modern Sculpture, Its Methods and Ideals*, London 1933.

Mauclair, Camille. *Paul Jouve*, Paris 1931.

Mayer, Marcel. *A. G. Perret*, Paris 1928.

McClinton, Katharine Morrison. *Art Deco, A Guide for Collectors*, New York 1972.

——. *Lalique for Collectors*, New York 1975.

Menten, Theodore. *Art Deco*, New York 1972.

——. *Advertising Art in the Art Deco Style*, New York 1975.

Morava, Claude. *L'Art moderne dans la verrerie*, Paris 1930.

Moreau, Charles. *Petits meubles du jour, 1923–1934*, Paris n.d.

Mourey, Gabriel. *L'Art français de la révolution à nos jours*, Paris 1922.

——. *La Manufacture Royale de Porcelaine de Copenhague à l'Exposition Internationale des Arts Décoratifs*, Paris 1925.

——. *La Vérité sur la Cour des Métiers. Ce qu'elle est . . . aurait dû être . . . pouvait être*, Paris 1925.

——. *Henri Sauvage*, Paris 1928.

Moussinac, Léon. *Etoffes imprimées et papiers peints*, Paris 1924.

——. *Intérieurs*, Paris 1924, 1925, 1926.

——. *Le Meuble français moderne*, Paris 1925.

——. *Etoffes d'ameublement tissées et brochées*, Paris 1926.

——. *Francis Jourdain*, Geneva 1955.

Muller, J. E. *Fauvism*, London 1967.

Naylor, Gillian. *The Bauhaus*, London 1968.

Neve, Christopher. *Leon Underwood*, London 1974.

Nordland, Gerald. *Gaston Lachaise, The Man and His Work*, New York 1974.

Novi, A. *Intérieurs modernes, mobilier et décoration*, Paris 1928.

Olmer, Pierre. *Le Mobilier français d'aujourd'hui*, Paris & Brussels 1926.

——. *L'Art décoratif français en 1928*, Paris 1928.

Ozenfant, Amédée. *Foundations of Modern Art*, London 1931.

Papini, Roberto. *Le Arti d'oggi*, Milan & Rome 1930.

Patout, Pierre. *L'Architecture officielle et les pavillons à l'Exposition de 1925*, Paris 1926.

Paulsson, Gregor. *Moderno Strömningar inom Europas Konstindustri*, Stockholm 1925.

Paulsson, Gregor (ed.). *Modernt Svenskt Glas*, Stockholm 1943.

Pazaurek, Gustav. *Kunstgläser der Gegenwart*, Leipzig 1925.

Percy, Vane. *The Glass of Lalique*, London 1977.

Perrot, Paul N.; Gardner, Paul V.; and Plaut, James S. *Steuben: Seventy Years of American Glassmaking*, New York & Washington 1974.

Pevsner, Nikolaus. *Pioneers of Modern Design*, London 1960.

Philippe, Joseph. *Le Val Saint-Lambert*, Liège 1974.

Plaut, James S. *Steuben Glass*, New York 1972.

Poillerat, Gilbert. *Ferronnerie d'aujourd'hui*, Paris n.d.

(c. 1947).

Poiret, Paul. *En Habillant l'Epoque,* Paris 1930.

Polak, Ada. *Modern Glass,* London 1962.

Poulain, Hervé. *L'Art et l'automobile,* Zoug 1973.

Prasteau, Jean. *La Merveilleuse Aventure du Casino de Paris,* Paris 1975.

Prouvé, Jean. *Le Métal,* Paris 1929.

Quenioux, Gaston. *Les Arts décoratifs modernes,* Paris 1925.

Rambosson, Ivanhoë. *Les Batiks de Madame Pangon,* Paris 1925.

———. *Esplanade des Invalides Le Pavillon de la Société de l'Art Appliqué aux Métiers,* Paris 1925.

Rapin, Henri. *La Sculpture décorative à l'Exposition Internationale des Arts Décoratifs,* Paris 1925.

———. *La Sculpture décorative moderne,* Paris 1936.

Régamey, Raymond. *Le Ferronnier d'art Edgar Brandt,* Strasbourg (Archives Alsaciennes d'Histoire de l'Art) 1924.

Reports on the Present Position and Tendencies of the Industrial Arts as Indicated at the International Exhibition of Modern Decorative and Industrial Arts, Paris 1925, London n.d. (1925).

Rickards, Maurice. *Posters of the Twenties,* London 1968.

Riotor, Léon. *Paul Follot,* Paris 1923.

Robinson, Julian. *The Golden Age of Style,* London 1976.

Rochas, Marcel. *Vingt-cinq ans d'élégance à Paris,* Paris 1951.

Rogers, J. C. *Modern English Furniture,* London & New York 1930.

Rosenthal, Léon. *La Verrerie française depuis cinquante ans,* Paris & Brussels 1927.

Roux-Spitz, M. *Bâtiments et jardins,* Paris n.d.

Saddy, P. *L'Exposition des Arts Décoratifs 1925,* Versailles 1966.

Salmon, André, *Marcel Vertès,* Paris 1930.

Sandoz, Gérard (ed.). *Objets usuels,* Paris n.d.

Saunier, Charles. *Les Décorateurs du livre. L'Art français depuis vingt ans,* Paris 1922.

Scarlet, Frank, and Townley, Marjorie. *Arts Décoratifs 1925,* London 1975.

Schaefer, Herwin. *The Roots of Modern Design,* London 1970.

Secrest, Meryle. *Between Me and Life, A Biography of Romaine Brooks,* London 1974.

Sedeyn, Emile. *Le Mobilier. L'Art français depuis vingt ans,* Paris 1921.

Spencer, Charles. *Erté,* London 1970.

———. *Léon Bakst,* London 1973.

Terrasse, Charles. *Paul Jouve,* Paris 1948.

Thomsen, Oluf. *Jais Nielsen,* Copenhagen 1931.

Thubert, Emmanuel de. *L'Exposition d'art décoratif français contemporain,* Paris 1912.

Tixier, Geneviève. *Les Années vingt, 1920–1930,* Paris 1970.

Uttenreitter, Poul. *Kai Nielsen,* Copenhagen & Flensburg 1925.

Vaillat, Léandre. *Un Grand Effort d'art décoratif moderne, 'le Paquebot Paris',* Paris 1921.

Valotaire, Marcel. *La Céramique française moderne,* Paris & Brussels 1930.

Van de Velde, Henry (Introduction). *Le Style Moderne, Contribution de la France,* Paris 1925.

Vellay, Marc and Frampton, Kenneth. *Pierre Charau,* Paris 1984.

Verne, Henri, and Chavance, René. *Pour comprendre l'art décoratif moderne,* Paris 1925.

Verneuil, M. Pillard. *Etoffes et tapis étrangers exposés au Musée des Arts Décoratifs,* Paris 1925.

Veronesi, Giulia. *Style 1925,* Paris 1968.

Viénot, Jacques. *L. Cappiello, sa vie et son oeuvre,* Paris 1946.

25 Ans d'affiches d'une imprimerie (1912–1937), Paris 1979.

Vitrail français, Le, Paris 1958.

Vitry, Paul. *Paul Manship, sculpteur américain,* Paris 1927.

Vox, Maximilien. *Cassandre, peintre d'affiches,* Paris 1948.

Walters, Thomas. *Art Deco,* London 1973.

Weiss, René. *La Participation de la ville de Paris à l'Exposition Internationale des Arts Décoratifs et Industriels Modernes,* Paris 1925.

Werth, Léon. *Meubles modernes, croquis de Francis Jourdain,* Esbly 1913.

———. *Chana Orloff,* Paris 1927.

Wettergren, Erik. *The Modern Decorative Arts of Sweden,* Malmö 1926.

White, Palmer. *Poiret,* London 1973.

Wollin, Nils G. *Modern Swedish Decorative Art,* London 1931.

Zadkine, Ossip. *Le Maillet et le ciseau: Souvenirs de ma vie,* Paris 1968.

Zervos, Christian. *Chauvin,* Paris 1960.

PERIODICALS

Contemporary:

Amour de l'art

Annuals of Advertising Art

Architectural Review

Art d'Aujourd'hui, L'

Art Décoratif, L'

Art et Décoration

Art et Industrie

Art et les Artistes, L'

Arts de la Maison, Les

Art Vivant, L'

Cahiers d'Art

Dekorative Kunst

Demeure Française, La

Deutsche Kunst und Dekoration

Echos d'Art, Les

Echos des Industries d'Art, Les

Esprit Nouveau, L'

Feuillets d'Art

Harper's Bazaar

Illustration, L'

Médecine de France

Mobilier et Décoration

Posters and Publicity Annuals

Renaissance de l'Art Français, La

Revue de l'Art Ancien et Moderne

Studio, The

Studio Yearbooks, The

Vogue

Wendingen

Post–World War II:

Connaissance des Arts

Connoisseur, The

Domus Estampille, L'

Jardin, des Arts

Oeil, L'

Réalités

EXPOSITION ALBUMS AND CATALOGUES

Album de l'Exposition Internationale des Arts Décoratifs (L'Art Vivant), Paris 1925.

Album Souvenir. Exposition des Arts Décoratifs 1925 (Papeghiri), Paris 1925.

Album Souvenir. Exposition des Arts Décoratifs Paris 1925 (Lévy de Neurduri), Paris 1925.

Arts Décoratifs Modernes, Les, Paris 1925.

Catalogue de la Compagnie des Cristalleries de Baccarat, Paris 1925.

Catalogue des Oeuvres de la Section des Pays-Bas, Haarlem, n.d.

Catalogue Général Officiel, Paris n.d. (1925).

Catalogue Illustré de la Section Japonaise, Paris (?) n.d.

Catalogue Officiel de la Section Belge, Brussels 1925.

Catalogue Officiel de la Section Danoise, Paris (?) 1926.

Catalogue Officiel de la Section Tchécoslovaque, Paris 1925.

Catalogue Section Polonaise, Paris (?) n.d.

Compagnie Royale Asturienne des Mines Zinc: Catalogue, Paris (?) 1925.

Exposition Internationale des Arts Décoratifs et Industriels (Paul Léon et al.), Paris 1925.

Exposition Internationale des Arts Décoratifs et Industriels Modernes: Programme, Paris 1924.

International Exhibition of Modern Decorative Art: British Section, London (?) 1925.

Italie: Catalogue, Paris (?) n.d.

Manufacture de Porcelaine: Copenhague, Copenhagen 1925.

Le Pavillon de Lyon et St. Etienne à l'Exposition Internationale des Arts Décoratifs et Industriels Modernes, Paris 1925.

Pavillon Officiel du Vitrail: Catalogue, Chartres n.d.

Rapport Général (Ministère du Commerce, de l'Industrie, des Postes et des Télégraphes).

Section de la Suède: Guide Illustré, Paris (?) n.d.

Section Serbe-Croate-Slovène, Paris 1925.

Suisse: Catalogue, Paris 1925.

Union des Républiques Soviétiques Socialistes: Catalogue, Paris 1925.

EXHIBITION CATALOGUES

Amsterdam

Stedelijk Museum: *Vijftig Jaar Zitten,* 1966.

Beauvais

Musée Départemental de l'Oise: *Auguste Delaherche*, 1973.
Berlin
Kunstbibliothek: *Plakate in München 1840–1940*, 1975.
Bonn
Stadtisches Kunstmuseum: *Alastair*, 1973.
Bordeaux
Hôtel de Lalande: *Céramiques de René Buthaud*, 1976.
Musée des Arts Décoratifs: *Bordeaux Art Déco*, 1979.
Brighton
Museum and Art Gallery: *The Jazz Age*, 1969.
Museum and Art Gallery: *Clarice Cliff*, 1972.
Brussels
Musées Royaux d'Art et d'Histoire: *Marinot*, n.d.
Société Générale de Banque: *Art Déco 1925*, 1975.
Palais des Beaux Arts: *L'Art Deco en Europe*, 1989.
Calais
Marinot, 1973.
Cambridge, Massachusetts
Carpenter Center for the Visual Arts, Harvard University: *The Other Twenties*.
Cologne
Kunstgewerbemuseum: *Französischer Keramik 1850–1910*, 1974.
Galerie Gmurzynska: *The 1920s in Eastern Europe*, 1975.
Dijon
Musée des Beaux-Arts *Pompon, sculpteur animalier*, 1964.
Düsseldorf
Kunstmuseum: *Leerdam Unica*, 1977
Erbach
Deutsches Elfenbeinmuseum: *Europaïsche Elfenbeinkunst vom Fin de Siècle bis zum Art Deco (1880–1940)*, 1978.
Frankfurt am Main
Museum für Kunsthandwerk: *Art Deco aus Frankreich*, 1975.
London
Royal Society of British Sculptors: *Modern British Sculpture*, n.d. (1921).
Victoria and Albert Museum: *English Pottery Old and New*, 1935.
Royal Society of British Sculptors: *Modern British Sculpture*, n.d. (c. 1939).
Editions Graphiques Gallery: *Van Dongen, Vertès, Foujita*, 1971.
Editions Graphiques Gallery: *Art Deco Costume Designs for Music Hall and Ballet*, 1973.
Editions Graphiques Gallery: *Chryselephantine Sculptures of the 20s and 30s*, 1973.
Arts Council, Hayward Gallery: *Pioneers of Modern Sculpture*, 1975.
Victoria and Albert Museum: *Art Deco*, n.d. (1975).
Victoria and Albert Museum: *Fashion 1900–1939*, 1975.
Arts Council, Hayward Gallery: *Neue Sachlichkeit and German Realism of the Twenties*, 1978.
Arts Council, Hayward Gallery: *Britain in the Thirties*, 1979.
Foulk Lewis Collection: *The Extraordinary Work of Süe et Mare*, 1979.
Foulk Lewis Collection: *Ruhlmann Centenary Exhibition*, 1979.
Lyons
Musée des Beaux-Arts: *Marinot*, 1965.
Milan
Galleria Milano: *Art Deco 1920–1930*, 1965.
Galleria del Levante: *Alastair*, 1968.
Minneapolis
Institute of Arts: *The World of Art Deco*, 1971.
Munich
Stuck Villa: *Objekte der Zwanziger Jahre*, 1973.
Stadtmuseum: *Plakate in München 1840–1940*, 1975.
New York
The Gorham Company: *Famous Small Bronzes*, 1928.
Museum of Modern Art: *Posters by A. M. Cassandre*, 1936.
Finch College Museum of Art: *Art Deco*, 1970.
Acquavella Art Galleries Inc.: *François Pompon*, 1971.
Whitney Museum of American Art: *The Sculpture and Drawings of Elie Nadelman*, 1975.
Delorenzo Gallery: *Jean Dunand*, 1985.
Nîmes
Marinot, 1972.
Paris
Les Cires de Pierre Imans, 1920.
Musée des Arts Décoratifs: *Exposition de céramiques d'Emile Decoeur*, 1922.
D.I.M. (Décoration Intérieure Moderne), n.d. (1925).
Musée des Arts Décoratifs: *1ère Exposition de l'Union des Artistes Modernes*, 1930.
Musée des Colonies: *Exposition Coloniale Internationale de Paris*, 1931.
René Lalique: *Lalique*, 1932.
Musée des Arts Décoratifs: *Rétrospective Ruhlmann*, 1934.
Musée des Arts Décoratifs: *Le Décor de la vie de 1900–1925*, 1937.
Musée des Arts Décoratifs: *Exposition A. M. Cassandre*, 1950.
Musée Galliéra: *Fastes et décors de la vie parisienne de 1909 à 1929*, 1957.
Musée Galliéra: *Paris 09–29*, 1957.
Musées Nationaux: *Robert Delaunay*, 1957.
Galerie Romanet: *Louis Süe et ses amis*, 1959.
Galerie Bernard Lorenceau: *Claudius Linossier 1893–1953*, 1962.
Marcel Sautier: *Bibliothèque reliée par Paul Bonet*, 1963.
Musée des Arts Décoratifs: *Les Années '25'*, 1966.
L'Enseigne du Cerceau: *Gustave Miklos*, 1967.
Musée des Arts Décoratifs: *Les Assises du siège contemporain*, 1968.
Hôtel de Sens: *Les Ballets Suédois et l'art décoratif des années 1920–1925*, 1970.
Depôt 15: *De Gallé à Marinot*, 1972.
Galerie du Luxembourg: *Illustrateurs des modes et manières en 1925*, 1972.
Galerie du Luxembourg: *Tamara de Lempicka*, 1972.
Hôtel Drouot: *Ancienne Collection Jacques Doucet (Studio, Neuilly)*, 1972.
Galerie du Luxembourg: *Jean Dunand, Jean Goulden*, 1973.
Knut Gunther: *Les Artistes Décorateurs des années 20 et 30*, 1973.
L'Enseigne du Cerceau: *Chauvin*, 1974.
Musée Jacquemart-André: *Poiret le Magnifique*, 1974.
Orangerie des Tuileries: *Juan Gris*, 1974.
Depôt 15: *Csaky*, 1975.
Musée Bourdelle: *Trois Sculpteurs des années 30: Gargallo, Csaky, Lambert-Rucki*, 1977.
Salon d'Automne, Catalogues.
Société des Artistes Décorateurs, Catalogues.
Société des Artistes Français, Catalogues.
Société Nationale des Beaux Arts, Catalogues.
Pforzheim
Schmuckmuseum: *Art Deco: Schmuck und Bücher aus Frankreich*, 1975.
Portland, Maine
The American Federation of Arts: *International Exhibition of Contemporary Glass and Rugs*, 1929.
Saint-Etienne
Musée d'Art et d'Industrie: *L'Art dans les années 30 en France*, 1979.
Saint-Jean-de-Monts
Joël et Jan Martel, sculpteurs 1896–1966, 1976.
San Francisco
California Palace of the Legion of Honor: *Contemporary American Sculpture*, 1929.
Sarrebruck
Moderne Galerie: *Les Années folles*, 1974.
Sèvres
Musée Nationale de Porcelaine: *L'Art de la poterie en France de Rodin à Dufy*, 1971.
Strasbourg
Ancienne Douane: *Les Ballets Russes de Serge Diaghilev 1909–1929*, 1969.
Ancienne Douane: *L'Art en Europe autour de 1925*, 1970.
Ancienne Douane: *André Mare et la Compagnie des Arts Français*, 1971.
Stratford, Canada (also Vancouver, Edmonton, Hamilton, Montreal, Quebec and Winnipeg)
Art Deco 1925–35, 1975.
Washington
Smithsonian Institution: *Archipenko*, 1968.
International Exhibitions Foundation: *Stage Designs and the Russian Avant-Garde (1911–1929)*, 1976.
Zürich
Kunstgewerbemuseum: *Die Zwanziger Jahre*, 1973.

INDEX

Figures in italics refer to pages containing illustrations; figures in bold type refer to pages containing biographies or brief histories.

ACKNOWLEDGEMENTS

I would like to thank all the institutions, galleries and private collectors who have allowed items from their collections to be reproduced, including Maria de Beyrie; Frederick R. Brandt, Curator of 20th Century Art and Howell W. Perkins of the Department of Photography Resources, Virginia Museum of Fine Arts, Richmond, Va.; François Braunschweig and Hugues Autexier; Barry Friedman; Laurence and Barlach Heuer; David Hughes; Barry Humphries; Donald Karshan; Bob Lawrence and Davis Inglesis; Alain Lesieutre; Nourhan Manoukian; Veronica Manoussis; Félix Marcilhac; Florence Camard; Valerie Mendez; Michel Périnet; Clara Scremini; Bob and Cheska Vallois; Mr. and Mrs. Robert Walker; Robert Zehil; as well as all those who prefer to remain anonymous. I should also like to express my gratitude to the many people who have helped me in the preparation of this book, including Frank Russell for his editorial work, Ann Bridges for her editorial assistance, Mario Bettella for his design assistance in this new edition, Judith Michael for designing the first edition, Andreas Papadakis for his steady support and encouragement, and my wife Gretha for her patient and devoted typing of my barely decipherable text, her fierce loyalty and the inspiration of her affection.

Sources of photographs, whether collections or individual photographers, are given at the end of each caption. In the majority of cases where no credit is given photographs are by Richard Ball, Academy Editions.